W9-BFS-218

Understanding God's World Series

Understanding God's World Series

Homelands

of

North America

The United States and Canada

Grade 5

Rod and Staff Publishers, Inc.
Hwy. 172, Crockett, Kentucky 41413
Telephone: (606) 522-4348

Acknowledgments

We are indebted first of all to God who created the world and who upholds all things by the Word of His power. We are grateful that He has enabled the many who have worked on this project. Brother David Martin wrote the basic text, the brethren John Yoder and Bennie Hostetler served as editors, Brother Dale Yoder drew the maps, Brother Lester Miller illustrated the Chapter 8 title page, and Sister Ruth Goodwin drew all the other art work except the old prints listed with photo credits. Others spent many hours writing exercises, reviewing the material, giving helpful suggestions, and preparing the manuscript for publication.

We are also grateful for the permissions that were granted for use of photos. See page 475 for credits.

The Publishers

Front cover: Last Dollar Road in Colorado offers a scenic view of the Rocky Mountains.

Copyright, 1994
by

Rod and Staff Publishers, Inc.
Hwy. 172, Crockett, Kentucky 41413
Printed in U.S.A.

Code no. 94-3-97
Catalog no. 19510

CONTENTS

Farmland near Petersburg, West Virginia.

CHAPTER 1

THE NORTH AMERICAN CONTINENT

1. Where Is North America?

Glossary Words

Arctic	hemisphere	time zone
continent	sphere	Torrid Zone
equator	Temperate Zone	Tropics
Frigid Zone		

Some people in the world know only about a few square miles around their homes. They have never heard of the hot equator, the icy South Pole, the oceans, or the *continents*. They do not even know what country they live in. Where you live, grown-up people are expected to know that and much more. This book should help you grow up in understanding your own continent of North America.

You know that God created the world we live on as a *sphere*, or ball.

Northern and Southern Hemispheres

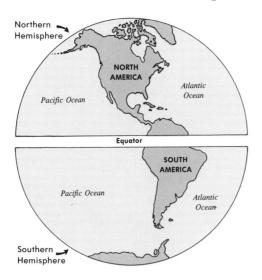

Sometimes we think of it as two *hemispheres* (half balls). An imaginary line, called the *equator*, runs around the earth and divides it into a "top" half, called the Northern Hemisphere, and a "bottom" half, called the Southern Hemisphere. Since we live north of the equator, we are in the Northern Hemisphere.

Because we often think of "up north" as being colder than "down south," you might suppose that the Northern Hemisphere is colder than the Southern. This is not really so. It is true that the farther north you go from the equator, the colder it gets until you reach the North Pole. But it is also true that the farther south you go in the Southern Hemisphere, the colder it gets until you reach the South Pole.

The Northern Hemisphere and the Southern Hemisphere both have summer and winter. But there is one difference; while we have summer, the people of the Southern Hemisphere have winter. And while we have winter, they have summer. In April,

The Seasons

When the North Pole is tilted toward the sun, the Northern Hemisphere has summer and the Southern Hemisphere has winter. When the South Pole is tilted toward the sun, the Southern Hemisphere has summer and the Northern Hemisphere has winter.

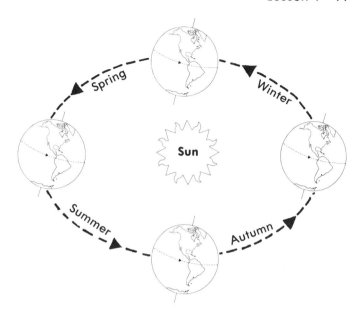

when you are enjoying spring, children in Australia are having autumn. This is because during our summer the northern part of the earth tilts toward the sun, and during our winter the southern part of the earth tilts toward the sun. God promised Noah: "While the earth remaineth, seedtime and harvest, and cold and heat, and summer and winter, and day and night shall not cease" (Genesis 8:22).

Map makers have divided the area between the equator and the North Pole into three zones. The map on this page shows them. The hot lands close to the equator are in the *Torrid Zone*, which is also called the *Tropics*. The cold lands close to the North Pole are in the *Frigid Zone*, which is also called the *Arctic*. Likely you live in between, where there are both warm summers and cool or cold winters. This is called the *Temperate Zone*. It is a good place to live. In the Temperate Zone, people do not spend most of their time trying to keep warm. Neither are they usually so hot they do not feel like working. Here is where people most easily get useful work done.

Climate Zones

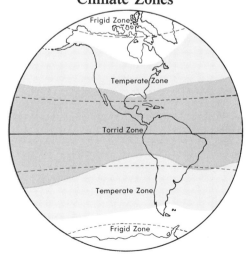

Eastern Hemisphere

Western Hemisphere

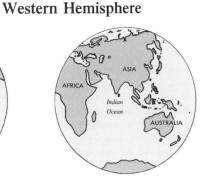

Map makers have also drawn an imaginary line from the North Pole to the South Pole and around the earth to the North again. Just as the equator divides the earth into a Northern and a Southern Hemi- sphere, this line divides the earth into an Eastern and a Western Hemisphere. North and South America are in the Western Hemisphere. Europe, Asia, Africa, and Australia are in the Eastern Hemisphere. Since you live

Time Zones of North America

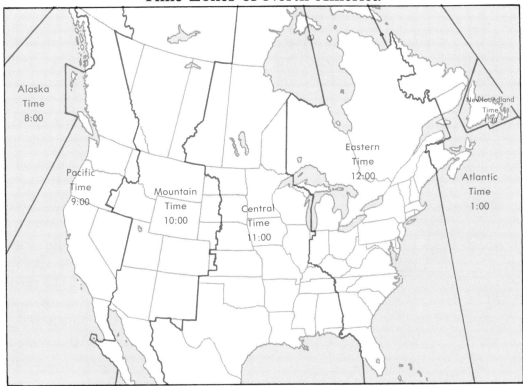

in North America, in which hemisphere do you live—Eastern or Western?

You probably know that imaginary lines crisscross the entire globe. Some of the most important are the twenty-four *time zone* lines that run from north to south, making the globe look like an orange cut into thin sections. The time zone lines help people to know how to set their watches. When people in eastern North America set their watches for 12 o'clock, people in the middle of North America set theirs for 11 o'clock. At the same time, people in the Rocky Mountains set theirs for 10 o'clock, and the people along the Pacific Ocean in the West set theirs for 9 o'clock.

Before the time zone lines were drawn, travelers did not know exactly what time it was when they came to a city. Today, travelers know that a new time zone will be exactly one hour different from the one they just left.

Study Exercises

1. Is the earth shaped like a dish or like an orange?
2. In which half of the earth would you find the weather becoming cooler as you travel south?
3. People living in southern South America would have to go in which direction to reach the equator?
4. If you are having autumn now, what season are people enjoying in the Southern Hemisphere?
5. Do you live in the Eastern or the Western Hemisphere?

Gaining Geographical Skills

Begin making a notebook of maps. There is a map section in the back of this book. Be sure to follow the rules given there for making neat maps.

1. Find Map A in the map section, and trace it. Above your map, write the title "North America."
2. Lightly shade in the Torrid and Temperate zones as they are done in the sketch in this lesson. Leave the Frigid Zone unshaded. Label the three zones.

Further Study

1. As the Northern Hemisphere tilts away from the sun, the days become shorter. What happens to the days at the same time in the Southern Hemisphere?

2. Which North Americans get up first in the morning—those who live in the East or those who live in the West?

2. *United States Geography*

Glossary Words

Appalachian Mountains   Great Valley of California
Atlantic Coastal Plain   Piedmont
Central Plains   Rocky Mountains
Coast Ranges   Sierra Nevada
Great Basin

The United States is the fourth largest country in the world. It has fifty states. Forty-eight states are in the main part, which stretches from the Atlantic to the Pacific Ocean. The largest state, Alaska, lies far to the north, and the state of Hawaii, made up of islands, lies to the west, in the Pacific Ocean.

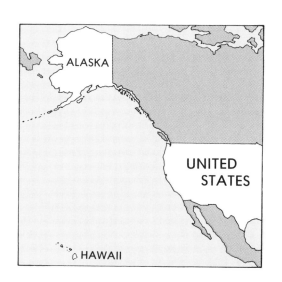

To describe United States geography quickly and easily, you could just say the United States is low in the middle and high at both ends. That is mainly true; in the middle of the United States lies a broad plain with hardly any mountains. At the east end are the Appalachian Mountains, and at the west are the Rockies and neighboring mountains. But such a description leaves out many details that you should know.

Let us imagine that you live in New Jersey and are traveling with your parents to visit someone in San Francisco, California. Leaving the Atlantic Ocean behind, you cross the level *Atlantic Coastal Plain*, with its many farms, towns, and cities. In New Jersey, the plain is fairly narrow, but if you were farther south, the plain would be much broader. You can see this on the United States map in this lesson.

Next you come to a hilly region called the *Piedmont* (PEED mont), where there are more farms and cities.

The *Appalachian Mountains* come next. Your road weaves back and forth through them. Though the

Relief Map of United States

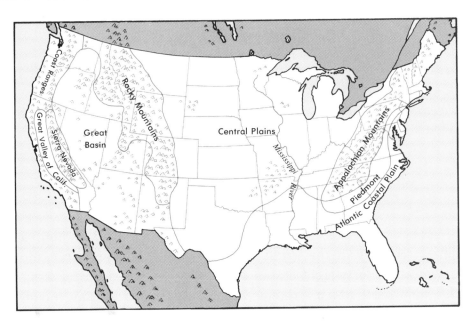

mountains are high, they are still low enough to be tree covered all the way to the top.

The mountains and hills go on for many miles. But at last they become fewer and you come out to the biggest region in the United States. This region is called the *Central Plains*.

Rivers from all over the Central Plains empty into the mighty Mississippi River, which is also known as the Father of Waters. Tugboats and barges use it for a highway.

Near Chicago, the biggest city of the region, you drive through a maze of highways. During the next few

An interstate highway stretches through level fields in the Central Plains.

An interstate highway winds through the Appalachian Mountains of eastern United States. Some Appalachian peaks are more than a mile above sea level, yet they are lower than western mountain ranges.

days you pass among hundreds of cornfields, then wheat fields, and then vast grasslands. Finally you come to the *Rocky Mountains*, so tall that their snowcaps might be in the clouds. Such mountains! Steep gray rocks rise higher than any mountains you have seen before. You marvel at the mighty works of God. "For, lo, he that formeth the mountains, . . . The Lord, The God of hosts, is his name" (Amos 4:13).

On the other side of the Rocky Mountains lies a dry region with broad valleys called basins. Its mountains are not so high as the Rockies. The largest area here is called the *Great Basin*.

This region ends when you cross the *Sierra Nevada* mountain range. Sierra Nevada means "snowy range." The range is so named because of the

Majestic peaks of the Rocky Mountains. Pioneers traveling to the west coast looked for the easiest places to cross these mountains. Some roads still follow the same routes.

The Coast Ranges run along the Pacific Ocean.

beautiful snowcapped mountains you can see here.

Finally, coming down into California, you see a great valley full of farms and orchards. It is called just that—the *Great Valley of California*. On the west side of the valley God placed still more mountains! These make up the *Coast Ranges*. The mountains crowd very close to the shore of the Pacific. There is no broad plain along the Pacific, such as the one you started from along the Atlantic.

The United States has many different kinds of climate. Some places are much colder or warmer or wetter or dryer than others. In some areas, Americans can grow cotton and oranges and sugar cane; in other areas they can grow apples and produce maple syrup. Americans appreciate the variety they find in their country. Much of the United States lies within the Temperate Zone. In most areas, people can live comfortably and raise crops and animals. Americans should thank God for giving "rain from heaven, and fruitful seasons" (Acts 14:17).

Study Exercises

1. Match these landforms with the descriptions given below them. One landform uses two descriptions.

   a. Atlantic Coastal Plain
   b. Piedmont
   c. Appalachian Mountains
   d. Central Plains
   e. Rocky Mountains
   f. Great Basin
   g. Sierra Nevada
   h. Great Valley of California
   i. Coast Ranges

   1. dry region west of the Rocky Mountains
   2. where rivers flow into the Mississippi River
   3. "snowy range"
   4. tree-covered mountains of the East
   5. full of farms and orchards
   6. largest region in the United States
   7. close to the Pacific Ocean
   8. hilly region east of the Appalachian Mountains
   9. high mountains just west of the Central Plains
   10. level land bordering the Atlantic Ocean

Gaining Geographical Skills

1. Trace Map B in the map section. Write the title "United States" above your map. Label these land regions: Atlantic Coastal Plain, Piedmont, Appalachian Mountains, Central Plains, Rocky Mountains, Great Basin, Sierra Nevada, Great Valley of California, Coast Ranges.
2. Make ∧ ∧ ∧ symbols where there are mountains.

3. Draw and label the Mississippi River.
4. Label the states of Alaska and Hawaii. They are not connected to the main part of the United States.

Further Study

1. How many countries in the world are larger than the United States?
2. Why is the Mississippi River called the Father of Waters?
3. From what you have learned about the Torrid, Temperate, and Frigid Zones, explain why people live in most areas of the United States.

3. *Canadian Geography*

Glossary Words

Arctic Islands	Canadian Shield	province
border	Interior Plains	territory

God has made another beautiful North American country, which is called Canada. Canada stretches about three thousand miles from east to west, covering most of the northern half of North America. People living on the eastern shore of Canada are closer to Europe than to the western shore of Canada. People on the west-

ern shore are closer to Japan than to the eastern shore. And Canada reaches almost as far from south to north as from east to west.

The *provinces* are big too. The state of Texas would easily fit inside the province of Quebec. Canada's ten provinces and two *territories* cover a greater area than all fifty states of the

Relief Map of Canada

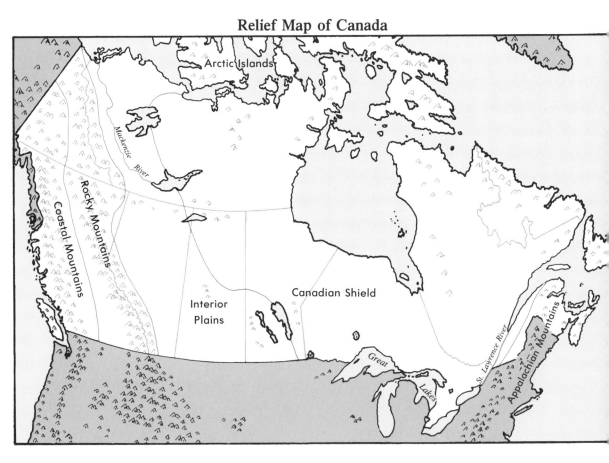

United States combined.

Although it is bigger than the United States, Canada has only one person for every ten Americans. This is because much of Canada is too cool and has poor soil. Because much of the land cannot be farmed, many square miles of Canada lie empty except for beautiful forests and lakes and rocks. On the average, there are about seven Canadians for every square mile of country.

But, of course, not every square mile has seven people living in it. Most Canadians live in cities, and most of them live less than two hundred miles from the southern *border*. That is not very far when you stop to think that Canada stretches almost three thousand miles north to south. Southern Canada is the warmest, most pleasant part to live in.

Hundreds of rivers flow through Canada. The St. Lawrence River in eastern Canada is one of the most important rivers in North America. It is about 800 miles long, the second longest river in Canada. The St. Lawrence connects the Atlantic Ocean with the Great Lakes. Early

A New Brunswick farm. Notice the dirt banked around the barn. This helps to keep the barn warm in the cool Canadian climate.

settlers and explorers discovered the river and used it for a major boat highway. Today, large ships carrying many tons of cargo use the St. Lawrence River.

The Mackenzie River in the great Northwest is about 1,070 miles long, the longest river in Canada. Many rivers and lakes drain into it. Although the Mackenzie runs through lonely northern lands, boats and barges use it when it is not frozen.

Along the border of Canada and the United States lie the Great Lakes. They too provide a huge water highway for ships sailing from the Atlantic far inland to cities such as Thunder Bay. Look at the map of the Great Lakes and the St. Lawrence River. Can you trace the route that ships take to go through the Great Lakes? Do you see which of the five Great Lakes does not touch Canada?

The Hudson Bay is a huge bay in northern Canada. It is over three times as large as the Great Lakes. The southern shores of the bay are covered with forests, but the northern shores are cold, flat, and treeless.

Three important mountain ranges in Canada are the Appalachians in the East, the Rocky Mountains in the

Winnipeg, a large Canadian city, sits about halfway between the Atlantic and Pacific oceans.

The Great Lakes and the St. Lawrence River

CANADA

Lake Superior

Lake Huron

Lake Michigan

Lake Ontario

St. Lawrence River

Lake Erie

UNITED STATES

West, and the Coast Ranges on the far western edge of Canada. The Appalachians in Canada are not as tall as the Appalachians in the United States. In some places, you could call them hills. But the Rockies are very tall and steep, and except for snow-caps, they are bare at the top.

About half of Canada is covered by the *Canadian Shield*. The Canadian Shield has low, forested hills and thousands of lakes. It does not reach all the way west to the Rocky Mountains. In between stretch the level, open *Interior Plains*. The Interior Plains are vast grasslands. Much grain is raised in the fertile black soil, and many cattle are grazed in the drier areas. North of the Canadian Shield, in the Arctic Ocean, are several hundred *Arctic Islands*. These islands are too cold and dry for trees to grow, and no people live there.

Canada lies to the north of the United States (not counting the state of Alaska), so its winters are cold. But not all of Canada has deep snow. Eastern Canada receives the most snowfall, often over one hundred inches per year. But the far northern regions, strangely, get only a few inches. And one small corner in southwestern Canada receives very little snow, if any. Temperatures are so mild that this area remains green the year round.

The Rocky Mountains pass through western Canada. Snow and ice cover their high peaks year round.

Study Exercises

1. How does the size of Canada compare with that of United States?

2. How does the number of Canadians compare with the number of Americans?

3. Why do most Canadians live less than two hundred miles from the southern border?

4. (*a*) Do you think the Mackenzie River is used more during the summer or during the winter? (*b*) Why?

5. Which of the five Great Lakes does not touch Canada?

6. What region covers about half of Canada?

7. Which of these are true about the Canadian Shield? (Choose more than one.)
   a. flat plains
   b. forested hills
   c. island in the Arctic Ocean
   d. thousands of lakes
   e. covers about half of Canada

Gaining Geographical Skills

1. Trace Map C in the map section. Write the title "Canada" above it. Label the Appalachian Mountains, the Rocky Mountains, the Coast Ranges, the Canadian Shield, and the Interior Plains.
2. Make ∧ ∧ ∧ symbols where there are mountains.
3. Draw and label the St. Lawrence River and the Mackenzie River.
4. Mark the route that ships take to go through the Great Lakes. Then mark the route they take to get from the Great Lakes to the Atlantic Ocean.

Further Study

1. A square mile is an area of land one mile long and one mile wide. Try to imagine an area near your school that covers a square mile. If all the Canadians were spread out evenly over Canada, about seven people would live in each square mile of land. Since the people are not spread out evenly and most Canadians live in cities, large areas in Canada have (more, fewer) than seven persons for every square mile.
2. Find out the average number of people living in each square mile in your area.
3. Why did the early settlers of Canada use rivers and lakes for much of their travel?

Chapter 1 Review

Reviewing What You Have Learned

A. *Write a glossary word for each definition.*

1. An object shaped like a ball.
2. One of seven large areas of land on the earth.
3. Hot region; another name for the Torrid Zone.
4. The region around the North Pole; another name for the Frigid Zone.
5. Half of the earth.
6. One of the divisions of Canada.
7. An imaginary line dividing the Northern and Southern hemispheres.
8. A part of a country that is not a state or a province.

B. *Choose the correct answer to complete each sentence.*

1. People living in the Southern Hemisphere are having —— while North Americans are having winter.
   a. spring
   b. summer
   c. autumn
2. North America is in the ——. (Choose two.)
   a. Western Hemisphere
   b. Eastern Hemisphere
   c. Southern Hemisphere
   d. Northern Hemisphere
3. Most of the United States is in the —— Zone.
   a. Frigid
   b. Temperate
   c. Torrid
4. The tree-covered mountains of the East are the ——.
   a. Appalachian Mountains
   b. Coast Ranges
   c. Rocky Mountains

5. The Mississippi River flows through the ———.
   a. Coastal Plain
   b. Great Basin
   c. Central Plains

6. The high mountains just west of the Central Plains are the ———.
   a. Piedmont
   b. Sierra Nevada
   c. Rockies

7. Canada is ———.
   a. larger than the United States and has more people
   b. larger than the United States and has fewer people
   c. smaller than the United States and has more people

8. Most Canadians live ———.
   a. less than two hundred miles from the southern border
   b. on farms
   c. near Canada's northern border

An Indian lady of southwestern United States, weaving blankets in the same way her ancestors did.

THE FIRST NORTH AMERICANS

—*Read Tree in the Trail*

4. Who Were the Indians?

Long before your grandparents or even your great-great-grandparents were born, Indians were living in North America. Compared to the many people who live in North America today, there were only a few Indians. Yet those Indians who lived in North America gave us gifts to remember them by.

Have you ever enjoyed maple syrup? What about pumpkins, tomatoes, or squash? Of course, you have eaten corn and potatoes. These were strange foods to the white man before the first explorers met the Indians. Indians also gave us moccasins, which some pioneers liked better for walking in the wilderness than

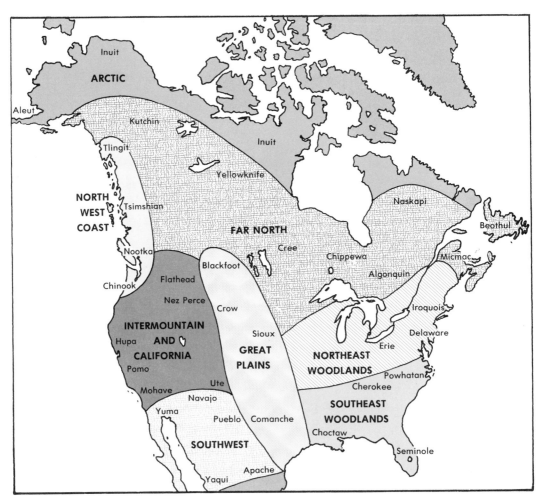

This map shows where the Indians of North America lived before white men came. The names of tribe groups appear in blue. The names of individual tribes appear in smaller black type. (The Far North tribes do not have a separate lesson in this book.)

Snowshoes
Moccasins
Parka
Potatoes
Corn
Toboggan
Tomatoes
Pumpkin

Gifts from the Indians

stiff-soled shoes. Indian snowshoes and toboggans were just right for traveling across deep, fluffy snow. Eskimos, who are related to the Indians, wore fur-lined parkas, and today many people besides Eskimos wear them.

Some of the words we use come from the Indians. The word *Canada* comes from an Indian word. *Mississippi* means "Father of Many Waters." Indians also named the caribou, the chipmunk, the raccoon, and the skunk.

The Indians loved the animals, the trees, and the countryside. Although they sometimes killed animals for food and clothing, they did not kill more animals than necessary or cut down more trees than they needed.

Indian medicine men were respected but also feared. No doubt many medicine men helped heal sick people, because they knew how to make medicines from plants. But

Some Indians made clothing and other items from animal skins. Preparing the skins took much time and hard work.

Indian mothers were fond of their children. In many Indian tribes, babies stayed in cradleboards most of the time. The cradleboard could be hung in a tree while the mother worked.

many medicine men also practiced witchcraft.

Many tribes believed in one Great Spirit, who created all things. But the Indians had never seen a Bible or heard of God or Jesus Christ. Their medicine men sacrificed to various spirits and asked them to heal the sick and bring animals to the hunters. Indians believed that a man's spirit lived on after his body was dead, but they did not know about eternal life in heaven.

Young Indians would sometimes go off by themselves, fast and pray, and wait for a vision. They hoped some spirit would appear to them and

A missionary preaching to Indians. Some Indians became Christians when they heard about Jesus.

from then on be their guide and helper through life.

When people do not know about God or His Word, they cannot enjoy the love of God or live holy lives as God commands in His Word. Sin caused the Indians much sorrow, just as it does for people today who do not serve the Lord. It was a wonderful day when they learned about Jesus. But many Indians died without ever hearing God's Word.

Study Exercises

1. Who lived in North America before white men came?
2. List at least ten things the white men learned to use from the Indians.
3. How did the Indians show their appreciation for nature?
4. What did the Indians believe about life after death?
5. Read Romans 10:13, 14. God knows people need ——— to help them learn about Him.

Further Study

1. (a) Why did the Indians fear their medicine men? (b) How did the medicine men help sick people?
2. List several things that show that the Indians realized there was a power greater than man, even though they did not know the truth about God.

5. *The Northeast Woodland Tribes— Farmers and Hunters*

Glossary Words

long house   palisade   wampum

In the days when all the northeastern United States was covered by forests, many Indian tribes made this area their home. One tribe was the Erie, after whom one of the Great Lakes was named. (In fact, all the Great Lakes but one have Indian names.) Another was the Miami, which has a city named after it in Florida.

Northeast Woodland Tribes

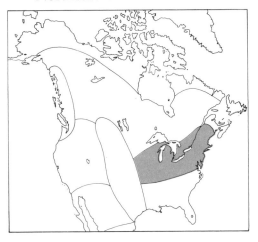

Some Indian tribes that lived here interest us because they were the first Indians that the French and English settlers met. The Delaware Indians sold land to early settlers in Penn-sylvania. Other Indians helped the first French explorers. The best-known of all the Indians in this area were the Iroquois (EER uh kwoy).

Iroquois houses were wooden frameworks covered with bark, like those of many other Indians. But instead of being round, as many Indian houses were in the Northeast, Iroquois houses were long. A *long house* could shelter ten families. Five family sections stood along either side. Fires were built down the center of the building. The families on either side of the aisle shared the fire between their rooms.

Besides all the foods they enjoyed from their orchards and the forests, the Iroquois often planted corn, beans, and squash. These three crops grow well together, and the Indians called them the Three Sisters. Indian men helped clear the land in the forest, but once the soil was ready, they turned it over to the women and children. Men were hunters.

The Iroquois were also some of the most feared fighters among the Indians in the Northeast. Any man captured by them could have expected one of three things to happen to him. He might have been killed outright, he might have been tortured to death, or he might have been adopted into the tribe.

One thing that made the Iroquois so strong was that they were not just one tribe, but five tribes banded together. Have you ever seen or heard any of the names Seneca (SEN ih kuh), Mohawk, Onondaga (ahn un DAW guh), Cayuga (kay YOO guh), or Oneida (oh NY duh)? A number of places and brand names have been called after their names. These five Iroquois tribes agreed to work together and not fight each other.

Indians of the Northeast made canoes of bark, which were light and easy to carry. White men from Europe found these canoes very handy for exploring much of North America.

The Iroquois were the best-known Indians of the Northeast.

Stripping Birch Bark

Building a Birch Bark Canoe

How many different activities can you see here? Why did the Iroquois build palisades around their villages? Why did they pile stones on the palisade platform? Where did the Iroquois get their building materials?

Around their villages the Iroquois and other Indian tribes built walls of logs stuck upright in the ground, like pickets in a fence but much closer together. This kind of wall is called a *palisade*.

Most Indians had no use for money. But in the Northeast, the Indians used shells to make beads, called *wampum*, which they sometimes used for money.

Study Exercises

1. Who were the best-known of all Indians in the Northeast?
2. Iroquois houses had (*a*) —— frames covered with (*b*) ——. (*c*) Why were the houses built so long?
3. (*a*) What were the Three Sisters? (*b*) Why were they called that?

4. Why were the Iroquois so powerful?
5. Name two things the Indians made from trees besides their houses.

Further Study

1. Why are Indian names still used?
2. Why did most Indians have no use for money?

6. *The Southeast Woodland Tribes—Woodsmen and Farmers*

Southeast Woodland Tribes

Cherokee (CHER uh kee) is quite a famous name in Indian history. You might also have heard Indian names like Choctaw (CHAHK taw), Creek, or Seminole (SEM uh nohl). The Powhatan (pow huh TAN) Indians saved the first white settlers in Jamestown, Virginia, from starving, and today a town in Virginia is named Powhatan. These are just a few of the tribes that lived in southeastern North America.

This is warm-weather country. Besides fishing and hunting for wild turkeys, deer, and bear, these Indians could do much farming and gardening. Next to meat, probably their most important foods were beans and corn. Also, they planted orchards in which peaches were favorites, and apples too if the tribes were not too far south for apples.

The southeastern tribes ate a variety of foods.

Indian women keeping birds out of their cornfield.

Like many other Indians, these people lived in villages surrounded by palisades. Many of their houses looked like Iroquois houses except that they were shorter and housed only one or two families. They were shaped somewhat like a loaf of bread.

Some of these Indians were quick to pick up white men's ways. They had neat farms, and they raised cattle, hogs, and horses. They even had their own schools.

The Cherokee Indians, especially, are remembered for this. One of them, named Sequoya (see KWOY uh), became interested in white men's reading and writing. He decided to invent an alphabet for the Cherokee

Sequoya developed an alphabet for the Cherokee language so that his people could learn to read and write.

language and worked at it for twelve years. After he finally finished in 1821, he taught it to other Indians. They became some of the first Indians to be able to read and write. They even published their own books and newspapers.

The Cherokee Indians are also remembered for the way they were later forced out of their homes by greedy white men who wanted their land. These ungodly men did not love their neighbors as themselves (Matthew 19:19). They made the Indians walk to other land west of the Mississippi River. Along the way, so many Indians died—over four thousand of them—that this journey became known as the Trail of Tears.

Study Exercises

1. Which Southeast tribe was very important to the early settlers in Virginia?
2. List eight foods the Southeast Indians ate.
3. (a) How were these Indians' villages similar to Iroquois villages? (b) How were they different?
4. How did Sequoya help the Cherokee?
5. What was the Trail of Tears?

Further Study

Indians are sometimes described as troublemakers for the white men. Find two things in this lesson that prove this was not always true.

7. The Great Plains Tribes— Buffalo Hunters and Tepee Travelers

Glossary Words

headdress	pemmican	travois
nomadic	tepee	

The Indians of the Great Plains lived in what is now southern Canada and the northern United States. They were the kind of Indian many people think of first when they think of Indians. They hunted buffalo, wore feather *headdresses*, and sometimes lived in *tepees*.

On the plains, one could look for miles without seeing a single tree. Not much rain fell. Summers were hot and winters were cold. How did the Plains Indians live here?

Great Plains Tribes

Buffalo herds such as these stretched as far as the eye could see.

Life was different for the Indians before white men came. The Indians got their food by farming and hunting. Once a year, the Indians had a big buffalo hunt. They knew how to use every part of a buffalo without wasting it. From the hides they made not only moccasins and robes but also covers for their boats and tepees. Buffalo shoulder blades were made into hoe heads.

In fact, buffalo even provided fuel. Since wood was so scarce, the Indians burned the dried manure. The Indians had learned to make good use of God's gifts, even though they did not know God Himself.

One interesting food the people ate was *pemmican*. They made it by pounding dried buffalo meat into powder and mixing it with animal fat and sometimes berries. Pemmican did not spoil, and it made a handy meal when the Indians were traveling.

Plains Indians did not always live in tepees. In fact, most of the time they lived in earth-covered houses that looked like upside-down bowls. Tepees were easy to move, however, and they could be used when hunting.

The Indians did not ride horses, but when they went hunting, they could walk, trot, or run ten to thirty miles a day. They did not use carts or

The Plains Indians lived in tepees, which they could easily move as they followed the buffalo herds. Notice the meat drying on the poles.

Blackfoot Indians moving. They carried their belongings on a travois, a platform fastened to two long wooden poles hitched to a dog or horse. Have these Indians done any trading with white men? Check the goods they have piled on the travois.

wagons, for they knew nothing of wheels. Their dogs helped to pull their loads. The Indians would make a *travois* (truh VOI) by tying two sticks together in the shape of a V and harnessing it to a dog with the point of the V over the dog's back. The ends of the sticks dragged on the ground behind the dog. The Indians could load this stick framework with tepees or food. A good dog often pulled more than a hundred pounds on a travois.

Things changed for the Indians after white men came. Now, for the first time, the Indians had horses and rifles. They could follow the buffalo herds and kill the buffalo easily. They began to neglect farming and lived mainly from the buffalo. Up to this time, they had used tepees only when hunting. Now they lived in tepees all the time. Moving from camp to camp like this is called a *nomadic* way of life.

Because they now could travel faster on horses, they met other Indians more often. Sometimes they fought with them. However, the Indians thought that a greater honor than killing an enemy was to touch a living one. And they had ways of making peace as well as of fighting. Sometimes they sat together and smoked a peace pipe as the Indian way of showing friendship. They also developed a sign language so that tribes who spoke different languages could talk to each other.

As more people moved onto the plains and began killing buffalo, the Plains Indians found it harder and harder to live as they always had. By the time your great-grandparents were born, the Plains Indians' way of life had ended.

But the Indian names remain. Have you ever heard or read of the Blackfoot tribe, or the Comanche, Crow, Pawnee, or Sioux (SOO) Indians? No doubt you have heard or read about the states of Iowa and Kansas. They are named after Indian tribes. So are some cities of the plains, such as Wichita, Kansas.

Study Exercises

1. Write the titles "Before White Men Came" and "After White Men Came" on your paper. Copy each of the following facts about the Plains Indians under the proper heading.
   a. had horses and rifles
   b. did some farming
   c. had one big buffalo hunt each year
   d. lived mainly from buffalo
   e. lived in tepees all the time
   f. lived in houses most of the time
   g. often met other Indians
   h. dogs pulled travois
   i. Indian way of life died out

Further Study

1. List seven products the Indians got from the buffalo.
2. (a) Describe a travois. (b) Explain how it helped the Indians.
3. What animal brought the biggest change to the Plains Indians' way of life?

8. The Southwest Tribes— Apartment Dwellers of the Desert

Glossary Words

adobe   pueblo   reservoir

Apartment houses are not new inventions. A number of Indians in the Southwest (where Arizona and New Mexico are now) lived in apartment houses hundreds of years ago. But their apartment houses, called *pueblos* (PWEB lohs), were different from the kind you see today. One of their favorite building materials was *adobe* (uh DOH bee), a kind of clay mixed with straw. The Indians did not try to make brick shapes out of the adobe. They just dried lumps of it in the sun and later plastered them into walls with more adobe.

Southwest Tribes

There were no doors on ground level. The Indians had to climb a ladder to the roof of the first floor and then climb another ladder down into the house. (Since there was no front door, they did not have to lock it. They just pulled their outside ladder up on the roof.) The roofs of the first-floor apartments were the front porches of the second-floor apartments, which were set back a little. The roofs of the second-floor apartments served as front porches for the third floor, and so on.

Some Pueblo Indian customs were different, not only from our customs, but also from the ways of other Indians. You may recall that Iroquois women did the farming. But among Pueblo Indians, it was the men who farmed. Iroquois men built the long houses, but Pueblo women helped to build the adobe houses.

In some ways, Pueblo Indians were like certain other Indian tribes. Women owned the property. Children belonged to their mother's clan (family) rather than their father's, and it was their mother's brother who

The Pueblo Indians built apartment houses long before white men built cities in North America. They used adobe because wood and skins were scarce in the Southwest. Adobe buildings were also cooler.

taught them. Although councils of old men governed the pueblos, they listened carefully to the women's advice. They did not follow God's plan for families. The Bible teaches that a husband is the head of his wife and that a father is to bring up his children in the nurture and admonition of the Lord (Ephesians 5:23; 6:4).

The Pueblo Indians wove religion into every part of their lives. For example, they had dances and ceremonies to help the corn grow and the rain fall. Men who danced at these ceremonies were called Kachina (kuh CHEE nuh) dancers. Christians know that every good and perfect gift comes from God (James 1:17). They pray to God about their needs instead of performing religious ceremonies.

Although Pueblo Indians would fight to defend their homes, they were not as warlike as their neighbors, the Navajo (NAV uh hoh) Indians. They did not like to fight among themselves. If they could not get along in peace, they preferred to separate and start a new pueblo. Any man who killed someone had to be purified with long ceremonies.

The Pueblos lived in desert country. Other Indians lived in deserts too, but they wandered from place to place rather than living in villages as the Pueblos did. The Pueblos used irrigation systems that included large *reservoirs* and long canals. This meant they could farm, staying in one place and building permanent houses. Some of the important foods they raised were beans, squash, and corn. They had six colors of corn: red, green, blue, purple, black, and yellow!

Their farms were large. Planting, irrigating, and harvesting the crops was hard work. Maybe that is one reason the Pueblo Indians were peaceful. Being busy, they did not have time for mischief. The Scriptures say, "He that tilleth his land shall be satisfied with bread: but he that followeth vain persons is void of understanding" (Proverbs 12:11). Neighboring Indians, such as the Navajo, learned some farming methods from the Pueblos.

Besides food, the people raised cotton and wove it beautifully. They

Southwestern Indians wove beautiful blankets from sheep's wool. Notice the baby on a cradleboard.

Shiprock Peak has been a familiar sight to Southwest Indians for hundreds of years. It is located in a Navajo Indian reservation.

also wove baskets and made decorative pottery.

The first white men to visit this area were the Spanish. They would not leave the Pueblo Indians alone. They broke into the pueblos in spite of the care the Indians had taken to make their walls strong. Finally the Indians were forced to go to caves high up on cliffs and to ledges of canyon walls. Here they built villages that were almost impossible to conquer.

Study Exercises

1. Describe a pueblo. Tell about
   a. the material used to build them.
   b. the first floor entrances.
   c. how each additional floor was added.
2. List four ways the Pueblo women were involved in tribal life.
3. How did the Pueblo Indians keep peaceful relations among themselves?
4. What made it possible for the Pueblo Indians to have permanent farms and houses in the desert?
5. How did the Pueblo way of life change when the Spanish moved into the area?

Further Study

1. List some ways the Pueblos were more like present-day North Americans than many of the other Indian tribes.
2. What might be one reason the Pueblos did not fight as much as other Indian tribes?

9. The Intermountain and California Tribes— Seed Eaters and Basket Makers

Glossary Words

pinyon nut   reservation

The Sierra Nevada (snowy range) stands just east of California. Winds from the Pacific Ocean bring rain and snow to these high mountains. To the east of the Sierra Nevada the air is dry. Here, in an area called the Great Basin, the mountains and valleys are desert.

Indians in these intermountain deserts probably lived more simply than any other Indians. The soil of the Great Basin was too dry to farm,

Intermountain and California Tribes

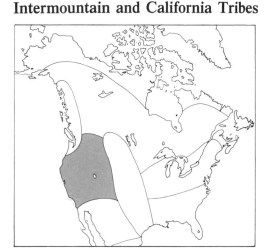

This woman is cooking acorns near her simple hut.

and there was little game (animals that could be hunted for food). Some of these Indians could scarcely find enough to eat. They ate rats, snakes, grasshoppers, grass seeds, weed seeds, and roots. Of course they ate larger animals when they could. Sometimes in the fall, they would band together to make rabbit or antelope drives. After such a drive (chase), they could feast awhile on meat. They could also use the animal skins for clothing or blankets.

The Intermountain Indians had to keep moving from place to place to find seeds as they ripened. They would stay at one place, hunting game and harvesting seeds, until food grew scarce, and then they would move on. If they lived where *pinyon nuts* could be found, they would gather them in the fall for the winter. They spent winters in sheltered valleys where they had stored away food.

Because life in the desert was so hard, the Indians felt that they could not support anyone who could not help himself. If a person became so old or so sick that he could not keep up with the group, he was left behind. These Indians did not fulfill the royal law according to the Scripture, "Thou shalt love thy neighbour as thyself" (James 2:8).

West of the Sierra Nevada lies the Great Valley of California. This valley has many sunny, mild areas where rain falls. Indians who lived here could easily raise vegetables in the rich soil. Nearby they could find fish and game. The Indians did not spend

The Pomo Indians made beautiful baskets.

all their time looking for food. Some of them were known for the beautiful baskets they made.

In the end, surprisingly, the Indians of the intermountain deserts fared better than the Indians of California. The desert Indians had to submit to white men's government and were placed on *reservations*, where they continued living much as they had before. But the Indians of California lived on land that white men wanted. So when settlers moved in and helped themselves to land, the California Indians had nowhere to go. Many of them starved.

Study Exercises

1. Why did the Intermountain Indians live more simply than most other Indians?
2. How did these desert Indians decide where to set up camp?
3. Why were some old or sick people left behind to die?
4. (a) Why did the California Indians not spend all their time looking for food? (b) How did some of them use their extra time?
5. (a) What happened to the Intermountain Indians? (b) What happened to the California Indians?

Further Study

1. List the foods that the Intermountain Indians ate. Have you eaten any of these?
2. Give some Bible verses that show God's disapproval of the way that Intermountain Indians treated their old and sick.

10. *The Northwest Coastal Tribes—* *Carvers and Boatbuilders*

Glossary Words

potlatch   totem pole

It might surprise you to learn that long ago some Indians lived in large wooden houses with peaked roofs. These Indians lived along the Pacific Coast, where Oregon, Washington, British Columbia, and Alaska are now. Here, because the Pacific Ocean is so close, the rainfall is heavy. Trees grow tall.

It was not hard for the Indians to find wood to make stout posts and beams for their houses. They made their walls of wooden planks. The peaked roofs kept out the heavy rains. The houses were as much as one hundred feet long, and they held as many as ten families.

Northwest Coastal Tribes

Felling trees by burning and chopping with a stone axe.

A Dug out Canoe was made by shaping a log, charring the inside, and then scraping it with sharp stones.

Northwest Coastal Indians called Ninstints skillfully carved out large canoes without any iron tools. The boxes on the poles may be burial boxes.

The Indians made other things of logs, such as canoes. They had no iron tools, so they hollowed out canoes by using stone hatchets and by lighting fires on the log to burn away the wood. They also made **totem poles**, on which they carved birds or animals. Often they considered these birds or animals to be sacred.

For meat, the Northwest Coastal Indians ate much fish, especially salmon. As the salmon swam and leaped upstream every summer, the Indians caught them, often with nets.

After the fish were caught, the Indians smoked or dried them. Dried or smoked fish lasted a long time.

The Indians also hunted bears and sea animals such as whales, seals, and otters. Along the seashore, when ducks and geese would fly in such numbers that they would darken the sun, the Indians strung nets between tall poles and caught these birds in midair.

For important times, such as naming a new chief or setting up a totem pole, the Indians had feasts that they

Some Northwest Indians covered the inside walls of their wood houses with carvings. The houses had only one entrance and no windows.

called ***potlatches***. They would invite neighboring villages to join them. They would gather a great amount of food and many gifts to give their neighbors. Sometimes they did this because they had so much and wanted to share with others. At other times they gave so much away because they wanted to show how rich they were, or because they hoped to receive gifts in return. It is true that "God loveth a cheerful giver" (2 Corinthians 9:7). But Jesus said that we must not give just to be seen of men (Matthew 6:1).

Study Exercises

1. Why did the Northwest Coastal tribes build houses with peaked roofs?
2. Which other Indian tribe built long houses?
3. Besides their houses, what other things did these Indians make from trees?
4. Name three kinds of animals the Indians caught with nets.
5. (a) What were potlatches? (b) Why did the Indians give food and gifts to their neighbors?

Further Study

1. List two things which show that totem poles were important to the Northwest Coastal Indians.

2. What modern inventions allow us to preserve meat without drying or smoking it?

11. The Arctic People—
Dwellers of the North Lands

Glossary Words

Aleuts	harpoon	Inuit
Eskimo	igloo	kayak

What people do you think of when you hear the word *igloo*? Likely you think of the kind of Indian we call Eskimos. The word *Eskimo* means "eater of raw flesh." Since the Eskimos had so little wood to burn, it was easier just to eat their meat raw. But the Eskimos themselves never thought anything was special about the way they ate. They called themselves "the people." Their word for "the people" was *Inuit* (IN yoo it).

The Inuit lived on the coast of Alaska, along Canada's northern coast, and around the coast of Greenland. In most of these sections, cold weather lasts for much of the year, and there are no farms. Trees do not even grow there. If we were suddenly placed in Inuit country, most of us would not be able to find food, clothing, or shelter. How could the Inuit live there?

The Inuit got much of their food and clothing by hunting animals—mostly caribou and seals. Usually they banded together to hunt caribou. Women and children chased the caribou toward the men, who were waiting to kill the caribou with spears or bows and arrows.

Hunting seals took patience. Out on the ice, a hunter would stand at a breathing hole with a stone-tipped *harpoon*. After hours of waiting, he might have a chance to harpoon a seal as it came to a breathing hole.

Animal blubber (fat) could be made into oil for lamps. And caribou skins made good, warm suits. In winter, the Inuit wore two layers of skins, the inner layer with the fur

Arctic People

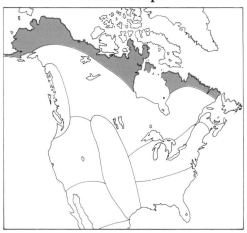

called huskies pulled their sleds in winter. For a time during the short summer, the snow melted, and sleds could not be used. But while the water was not frozen, the people could use boats covered with skins. One kind of boat was called a *kayak* (KY ak). It was big enough for one or two men. Skins closed in the top of the boat as well as the bottom. The man who rode in it could draw the opening in the top of the boat tight around his

An Eskimo hunting seals. He did not need to chop a hole in the ice. Seals will come to the open water to breathe.

turned in, and the outer layer with the fur turned out.

The Inuit sometimes killed and used other animals, such as fish, birds, or whales.

No doubt you already know that for shelter the Inuit built igloos of snow. Some Inuit built snow igloos only when they were on hunting trips. Two men could build one in about an hour. Some people built igloos of sod. In summer, the Inuit used tents of seal or caribou skins.

How did the Inuit travel? Dogs

Eskimos wore parkas to keep warm. During the long winters, they carved tools and other items from driftwood, whale bones, and walrus tusks.

An Eskimo hunter in a kayak. With this little boat he could quietly stalk his prey. His white clothing made him difficult to see against the snow and ice.

waist. This made the boat watertight, even if it tipped.

Another group of people who lived in the north were the **Aleuts** (AL ee oots). They lived on the Aleutians (uh LOO shuns), a string of islands that run out into the Pacific from Alaska, toward Russia. The Aleuts' homes were huge pits often large enough for a whole village. A ladder went up through a hole in the roof that also served as a chimney.

One reason they lived underground year round was to find protection from the wild storms. With the wind might come hail, snow, rain, or even all three.

The Aleuts hunted whales, as some Eskimos and Indians did. But there was one difference: they put poison on their harpoons to help kill the whales. So whale hunting was not as dangerous for them as for other Indians.

The north lands would seem very cold and barren to those living in warmer lands. But to the Inuit and Aleuts, these Arctic lands were home.

By using the ability that God has given, man can learn to live in almost all parts of the earth.

Study Exercises

1. *Eskimo* means "———."
2. Why did the Inuit eat their meat raw?
3. Tell how the Inuit provided for their need of (*a*) food, (*b*) clothing, and (*c*) shelter.
4. Name the two kinds of transportation the Inuit used.
5. On what islands did the Aleuts live?

Further Study

1. What did the Eskimos call themselves in their own language?
2. Name two ways the Aleuts were different from the Inuit.

Chapter 2 Review

Reviewing What You Have Learned

A. *Write a glossary word for each definition.*

1. A feast given by the Northwest Coastal Indians.
2. Land set aside for Indian use.
3. A protective wall made of logs.
4. A spear used for hunting.
5. Clay used to make bricks.
6. Wandering from place to place.
7. A body of water stored for future use.
8. Beads used for money by some Indians.
9. A two-pole sled pulled by a dog or a horse.
10. A dome-shaped Eskimo house.

B. *Choose the correct answer to complete each sentence.*

1. The Indians believed ——.
   a. that there was no life after death
   b. that only Indians could go to heaven
   c. that a man's spirit lived on after his body was dead
2. The Northeast Woodland tribes were ——.
   a. the first Indians to meet the English and French settlers
   b. always enemies of the white men
   c. unknown to the early English settlers
3. Five tribes banded together to form the ——.
   a. Iroquois
   b. Northeast Woodland tribes
   c. Cherokee
4. The Trail of Tears was caused by ——.
   a. Indians
   b. white men
   c. neither the white men nor the Indians

5. After the white men came, the Plains Indians ——.
   a. farmed more
   b. lived mainly in houses
   c. traveled more

6. Pueblos were built ——.
   a. by the men
   b. with no first-floor entrances
   c. with rock and mortar

7. The Pueblo Indians prospered because they ——.
   a. had large, irrigated farms
   b. were fierce fighters
   c. had good relations with the Spanish

8. The Intermountain Indians ——.
   a. carefully cared for each member of the tribe
   b. did not spend all their time looking for food
   c. lived very simply

9. The California Indians ——.
   a. lived in the Great Valley of California
   b. were placed on reservations
   c. lived in the Sierra Nevada

10. The Northwest Coastal tribes ——.
    a. lived in a dry area
    b. made houses, canoes, and totem poles from the plentiful trees in
       their area
    c. had large gardens

11. The word *Eskimo* means ——.
    a. "the people"
    b. "eater of raw meat"
    c. "dweller of the North"

12. The Inuit traveled by ——.
    a. kayaks and travois
    b. canoes and horses
    c. kayaks and dog sleds

C. *Copy the list of Indian tribes on the left. After each one, write the correct description from the list on the right.*

1. Northeastern	lived on Alaskan islands
2. Southeastern	made beautiful baskets
3. Great Plains	hunted buffalo
4. Southwestern	caught salmon with nets
5. Intermountain	also known as Eskimos
6. California	first tribes to meet English and French
7. Northwest Coast	lived in deserts
8. Inuit	quick to pick up white man's ways
9. Aleuts	built apartment houses

Gaining Geographical Skills

1. Trace Map A in the map section, and label it "The First North Americans."

2. Use the map in Lesson 4 to draw lines showing the approximate areas where each of the following groups lived.

    Northeast Woodland tribes

    Southeast Woodland tribes

    Great Plains tribes

    Southwest tribes

    Intermountain and California tribes

    Northwest Coast tribes

    Arctic people

3. Label the areas and color each one a different color. Notice that most of the tribes lived in the comfortable Temperate Zone.

So Far This Year

Choose the correct answers. See how many you can give without looking back.

1. North America is in the (Northern, Southern) and (Eastern, Western) Hemispheres.

2. Seasons in the (Southern, Eastern) Hemisphere are opposite from those in the Northern Hemisphere.

3. Temperatures are mild or moderate in most areas of (Canada, the United States).

4. Canada is (smaller, larger) than the United States, but it has (fewer, more) people.

5. Match.

    a. Northeast Indians
    b. Southeast Indians
    c. Great Plains Indians
    d. Southwest Indians
    e. Intermountain and California Indians
    f. Northwest Coastal Indians
    g. Arctic peoples

    1. made large wooden houses, totem poles, and log canoes.
    2. included Inuit and Aleuts.
    3. included the best-known Indian tribe—the Iroquois.
    4. built pueblos and irrigated crops.
    5. were quick to learn white men's ways.
    6. lived in teepees and hunted buffalo.
    7. gathered seeds and nuts and made baskets.

The early settlers and explorers were glad to see land after their long, dangerous voyage.

1490

1492
Columbus discovers America

1497
Cabot claims North
America for England

1520

Anabaptists start a *1525*
church in Switzerland

Cartier claims eastern *1534*
Canada for France

1550

EUROPEANS
COME TO
NORTH AMERICA

1580

Jamestown founded *1607*
Quebec founded *1608*   1610

Pilgrims land at Plymouth *1620*
New Amsterdam founded *1625*

Boston founded *1630*

1640

1670

Pennsylvania granted
to William Penn *1681*
1683
Mennonites settle in Germantown

1700

1730

1733
James Oglethorpe
arrives in Georgia

1760

12. *Europe—Crowded Land of Troubles*

Glossary Words

Amish	Mennonite	state church
Anabaptist	persecution	

Can you imagine what it would be like to leave your friends and the countryside you have always known, and move to a land of wild animals, unfamiliar plants, and strange people? That is what people from Europe did when they moved to America.

Why would anyone leave a well-settled country and go to the American wilderness where there were no roads, no church buildings, and no schools? One reason people

Almost everyone who left Europe to move to America left someone dear behind in the old country. Most never expected to see their loved ones again.

The landowner has come to take away this family's possessions because they could not pay their rent. Troubles like this caused many to look for a better life in the New World.

came to America was to escape *persecution* in Europe. In countries such as France, Spain, and England, the rulers decided which church their people should belong to. Anyone who joined another church could be fined, imprisoned, or even killed.

But many who came to America did not come for religious reasons at all. Some were forced to come. When kings and rulers were looking for people to send to America, they sometimes gathered up those whom they did not want in their own country, such as prisoners, orphans, and beggars. These people were loaded on ships and sent across the ocean.

Others who came were not beggars yet, but they knew they soon would be. Some were farmers who had

North America in the 1400s

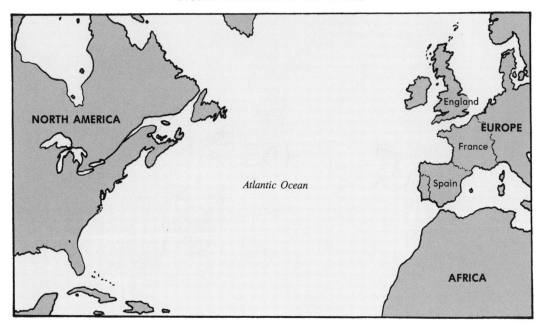

rented their land from rich land-owners. The landowners discovered that they could make more money by raising sheep, so they turned their acres into grazing land. Suddenly the farmers had no land. They were too poor to buy land for themselves, but they heard that thousands of acres lay waiting in America, ready for anyone who was willing to work. This chance to get land and enjoy a more comfortable life drew many people across the ocean.

Some people crossed the Atlantic with dreams of glittering riches floating in their heads. They had heard of the piles of gold that Spaniards had brought back from South America, and they hoped to find the same. Most of them were disappointed. More sensible people wanted to make money by bringing things from Europe and selling them. Merchants knew they could sell tea, silk, iron kettles, and many other things that no one made in the New World.

So you see, it is not surprising that people left the towns and countryside they had always known to go to the New World.

Reasons Europeans Came to America

True Christians in the 1500s

Did any true Christians live during the time of early American explorers? Yes, God has always had some faithful believers, though only a few true Christians lived in western Europe in the early 1500s. At that time, most churches were controlled by the government. Everyone in the country had to belong to the *state church*, and parents had to have their babies baptized into the church. Rulers persecuted anyone who disagreed with the official religion. But many church members and even church leaders lived ungodly lives, swore oaths, and went to war.

Some men began studying the Bible, and they saw that these practices were wrong. In January of 1525, Conrad Grebel, Felix Manz, George Blaurock, and other brethren started a new church of true believers. These brethren baptized only those who believed with all their hearts (Acts 8:37). Because most of the people they baptized had been baptized as babies, the brethren were called *Anabaptists*. Later, the Anabaptists led by Menno Simons became known as *Mennonites*, and those of Moravia became known as Hutterites.

The Anabaptists spread through Europe, preaching the Gospel, baptizing believers, and "teaching them to observe all things" that Jesus commanded (Matthew 28:20). They lived "soberly, righteously, and godly, in this present world" (Titus 2:12). They followed Jesus' command to "love your enemies" (Matthew 5:44). For many of them, this meant dying for their faith rather than fighting to defend themselves.

Did the early Anabaptists know about North America? Yes, some of them even thought of going to America to escape persecution. Although the first Anabaptists never left Europe, many Mennonites and *Amish* did move to America in the 1700s. There they enjoyed God's blessing of freedom to obey the Bible without persecution from a state church.

Some people say North America has freedom of religion because of wise government leaders and brave soldiers. This is partly true, for God does use government leaders to bring good to His people (Romans 13:4). But if the Anabaptists had not started a church of true believers, state churches might still control religion today—even in the United States and Canada.

===== **Study Exercises** =====

1. List five reasons Europeans moved to America.
2. What often happened in countries where a church and the government worked together to control religion?
3. Why did some of the poor farmers in Europe have trouble finding land to rent?
4. (a) Why did some Europeans think they could find gold in North America? (b) Why was selling products in the New World a better way to make money?
5. When did the Anabaptist church begin?
6. What kind of people did the Anabaptists baptize?

Further Study

1. (a) Do you think many Europeans would have come to America if there had been no major troubles in Europe? (b) Explain why you think that way.
2. Name some practices of the state churches that the Anabaptists found did not agree with the Bible.

13. *Europeans Come to America*

Glossary Words

America   Vikings

No one knows for sure who were the first white men to come to North *America*. They may have been *Vikings* from northern Europe. The Vikings were bold people who loved the sea. They would sail far out of sight of land in tiny ships. They traveled between Norway, Iceland, and Greenland without even a compass to guide them. A Viking legend tells about a ship that was blown off course in a storm and landed on the shores of North America, near Newfoundland, around A.D. 1000.

For a while some of the Vikings were interested in living in Newfoundland. But they found that the

The Vikings may have been the first white men to see North America.

Possible Route of the Vikings to North America

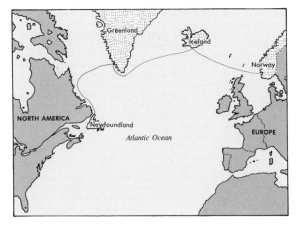

climate in Newfoundland was not favorable, and they finally gave it up. It seems this was not God's time for European people to settle in North America. However, from time to time the Vikings did return to cut the tall trees for lumber to build their ships.

For several centuries after the Vikings left, no one did important exploring in North America. Then in the late 1400s, a European named

Christopher Columbus had an idea. He knew that merchants were going to India and China to bring spices, silk, diamonds, and perfume back to Europe. But the journey was long and hard. Merchants traveling by land had to cross mountains and deserts. Robbers sometimes attacked them. Columbus also knew that other men were trying to reach India and China by sailing all the way around Africa. But sailing around Africa was long and dangerous too.

Columbus's idea was something like this, "Since people must travel so far east to reach China, could it be that when they have arrived there, they have traveled over halfway around the world? If so, they might as well keep going east around the world and return to Europe more quickly. Then why not take the short way to China in the first place? Why not sail west to reach the Far East?"

After receiving three ships from the king and queen of Spain, Columbus sailed across the Atlantic in 1492. The journey took more than two months. His men were not as sure as he was that they would ever find land. They were not even sure that the earth is round. The winds that sped them along were helpful but also frightening. How would they ever get back home? They begged Columbus to turn back.

Routes to the Far East

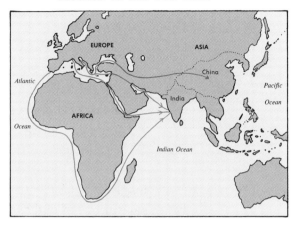

Finally, after Columbus promised that he would turn back in three days if they saw no land, they began to see signs that land was near. Birds flew overhead. A branch covered with berries floated nearby.

A night or two later, a sailor cried, "Land!" When they went ashore the next day, October 12, 1492, Columbus set up a cross and declared that the land belonged to the king and queen of Spain.

Columbus thought his experiment had worked. Thinking he had reached India or an island near it, he called the people *Indians*. Actually, he had arrived at an island near America, thousands of miles away from India. But the name *Indian* stuck. The natives of America are still called Indians today.

Since we think of Columbus as the discoverer of the New World, why not

Early Explorers

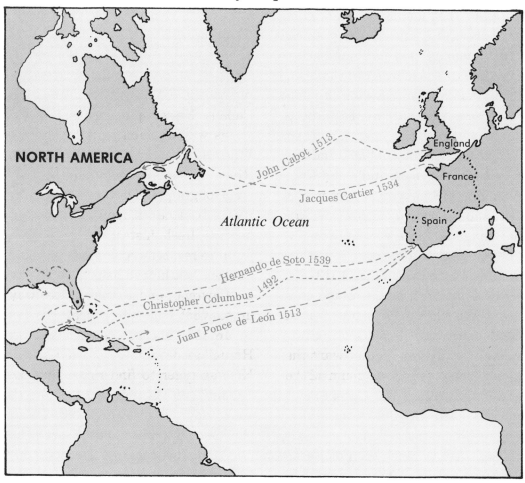

call it Columbia, after his name? A man named Amerigo Vespucci received that honor. He also explored the New World and wrote about his adventures. A mapmaker who read Amerigo's story began to label the new lands after Amerigo's name. As time went on, more and more people began to call the new land America.

Other men had the same idea as Columbus. Five years after Columbus's first trip to America, John Cabot sailed in an English ship across the Atlantic, but farther north than Columbus had sailed. He too hoped to reach China or India by sailing west. But like Columbus, he found a huge, strange land blocking his way before he reached the Far East. Cabot explored along the shore of North

America and claimed it for England, but he returned home without finding a way around it.

A number of Spanish explorers soon came to America. They did most of their exploring in the warmer parts of the New World. One of the best-known was Juan Ponce de León (PAWN say day lay AWN). Indians told him about a fountain of youth, whose waters would make him young again. Ponce de León never found that fountain. However, he was impressed by all the flowers he saw in the land he discovered in 1513. He called the area Florida, which means "full of flowers." It has been called that ever since.

The French king did not want the English and Spaniards to claim all the New World for themselves. In 1534 he sent a man named Jacques Cartier (zhahk car TYAY) to claim some of it and also to find a passageway through it, if he could. Cartier explored the area we now call eastern Canada. He set up crosses on the land as his way of claiming it for France. When he discovered the St. Lawrence River, he hoped this would be the long-sought passageway. But no! The river became narrow, its water became fresh instead of salty, and when he reached rapids, he finally had to stop. But he had helped to put the St. Lawrence on the map, all the way up to what is now Montreal.

In 1539 another Spaniard named Hernando de Soto explored Florida. He was eager to find riches like the

The Spanish, led by Hernando de Soto, explored what is now the southeastern part of the United States.

gold that Spanish explorers had been finding in South America. After exploring Florida and nearby areas, he led his men west. He kept hearing Indian tales about gold just a few days further on. Finally he stood on the shore of the Mississippi River. He was the first explorer to see this mighty waterway. Before his trip ended, he died, and his men buried him in the waters of the river he had discovered.

By the late 1500s Spanish people were making their homes in Florida. Before long, English and French people would be settling farther to the north. God was allowing Europeans to open up a country that would become a land of freedom for His children.

Study Exercises

1. According to a Viking legend, the Vikings came to America around (a) A.D. —— (b) How did they make this discovery?
2. Why did Columbus want to find a new way to reach the Far East?
3. Columbus landed in America on ——. (Give the month, day, and year.)
4. Copy the list of explorers on the left. After each one, write the correct description from the list on the right.
   a. Christopher Columbus   looked for a fountain of youth
   b. Amerigo Vespucci   discovered the New World
   c. John Cabot   explored the St. Lawrence River for
   d. Juan Ponce de León   France
   e. Jacques Cartier   claimed North America for England
   f. Hernando de Soto   the New World was named after him
                                first explorer to see the Mississippi
                                   River

Further Study

1. Explain why sailing across the Atlantic Ocean was a frightening experience for Columbus's men.
2. Which European nation began settling the New World first?

14. Jamestown—the English in America

Glossary Words

colony   represent   representative

In December of 1606, three ships slid from the wharves of London and sailed down the Thames River. They would try to do what others had tried before. Nearly twenty years earlier, a group of people had gone to America and settled on Roanoke Island, off the shore of what is now North Carolina. But every person in that little settlement had disappeared; no one knew what had happened to them. The men on these three ships would go to the same general area and make a new try. These men were not fleeing from persecution. Many of them were going to the New World to find adventure or to get rich.

The beginning of their voyage was not very encouraging. Storms delayed them. After two months they had sailed no farther than some islands that were closer to Europe than to America. Finally, in April, they reached Virginia. After searching for three weeks to find a good spot to settle, they chose a peninsula on the James River. The town they built was close to a river channel so deep that ships could be tied to trees on the shore. They called their settlement

Jamestown Settlement

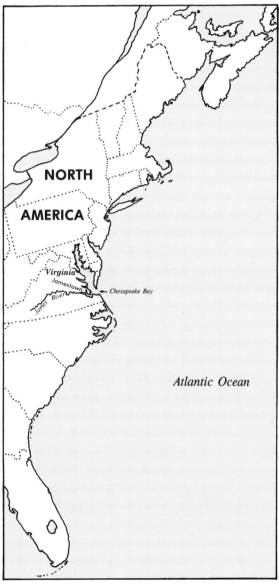

NORTH

AMERICA

Virginia
Jamestown
James River
← Chesapeake Bay

Atlantic Ocean

Jamestown, after their English king, James.

After the ships left for England, hardly two weeks passed before most of the men were sick. They had made the mistake of building their town on a low spot, close to swamps. Disease-carrying mosquitoes from the swamps were biting them, and the drinking water was impure. Besides, the men had little food because they had used it during the long voyage. Before long, two thirds of the men were dead.

There was another problem. A number of the men had grown up in wealthy families and were not used to working with their hands. Pulling weeds in fields was not for gentlemen, they thought. The only work they felt like doing was looking for gold. No one made them work until finally Captain John Smith was given control of the town. He made a law that no one would be given food if he did not work. Perhaps he had read what the apostle Paul wrote to the Thessalonians: "If any would not work, neither should he eat" (2 Thessalonians 3:10). Soon even the "gentlemen" were helping to chop logs, thatch roofs, and work among the crops.

One day when Captain John Smith was exploring the James River,

With so few people working, can you see why Jamestown got off to a poor start?

the Indians captured him and took him to their chief. After discussing the matter for quite a while, the Indians decided that Smith must die. The story goes that just as the Indians were about to kill him, the chief's favorite daughter, Pocahontas, begged that Smith be allowed to live. Whether the story is true or not, there was a real Pocahontas.

Smith was not altogether a hero. He got into quarrels with other men in the *colony*. When he was accidentally wounded by an explosion of gunpowder, he returned to England and never came back to Jamestown.

But his departure put the colony in great danger. When the Indians knew that the strong colony leader was gone, they began killing the colonists. Besides this, food was running so low that the people called that winter "the starving time." Five hundred people were living in Jamestown when Smith left for England. Within six months, only sixty people remained. Finally they decided to leave the settlement and sail for England. As they left, some of them even wanted to burn the buildings down, but they were persuaded not to. And then, just as their ships were heading out the James River, other ships met them! A new governor was coming, with more people, supplies, and food. The new governor ordered everyone

Early settlers in Jamestown lived in houses like this one.

back to the deserted colony. When they arrived, he and the men had something very important to thank God for. The buildings the settlers had wanted to burn were still standing, ready to receive them.

Up to this time, the colony had not found a good way to earn money. One of their first failures had been to think the earth beneath them was full of gold. They had sent a load of what they thought was gold back to England, only to discover that it was worth nothing. They also tried

The settlements in eastern Virginia grew and became more civilized during the 1600s. These settlers have met at the Old Burton Parish Church in Williamsburg.

making glass and wine, and they even tried raising silkworms. But all these failed too. Then a colonist named John Rolfe began raising a new type of tobacco and improved the way of curing the leaves. When the tobacco was shipped to England, people bought it eagerly.

King James hated to see people smoking. He talked and wrote against it. But the tobacco habit spread among the people. It did not seem to bother them that tobacco cost money, that it made their houses smell unpleasant, and that people with discernment did not like it. It did not seem to bother the Jamestown people either. Even today, some people earn much money from tobacco, while others spend much money for it and ruin their health. God wants us to avoid tobacco and other harmful products. A Christian's body is the temple of the Holy Ghost (1 Corinthians 6:19).

To help the farmers raise tobacco, ships began bringing black people from Africa. At first the colonists treated them like servants and allowed them to go free after a while.

But in later years, they treated them like slaves. This was the beginning of slavery in America.

At first only men lived in Jamestown. But later a shipload of ninety women came. Now the settlers could have homes, bring up children, and feel settled and happy at Jamestown. Their settlement grew into the colony of Virginia. Jamestown was the beginning of the first permanent English colony in the New World.

As the colony of Virginia grew, the leaders decided to let the people send two men from each part of the colony to discuss matters and make laws. They called this group of men the House of Burgesses. Each burgess *represented* the people in the area he came from. He knew how the people thought the colony should work and what laws they thought the government should make. The House of Burgesses was America's first *representative* government.

─────── **Study Exercises** ───────

1. Jamestown was founded in April of ──. (Read carefully!)
2. List three problems these early settlers faced after leaving England.
3. How did Captain John Smith help the colony?
4. (*a*) After John Smith left, the colony became (weaker, stronger). (*b*) A new ── arrived just in time to keep the remaining settlers from returning to England.
5. Why did the Jamestown settlers begin raising tobacco?
6. What helped the Jamestown settlers to feel like staying and working in the New World?
7. (*a*) The House of Burgesses was America's first ── government. (*b*) Whom did each burgess represent?

Further Study

1. (*a*) Why did the first settlers of Jamestown come to the New World? (*b*) Why did this goal have to change before the settlement could prosper?
2. What was King James's feeling toward tobacco?
3. How did slavery in America begin?

15. *Quebec—Beginning of the New French Empire*

Glossary Words

friar   scurvy   trading post

The first French explorer you studied about was Cartier, who reached the place on the St. Lawrence River where Montreal now stands. Cartier's adventures helped to interest the French in the furs they could buy from North American Indians. Beaver furs made good hats.

One of the French king's officials in the New World told Samuel de Champlain (sham PLAYN) to set up a new *trading post* on the St. Lawrence River. The trading post would also serve as a fort. It would allow only French ships to sail up the river to trade with the Indians.

With two ships, Champlain sailed up the St. Lawrence. They traveled only part of the way that Cartier had gone when they came to a place where the river narrowed. Here Champlain founded Quebec in 1608, a year after

Early French Settlements in the New World

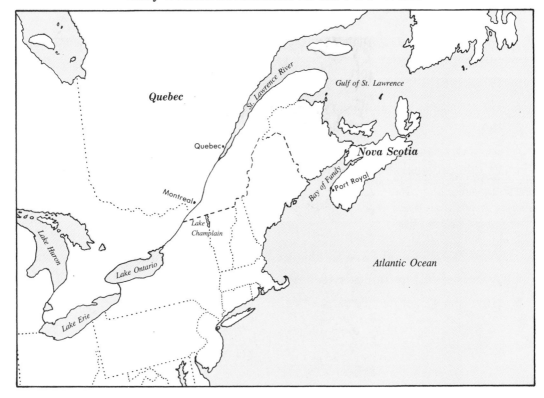

Jamestown was founded. It was North America's first permanent French colony. Indians heard of the fur-trading fort at Quebec. They were glad to trade their furs for the kettles, hatchets, knives, guns, and blankets the Frenchmen offered.

By fall, the men had loaded the ships with furs for France. The ships sailed away, leaving Champlain and twenty-seven other men behind at Quebec. When winter came, ice clogged the river. Because the men had no fresh fruits or vegetables, they began to get sick with *scurvy*. By the time spring had turned the forest green again, twenty of the twenty-eight men had died.

But Champlain stayed on. He kept trying to make friends with the

Beaver hats and other fur garments sold for good prices in Europe.

Indians in order to encourage them to sell furs to him. Besides, he wanted to explore areas beyond the St. Lawrence, and he knew he would need the help of his Indian neighbors. So when they asked him if he would go with

A camp on the bank of the St. Lawrence River. The French mingled more freely with Indians than the English did.

them to fight their enemies, the Iroquois Indians, he agreed.

That summer, Champlain and two other Frenchmen traveled with friendly Indians down the long lake we now call Lake Champlain. When Champlain and his friends met and fought against the Iroquois, the enemy Indians fled in panic. Their bows and arrows were no match for the white men's guns.

Champlain's Indian friends were happy. But Champlain had made enemies of the Iroquois Indians. From then on, the Iroquois counted Frenchmen as their enemies. They took revenge on them whenever they could. The Scriptures teach a better way to deal with enemies: "Therefore if thine enemy hunger, feed him; if he thirst, give him drink: for in so doing thou shalt heap coals of fire on his head" (Romans 12:20).

More Frenchmen came. Some of them stayed close to the trading posts, but others paddled canoes out into the wilderness, seeking furs. These adventurers lived a rough, hard life. Sometimes when they were rowing up streams, they came to waterfalls.

The French traveled far up the rivers, trading with Indians. These traders are carrying their canoes around a waterfall.

Then they had to unload their canoes and carry everything to where they could get back into the water again. Sometimes, coming downstream, they foolishly tried to run their canoes through rapids. Those who upset were often hurt or killed. Yet these men loved the challenge the wilderness gave them. Often they sang as they paddled along.

The French had not given up trying to find a waterway through North America to the Pacific Ocean. Like others, they did not realize how big North America was. But by trying to find a way through the land, they learned more about the land itself. One Frenchman, La Salle, explored far into the continent. Other explorers, who had found the Mississippi River, told him it would not lead to the Pacific. But La Salle explored it anyway, all the way to its mouth on the Gulf of Mexico. He arrived there in 1682 and claimed for France all the land whose rivers drained into the Mississippi.

Many Catholic *friars* came to Quebec and lived among the Indians. They baptized many Indians into the Catholic Church, which was the state church of France. The friars also tried to teach the Indians the European way of life, but most of them continued to live in the forests as they always had.

Quebec grew slowly because the French were interested mainly in furs, not in farms or towns. Besides, the French government allowed little freedom to settlers in New France, and for this reason few people wanted to settle there. For a long time Quebec was not big enough to be called a city. It was only a trading post and a Catholic mission station. More than thirty years after its founding, only three hundred French people were living at Quebec.

―――――――――― Study Exercises ――――――――――

1. (a) Samuel de Champlain founded Quebec in ――. (b) Quebec was the first ―― in North America.

2. Give two reasons why Champlain wanted the neighboring Indians to be his friends.

3. (a) How did Champlain try to help his Indian neighbors? (b) What was the result of his "help"?

4. The French never found a waterway through North America to the Pacific Ocean. (*a*) What did they gain from their exploration? (*b*) Who claimed for France all the land that drains into the Mississippi River?

5. Give two reasons why Quebec grew so slowly.

Further Study

1. List some things the French gave the Indians for their furs.

2. Why did the French want to find a waterway through North America? (Lesson 13 might help you.)

3. Why were settlers attracted to the Virginia colony more than to Quebec?

16. Plymouth Colony— the Beginning of Massachusetts

Glossary Words

independent   Pilgrims

At Jamestown and at Quebec, men came first to establish the settlements. Women came later. But the *Pilgrims*, who landed where Massachusetts is today, included men and women who brought their families with them. They did not come to the New World to get rich or to help build an empire. They came to find freedom to worship God in the way they believed was right.

The Pilgrim's story began in England. There they were called *Separatists* because they could not agree with the Church of England and had separated from it. Soon they were persecuted, and some fled to the nearby country of the Netherlands where they could worship as they chose. But there they faced a number of other things that they did not like. Being country people, they were disappointed when they were not allowed to own land and had to live in Dutch cities. They also did not want their children to lose their English ways. Even worse, they were afraid their children would be lost to the world if

Journeys of the Pilgrims

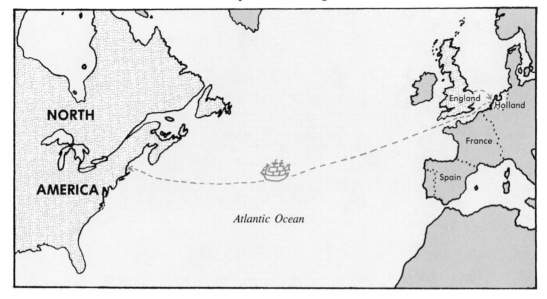

they stayed in the Netherlands.

Finally a group of Separatists decided to move to America. Besides having freedom of religion and a chance to make a good living, they would perhaps be able to convert the Indians to their faith.

In September of 1620, about a hundred men, women, and children squeezed into the little ship called the *Mayflower*. For a while they had favorable weather. But when they were halfway across the Atlantic, storms began to rock the ship. In spite of being tossed about, only one

Plymouth Colony

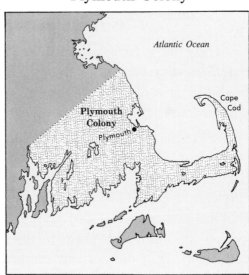

The landing of the Pilgrims at Plymouth, Massachusetts, in December 1620.

of these Pilgrims died during the two-month voyage. One child was born on the way.

When they reached land, they were farther north than they had intended to be. More storms came, forcing them to stay close to where they had landed. The king had given them permission only to settle farther south, in the Virginia colony. If they stayed where they were, who would govern them?

The men decided they would have to form their own government. Before leaving the ship, they drew up a paper stating that they would make fair laws and obey them. Forty-one men signed it. This agreement was called the *Mayflower Compact*. It gave the Pilgrims the first **independent** government in the New World. Their government did not depend on any other government.

The ship waited while the Pilgrims searched for a good place to build and to plant fields. During their exploring, they found buried treasure—not gold, but corn! Indians had stored it here. Even though the corn helped to feed the Pilgrims, they needed other kinds of food as well. In the five weeks that passed while the men searched for a good planting place, four more passengers died.

Finally, near the end of December, the *Mayflower* anchored in Plymouth

A drawing titled "Doling Out the Five Kernels of Corn"

Bay. Here they found a good, flowing spring and fields that had already been cleared. The men began building houses.

But such cold! These Englishmen were not used to it. Besides, the food supply was running low. And many of the people, sick with scurvy and other illnesses, could hardly work. At the worst time, only six or seven people were well enough to tend the sick. Nearly half the people died.

And yet by March, the thatched-roof houses stood ready for people to live in them. The men began to think of getting fields ready for planting. When the time came for the *May-flower* to return to England, the people stayed. Their life was hard, but they liked the freedom here.

All this time, the Pilgrims had not made friends with the Indians. They always had guns handy, even during church, lest Indians attack them. They had separated from the worldly Church of England, but they continued to use the weapons of this world (2 Corinthians 10:4). Then one day an Indian walked up and greeted the Pilgrims with "Welcome"—in English! His name was Samoset. He had learned a little English from fishermen who had visited New England.

Later Samoset brought his friend Squanto to the colony. Squanto knew English quite well. He had lived in Europe for a number of years. When he finally had returned to his village, eager to see his family and friends again, he was shocked. Disease had swept through the village, and everyone had died.

Squanto was happy to find that new friends had come to where his tribe had lived. He showed them how to catch fish, how to fertilize the Indian corn they planted by burying fish with it, and how to keep animals

A group of Pilgrims, always on guard, walk to church. Their muskets and Bibles carry two different messages. The guns speak of distrust and fear. The Bible teaches us to love our enemies.

from damaging their newly-planted fields. His help probably saved the Pilgrims from starving. Samoset and Squanto showed more love and trust toward the white men than the Pilgrims had showed toward the Indians.

When the Indian chief, Massasoit, came to see the governor, John Carver, Squanto served as interpreter. Massasoit and Governor Carver worked out a long-lasting peace treaty. The Indians returned tools they had stolen from the Pilgrims. The white men paid for the corn they had taken from the Indians' buried store. A friendship was started between the two groups.

That fall, when the first harvest was gathered, the Pilgrims set aside several days to rejoice and thank God for His goodness. The Indians came, bringing turkeys and venison (deer meat), and they all feasted together. Other people had kept days of thanksgiving before the Pilgrims, but the Pilgrims' Thanksgiving feast with the Indians is the one that we remember best.

Study Exercises

1. (a) Why did the Pilgrims leave England? (b) What things did they dislike about the Netherlands?
2. After sailing across the Atlantic on the (a) ——, the Pilgrims reached North America in December of (b) ——.
3. Why did the Pilgrims decide to form their own government?
4. (a) Which was worth more to the Pilgrims: gold, or the buried corn they found? (b) Why?
5. (a) What had happened to Squanto's tribe? (b) List three things Squanto helped the Pilgrims to do.
6. How did the Pilgrims show their thankfulness?

Further Study

1. How long had the settlers been at Jamestown before the Pilgrims landed at Plymouth?
2. (a) The Pilgrims signed the —— before they left the ship. (b) Why did they want an agreement before they started their colony?

17. Boston and Providence— Growing Pains in New England

Glossary Word

Puritans

The story of how Boston began is quite different from the story of Plymouth and the Pilgrims. Instead of a hundred poor people crossing the Atlantic in one ship, a thousand prosperous people came to Boston. The town they founded in 1630 was tiny compared to Boston today, but it was a strong settlement. Though the people faced hardships, and some died, they never endured terrible times of sickness and hunger such as the Pilgrims had.

The people of Boston called their settlement the Massachusetts Bay Colony. The Pilgrims now had neighbors only a few dozen miles away. Today both Boston and Plymouth are in the state of Massachusetts.

The newcomers in Boston had a religion much the same as that of the Pilgrims. However, they were not

Massachusetts Bay Colony and Providence Plantation

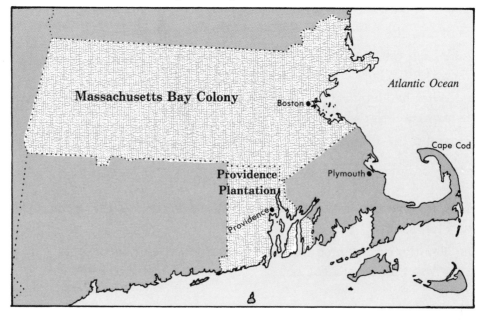

Separatists, as the Pilgrims were, but *Puritans*. This means they wanted to purify the Church of England, not separate from it. Since the Church of England had not agreed with their ideas, they had decided to come to America and have a purer church here. But like the Pilgrims of Plymouth, the Puritans saw nothing wrong with using guns to protect themselves.

In Boston, only church members could serve as colony leaders. Although not everyone in town had to be a church member, everyone had to attend the Puritan church services. For a time, things went well for the Puritans.

Then a young preacher named Roger Williams came to Massachusetts in 1631. At first the Puritans welcomed him gladly. They needed more ministers, and he was invited to preach or teach at various churches.

But within half a year, colony leaders began to frown on what Roger Williams was teaching. The people in the Plymouth and Massachusetts colonies had not paid the Indians for the land on which they settled. They had just moved in and called themselves the owners. Roger Williams thought this was wrong. He said that the colonists had no right to claim the land just because the king had given it to

Boston quickly grew into a thriving community. During the early years, people who broke the law were punished publicly.

them. The king of England did not own the land—the Indians did!

Roger Williams also taught that the colony should give the people more religious freedom. He said people of different religions should be able to worship as they believed God wanted them to, and not be forced to attend a certain church.

The Scriptures teach that the church should be separate from the government. God expects earthly rulers to keep law and order using force if necessary: "He . . . is a revenger to execute wrath upon him that doeth evil" (Romans 13:4). But Jesus said, "My kingdom is not of

The Indians received Roger Williams when he fled from Boston. Does he look prepared to live in the wintery outdoors?

to arrest Roger Williams and send him back to England. When Williams heard of this, he left his family and fled into the forest. It was a cold, snowy day in January. But he found shelter with his friends, the Indians. Later he wrote,

Lost many a time, I have had no guide,
  No house but a hollow tree!
In stormy winter night no fire,
  No food, no company.

Roger Williams and his followers finally bought land from the Indians and called their new settlement Providence Plantation. Today Providence is the capital of Rhode Island.

At Providence Plantation, anyone was welcomed regardless of his religion. Quakers, Catholics, and Baptists all could have their own churches there. Men did not have to be church members to fill government offices. In 1636, for the first time, there was a colony in America where people were not told by the government how to worship.

this world" (John 18:36). True Christians live holy lives according to God's Word, even when government leaders tell them to do otherwise (Acts 5:29).

In 1635, the leaders of the Massachusetts Bay Colony decided

Study Exercises

1. (*a*) A large group of prosperous people founded the town of ——. (*b*) What did they call their colony?
2. How were the Puritans' ideas different from the Pilgrims' ideas?
3. Name two things the Puritans did not like about Roger Williams' teaching.

4. (a) What did the Puritan leaders decide to do with Roger Williams? (b) How did he prevent them from doing this?

5. How was the Providence colony different from the Massachusetts colony?

Gaining Geographical Skills

1. Trace the outline of eastern North America from Map D in the map section. Label it "Early American Settlements."

2. Label these early settlements: Jamestown, Quebec, Plymouth, Boston, and Providence.

Further Study

1. Both the Pilgrims and the Puritans had once been part of what church?

2. Explain why Roger Williams and the Indians were good friends.

18. New Netherlands, New Sweden—New York and Log Cabins

Glossary Words

gulden   harbor

"The river hath an excellent *harbor*. There rise on either hand fertile green hills." About ten years before the Pilgrims came to America, Henry Hudson had brought this glowing report back to the Netherlands. The Hudson River he had explored empties into the Atlantic, where New York City stands today. Because of Hudson's explorations, the Dutch claimed the area and called it New Netherlands.

Five years later, in 1614, the Dutch built their first trading posts. They started buying furs from the Indians and were soon sending hundreds of beaver and deer skins back to Europe. They were more interested in getting furs than in building settlements. People were not suffering much or being persecuted in the Netherlands, so ten years passed before any families moved from the Netherlands to this fur-rich wilderness.

An artist's idea of New Amsterdam in 1643. What in the picture reminds you that New Amsterdam was founded by people from Holland?

Modern skyscrapers crowd the southern part of Manhattan Island, where New Amsterdam once began in a forest.

In order to keep up their fur trade, the Dutch tried to stay on good terms with the Indians. They paid for the land they settled on. One of the most famous purchases ever made took place in 1626 when the Dutch bought Manhattan Island for sixty *guldens* worth of trinkets. That island has thirty-one square miles of land. Today New York City's tallest skyscrapers stand on it, and no one could buy it even for billions of dollars.

The Indians probably did not realize what it meant to sell the land. But the Dutch knew they were buying a valuable island. It had an excellent harbor where ships could safely anchor. Because it was centrally located, traders from the Connecticut River Valley to the north and from the Delaware River Valley to the south would be able to meet at Manhattan Island with traders who came

New Netherlands and New Sweden

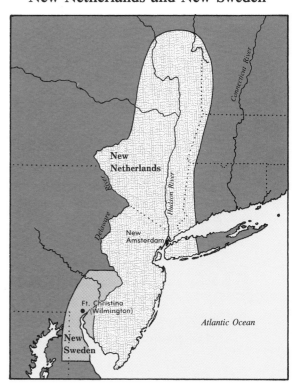

down the Hudson River. The Dutch called their new town New Amsterdam.

The Dutch were growing rich from their trade when settlers from Sweden moved into the Delaware River area. They settled the area that is now Wilmington, Delaware. The Swedes had come from a country of forests and knew how to clear timber off the land. They built little log houses like the ones they had left in Sweden. Within several years, settlers in other colonies were building log cabins of their own.

The Swedes were the first settlers in America to build log cabins.

The Dutch did not like having Swedish settlers claim land on the Delaware River. They were not pleased that the Indians began trading furs with the Swedes rather than with themselves. So they came and took control of the Swedish settlement along the Delaware. The Swedes settled down to making a living and let the Dutch rule.

But less than ten years later, in 1664, the Dutch lost control of their own colony. English warships came to New Amsterdam and demanded its surrender. The governor of New Amsterdam was Peter Stuyvesant (STY ves unt), whom people remember today for his wooden leg and hot temper. Nearly everyone in New Amsterdam thought it best to yield peaceably. They knew the great damage war would do to their town. Besides, they did not much appreciate the governor they had. Although Peter Stuyvesant declared that he would rather die than surrender, he finally gave in. Thus, New Netherlands became New York, the name we call it today.

Study Exercises

1. (*a*) Henry Hudson explored the ——— River for the Dutch. (*b*) Why were the Dutch interested in America?

2. Why did the Dutch buy Manhattan Island from the Indians instead of just claiming it for themselves?

3. Name two reasons why Manhattan Island was valuable to the Dutch.

4. (a) The ——— are known for introducing log cabins to America. (b) They settled along the ——— River.

5. (a) The ——— took over the Swedish settlement. (b) Later, the English demanded that the Dutch town of ——— surrender to them. (c) They renamed this town ———.

Further Study

1. How were the Dutch more like the French than like the English in their reasons for coming to the New World?

2. Why did the European countries try to conquer each other's colonies?

19. *Pennsylvania—Peaceful Refuge*

Glossary Words

Quakers   treaty

Quakers seemed strange to many people in England. They wore simple clothes without bright colors, and they were careful with their speech. They would not fight in the army or join the Church of England. Because of the stand they took, the Quakers were persecuted. They longed for a place where they could hold worship services in peace.

William Penn was a leader among the English Quakers. He had been thinking about starting a Quaker colony in America. Then came his opportunity. King Charles of England had owed William Penn's father a large sum of money. After William's father died, the king owed the debt to William, but his treasuries did not have enough money to pay the debt. So William Penn suggested that instead of money, the king give him land in the New World. Then William would have a place for the colony he was dreaming of.

William Penn wanted to call the area *Sylvania*, which means "woods." But the king insisted that it be named after William's father, who had been his good friend. Finally the two men agreed on *Pennsylvania*.

When the Quakers arrived in the New World in 1681, they built a little town called *Philadelphia*, which means

Quakers did not have preachers. Anyone could stand up during a service and give a message he or she believed was from God.

"brotherly love." They planned their town carefully, with broad streets that divided the town into blocks, like a checkerboard. They wanted no narrow, crooked streets like many in English cities.

William Penn respected the Indians. Even though the English king had said that William had a right to the land, William knew the Indians had been living on the land first. So he made *treaties* with the Indians and paid them for the land he wanted. William Penn wanted to "follow peace with all men" (Hebrews 12:14). The Indians knew from this fair treatment that Penn would not cheat them, and they respected him in turn.

The first settlers to come to Pennsylvania in large numbers were English people. This happened in neighboring colonies too. That is why we speak English today, and many of us live in towns with English-sounding names. It has also helped to decide what kind of clothes we wear and houses we live in.

William Penn advertised in Europe for settlers. He invited not only Englishmen like himself, but also people from other countries. He gave a special invitation to Germans, who were known as quiet, hard-working farmers. Lutherans, Moravians,

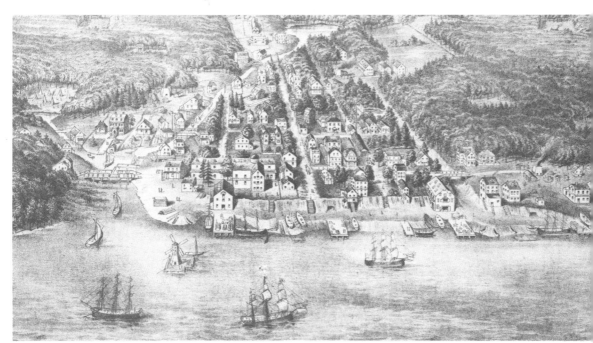

Philadelphia in 1702, twenty-one years after it was founded.

William Penn bought land from the Indians instead of taking it by force.

Early Pennsylvania Settlements

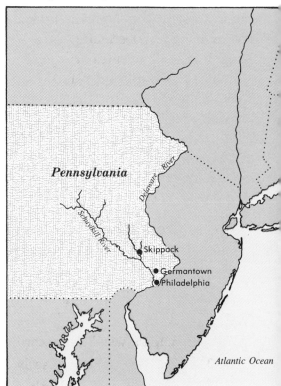

Amish, Mennonites, and many other Germans came eagerly.

In 1683, thirteen Mennonite families from Germany helped to start the settlement of Germantown near Philadelphia. At first the Mennonites worshiped with Quakers, and some of them became Quakers. But by 1690, the Mennonites at Germantown were having their own services. That year they chose William Rittenhouse as the first Mennonite minister in America.

The Mennonites who settled at Germantown had grown up in towns. Many of them were weavers or other tradesmen. In the early 1700s, Mennonite and Amish farmers from the Palatinate region of Germany arrived. These Mennonites traveled beyond Germantown and bought land to the west and north. More Mennonites settled in what is now Lancaster County, Pennsylvania, than in any other area. Descendants of the Pennsylvania Mennonites have spread to many different places in the United States and Canada.

Scotch–Irish people also came to Pennsylvania. Most of them did not care to settle near where other people already lived. They soon moved far out into the forest and cleared little farms for themselves.

Each of these groups of people, and other groups besides, brought ideas that their neighbors could learn from. This made the colonies a better place to live than if people from only one country had come to America.

Study Exercises

Answer true *or* false.

1. Quakers refused to fight in the army.
2. The Quakers were free to worship as they wanted in England.
3. The king of England paid William Penn with land in the New World.
4. *Sylvania* means "Penn's land."
5. Philadelphia was built according to a carefully made plan.
6. The Indians treated the early Pennsylvania settlers well.
7. William Penn accepted only Quakers into his colony.
8. Germantown was the first settlement in Pennsylvania.
9. Before 1690, the Mennonite ministers at Germantown preached for the Quakers.
10. More Mennonites settled in Lancaster County than at Germantown.
11. The Scotch-Irish people usually lived far away from towns.
12. Each group of people who came to America brought some valuable ideas.

Further Study

1. List several ways the Quakers were different from other Englishmen.
2. (*a*) Do you think William Penn was glad to get land instead of money? (*b*) Why?
3. Why did William Penn give a special invitation to the Germans?

20. Georgia—New Home for the Poor

No matter where you looked in England, there were poor people. Some could be seen begging at the back doors of country cottages. Some huddled in the warmth coming from open tavern doors. Tattered children played in the streets. Poor men were often in prison because they could not pay their bills.

James Oglethorpe thought this was a shame. One of his friends had been put into a prison because of debts he could not pay. James

Oglethorpe had not heard about this until it was too late to help him, and his friend had died in prison. Oglethorpe wanted to do what he could to keep such things from happening. He thought, "Wouldn't it be wonderful if poor people, especially prisoners, could go to the New World and earn a good living there?"

Many people had gone to the New World since Jamestown had begun more than a hundred years before. But the people James Oglethorpe

A gate to the Tower of London, where some English prisoners were kept. Debtors were usually kept in other prisons.

Georgia Colony

Georgia

Savannah

Atlantic Ocean

Gulf of Mexico

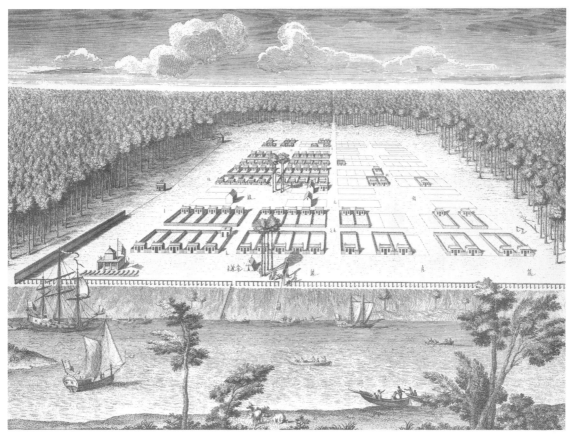

A view of Savannah in 1734, one year after its founding. The town was laid out in four sections, each with forty house lots and four sites for public buildings.

wanted to help were too poor to pay their way across the ocean. Hearing about James Oglethorpe's plan, a group of men in London agreed to pay for the expenses. They hoped that the people they helped would send enough goods back from the colony to repay them for the money they spent.

The new colony was named Georgia, after King George, who was then ruling England. The English made a treaty with the Cherokee In- dians of Georgia so that they could settle there peacefully.

Then, in 1733, James Oglethorpe arrived in Georgia with his first set- tlers. Not so many people were from debtors' prisons as he had first hoped, but there were many other poor people.

Much hard work awaited them. The settlers were given fifty-acre lots to farm. Soon it was easy to see which people were poor because they had not had work, and which ones were poor because they were lazy. The settlers with a mind to work chopped down the trees and planted Indian corn, rice, potatoes, peas, and pumpkins. But others left Georgia for settlements farther north, where life was easier.

The Bible offers no comfort to those who are poor because of laziness. "Slothfulness casteth into a deep sleep; and an idle soul shall suffer hunger" (Proverbs 19:15). But some people are poor even though they have been diligent. The Bible also says, "Whoso mocketh the poor reproacheth his Maker" (Proverbs 17:5). God commands us to work with our hands so that we may have something to give to those in need (Ephesians 4:28).

Study Exercises

1. What class of people was Georgia especially founded for?
2. (a) —— took pity on this class of people. (b) How did he want to help them?
3. (a) What kept these people from moving to the New World earlier? (b) Who agreed to help James Oglethorpe pay the expenses involved with his plan?
4. Why did the English not fight with the Indians in Georgia?
5. The first settlers arrived in Georgia in ——, over one hundred years after Jamestown was founded.

Gaining Geographical Skills

On the map that you traced for Lesson 17, add labels for these early settlements: New Amsterdam, Philadelphia, the colony of Georgia, and the Swedish settlement along the Delaware River.

Further Study

1. Men in Europe who could not pay their debts were often put into prison. Why would this cause an additional problem for them and their families?
2. Why were the men in London willing to give money to help start the colony?
3. (a) Was everyone that went to Georgia glad for a chance to live there? (b) Why or why not?

Chapter 3 Review

Reviewing What You Have Learned

A. *Write a glossary word for each definition.*

1. A settlement started by another country.
2. A protected place for ships to anchor.
3. Free from the control of others.
4. A Dutch unit of money.
5. To mistreat someone for his beliefs.
6. To speak or act for someone.
7. An agreement between two groups of people.
8. A store where goods can be bought and sold.
9. A group of people who separated from the Church of England.
10. A group of people who wanted to purify the Church of England.
11. A church that is controlled by the government.
12. Christians who baptized only believers and who later became known as Mennonites and Hutterites.

B. *Choose the correct answer to complete each sentence.*

1. Many Europeans came to America because ——
   a. life in America was very easy
   b. they wanted a chance to have a better life
   c. they knew they could find gold in America
2. The Vikings discovered America ——.
   a. while they were searching for a better route to the Far East
   b. when a storm blew one of their ships off course
   c. soon after Columbus discovered America
3. Columbus discovered America on ——.
   a. October 12, 1492
   b. April 21, 1607
   c. November 11, 1620

4. Captain John Smith helped the Jamestown settlement by ——.
   a. moving the town to a better location
   b. introducing tobacco raising
   c. requiring everyone to work for their food

5. —— became the New World's first permanent English settlement.
   a. Quebec
   b. Plymouth
   c. Jamestown

6. The —— settlers were mainly interested in trading with the Indians.
   a. French and Dutch
   b. English and Spanish
   c. Swedish and German

7. The Pilgrims left Holland because ——.
   a. they were persecuted there
   b. they did not want their children to learn worldly ways
   c. they wanted to form a government of their own

8. The Puritans disliked Roger Williams because he ——.
   a. said they should give more religious freedom to the people
   b. said they did not need to buy the land from the Indians
   c. had belonged to the Church of England

9. Providence Plantation was ——.
   a. founded by Henry Hudson
   b. the first colony in America to welcome people of any belief
   c. the first colony in America to have a representative government

10. The Dutch ——.
    a. bought Manhattan Island from the Indians because of its good location
    b. introduced log cabins to America
    c. captured New Amsterdam and renamed it New York

11. The first people to come to Pennsylvania in large numbers were the ——.
    a. German Mennonites
    b. Scotch–Irish frontiersmen
    c. English Quakers

12. Georgia was meant to be settled by ———.
    a. poor people
    b. only those who could pay for their trip to America
    c. groups of persecuted Christians

C. *Match the following dates with the events that took place during each year.*

1000,   1492,   1525,   1607,   1608,   1620

1. Columbus discovered America

2. The Pilgrims landed at Plymouth

3. Jamestown was founded

4. The Vikings landed in America

5. Quebec was founded by Champlain

6. The Anabaptists started a church of true believers

So Far This Year

Choose the correct answers. See how many you can give without looking back.

1. North America is in the (Northern, Southern) and (Eastern, Western) hemispheres.

2. Canada is (smaller, larger) than the United States, but it has (fewer, more) people.

3. Match.

   a. Northeast Indians
   b. Southeast Indians
   c. Great Plains Indians
   d. Southwest Indians
   e. Intermountain and California Indians
   f. Northwest Coastal Indians
   g. Arctic peoples

   1. made large wooden houses, totem poles, and log canoes.
   2. included Inuit and Aleuts.
   3. included the best-known Indian tribe—the Iroquois.
   4. built pueblos and irrigated crops.
   5. were quick to learn white men's ways.
   6. lived in teepees and hunted buffalo.
   7. gathered seeds and nuts and made baskets.

4. (Christopher Columbus, Amerigo Vespucci) discovered America while trying to find a new route to the Far East.

5. Jamestown was the first lasting (Dutch, English, Spanish) settlement in North America.

6. The Pilgrims, Quakers, and many other groups moved to America in search of (an easy life, freedom of worship, gold).

Most of the early North American settlers lived on farms. Farming in the new land was hard work, but the settlers were free and able to own land.

Chapter 4

LIFE IN COLONIAL AMERICA

Early North American Settlements

Quebec

Quebec

Montreal

Nova
Scotia

Port
Royal

Boston
Plymouth
Providence

Pennsylvania

Skippack
New
Amsterdam
Philadelphia
Germantown
Ft. Christina
(Wilmington)

Jamestown

Virginia

Georgia

Savannah

21. French Canada—
Rugged Life and Rented Farms

While the English were settling lands from New England to Georgia, what were the French doing? They were settling lands farther to the north, where Champlain and other Frenchmen had explored.

Some of these lands lay along the St. Lawrence River. The French farmers each wanted some land along the river because the river was the main highway for everyone. So they agreed that everyone should have a long, narrow farm, with one end touching the river. Then they built their houses along the river, where they could be close together. This helped the families to feel more neighborly and secure. Even today, long, narrow fields stretch away from the St. Lawrence River, just as they did hundreds of years ago.

Other lands the French settled lay where Nova Scotia, New Brunswick, and Prince Edward Island are today.

The early French settlers each farmed a long, narrow strip along the St. Lawrence River. Many of these narrow fields are still in Quebec today.

An old French house. Only important men in the early French settlements could afford a large, stone house such as this.

In these settlements, Frenchmen also farmed land near the water's edge, for there were no good roads across the country.

Winters are long and cold in French Canada. Colonial families banked their houses with hay to keep out the cold. They built steep roofs to shed the heavy snow.

French colonial homes were small, having only one or two rooms. The great stone fireplaces looked cozy, but did a poor job of heating the house. Though the area in front of the fireplace was very warm, the opposite end of the room was chilly. At meal times, adults usually sat on home-made wooden chairs. Children often sat on pine chests that served as benches. Meals were simple—potatoes and cabbage from the black pot in the fireplace, a crock of milk, and a loaf of brown bread.

The French were Catholics. They respected their priests and often asked them for advice. Usually a priest was the only educated man in a settlement. He would write things for the people and read public announcements that came.

The French settlers were not as free as the English settlers. The land belonged to the king, who appointed a man to keep charge of each settlement. This man built a mill and a large bake oven for the settlement. He set apart land for church use. The rest of the land was for the settlers' use—but they could only rent it, not buy it. However, the settlers owned their houses and animals. And they were glad that the rent was easier to pay than the rent they would have paid in France.

The early French used simple, homemade furniture. Corn hangs from the ceiling to dry.

=== Study Exercises ===

1. (*a*) The French settled lands —— of the English colonies. (*b*) Some of them settled along the —— River. (*c*) Why did these Frenchmen make their farms long and narrow?

2. Other Frenchmen settled lands that are now (*a*) ——, (*b*) ——, and (*c*) ——.

3. Name several ways the French prepared for the hard winters.

4. (*a*) The French were of the —— religion, and they respected their priests. (*b*) The priest was often the only —— man in a settlement.
5. What were the English settlers allowed to do that the French settlers were not?

Further Study

1. The early French settlements began slowly. What did the French settlers begin doing that helped their settlements grow? (Lesson 15 might help you.)
2. Name two things that show the French took their Catholic beliefs seriously, even though the beliefs were not based on the Bible.

22. New England—Farming Fishermen

Glossary Words

hornbook   indentured servant

New England! The name reminds many people of calendar pictures showing little towns and farms nestled among beautiful, green hills. Beautiful as the pictures are, farming on hills is not easy. Besides, the soil in much of New England is poor. Not long after the first settlers came to New England, they began turning to other work besides farming to make a living.

The people discovered that the Atlantic Ocean near their shores had rich fishing areas. One reason for this is that along the shore of New England the ocean is shallow many miles out from the coast. Many fish live in this area of shallow ocean. The New Englanders caught more fish than they could eat. They dried and salted the extra fish and shipped them to England.

New England men who continued farming found that their best crop was grass. They could raise many cows and sheep. New England still produces much milk and butter, as well as eggs.

Making animal products was not easy. To produce butter in those days,

New Englanders found good fishing along their coasts.

everything from milking the cow to churning the butter had to be done by hand. In the same way, hours and hours were needed to turn wool into good cloth. People had to clean dirt out of it, comb it to straighten the fibers, spin it into thread, wash it, and then either weave it or knit it.

Like the people in Georgia, some who lived in New England had not been able to afford their passage there. They had depended on other persons to pay their way across the ocean. Now these settlers owed a debt to those persons. To pay it off, the debtors would work for them, usually from four to seven years. Anyone who came to America under such an agreement was called an *indentured servant.*

An indentured servant was not a slave, but neither was he free to leave his master and work for anyone else. Some indentured servants were treated better than others. A master who treated his servant well gave him food, clothing, a place to live, and even some schooling during the winter.

Schools were important to the people of New England. They wanted everyone to be able to read the Bible for himself. They required all villages, if they were big enough, to have a school. However, life was hard in New England, and the children had much work to do at home. They could not spend as much time in school as children do today. Also they did not

A colonial New England kitchen. Find the following items in the picture: butter churn, spinning wheel, candlesticks, broom, irons, mirror, drinking gourd, snowshoes, onions, and musket. Notice beside the fireplace the iron door to a bake oven, where pies and bread are baked. The little metal box with a door is a foot warmer. Filled with hot coals, it helped keep feet warm at home, in the sleigh or carriage, and at church.

have many books and papers to read. Since paper was scarce, children beginning to read were given a **hornbook**, which was actually a piece of wood with a sheet of paper pasted onto it. A clear covering of horn protected the paper. From it the children learned the ABCs.

Religion was also important in New England. Often the people would sit listening to a sermon two or three hours long. And no one was supposed to whisper or fall asleep. Men were appointed to watch over the congregation. If anyone fell asleep, one of those men would wake him up. Although the services might seem long to many people today, we should not think the New Englanders suffered because of it. They expected long sermons, and they did not think a preacher should wear out after just half an hour!

During this time, one of New England's most able preachers was Jonathan Edwards. People still study a sermon he preached called "Sinners in the Hands of an Angry God." During the sermon, people all over the church could be heard weeping. But Jonathan Edwards could also speak warmly of God's kindness and love. Because he was a man of much prayer, he helped to start a revival that is now called the Great Awakening.

A hornbook

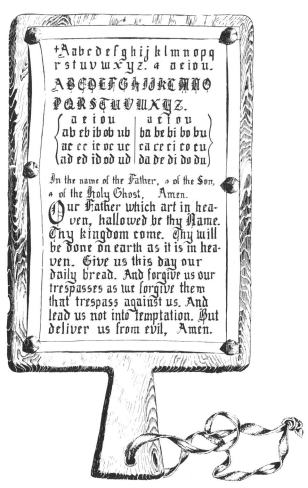

George Whitefield (HWIHT feeld) came from England in 1740 to stir up the revival. He was a lively preacher who spoke not only in churches but also in fields, in barns, and from farm wagons. His loud, clear voice carried surprisingly far across the open air. People everywhere gave their hearts to the Lord. Other praying people, and preachers less famous than

Whitefield, also helped to spread God's Word. The Great Awakening was still growing!

In fact, people began to get so noisy and excited at meetings that sensible Christians began to be concerned. "Will people soon begin to think that excitement is the most important part of religion?" they asked. Jonathan Edwards, trying to be fair, said that people should not be too emotional in their meetings. But he also said that the power of God does stir people's feelings.

Jesus told a parable about a sower to show how different people respond to God's Word. Some people refuse to listen at all. Some get excited when they hear the Word, but they lose interest when troubles come. Some hear the Word, but they are too busy with the things of this world to obey. God wants all people who hear His Word to become useful, obedient servants.

New England farmers lived in villages, but each had his own farm buildings such as these. Can you identify each building? The fields belonging to this farmer may not be close to his buildings. The countryside was divided so that good and poor land would be shared.

============ Study Exercises ============

1. (a) Why did some people of New England need something besides farming to make a living? (b) Why did they choose fishing?
2. What kind of products did most of the New England farmers produce?
3. What was an indentured servant?
4. (a) Why were schools important to the New England settlers? (b) Why did their children have less time to go to school than you have?
5. (a) —— was a preacher who helped to start the Great Awakening. (b) What other preacher helped the Great Awakening to spread?

Further Study

1. Why were animal products harder to make during the time of the early settlers than they are today?
2. How did the sermon "Sinners in the Hands of an Angry God" affect the listeners?
3. (a) What began to concern some Christians? (b) How did Jonathan Edwards try to take care of the concern?

23. *Pennsylvania—Life in the Middle Colonies*

Pennsylvania and nearby colonies—New York, New Jersey, Delaware, and Maryland—were called the middle colonies. Life in the middle colonies was never as difficult as it had been for the first settlers in New England. The soil was more fertile, and summers were longer. Also, in Pennsylvania the Quakers kept peace with the Indians so that no fighting took place for many years. Still, for most people, life was not easy.

Living in a log cabin might sound exciting to you, but it really was not. A cabin, with its small windows, was dark. If it had no wooden floor, it was dirty and damp. Most of the heat from the fireplace went up the chimney. Families were glad to move into a better house when they could.

The better houses were simple too, with perhaps two rooms upstairs and two downstairs. These houses were heated with stoves, which did a better job than the fireplaces. Dishes and spoons were often made of wood. A few things, such as the big cooking pot, were made of brass or iron.

The people who had a spring near their house built a springhouse to serve as a kind of refrigerator. The cold spring water kept their food cool. Many of them built a smokehouse where they could smoke meat to

The Christian Herr house in Lancaster, Pennsylvania, is the oldest Mennonite meetinghouse in America. Christian Herr, the son of Hans Herr, built this house in 1719. Hans Herr was the leader of the congregation that met here for Sunday worship.

preserve it. Most people also had a woodshed and an outdoor bake oven.

Without canning or freezing, people had a hard time getting good, fresh food all winter long. Besides smoking food, they sometimes salted it, because salt is an excellent preserver. They dried some foods such as apples and beef.

The clothing of most people was simple. They often wove linen and wool into a homemade cloth called linsey-woolsey, and then they made clothes from it.

Many of the people were farmers.

They did most of their sowing, harvesting, and other work by hand. For work that animals could do, they often used oxen. An ox was slow but strong, and ate only half as much as a horse.

Life was hard. But then, in any other country of the world, people had a hard life too. Most Pennsylvanians were glad that they or their parents had left Europe and had come to this land. Here, if they worked hard, they could offer their children a better life than they would have had in Europe.

Like the people of New England, many people in Pennsylvania were interested in sending their children to school. Schools were operated by the church or the parents. Often the minister taught school during the week, and on Sunday he used the schoolhouse as a church building. Schools were not operated by the government until much later. Schools were one-room buildings made of logs notched at the corners, just like people's houses. The children sat on backless benches. Drinking water

Schools were important in colonial days. The children standing in front of the teacher will recite the lesson they have memorized. Notice the backless benches, the log walls, and the large fireplace.

came from a bucket carried from the well, and everyone drank from the same tin dipper. In winter, the classroom was hot near the fireplace and cold on the other side of the room. But learning to read and write made the discomforts worthwhile. Books were special treasures in those days, because there was not a big supply of books, as you would find in a modern school.

One of the best-remembered teachers in early Pennsylvania was Christopher Dock. He taught differently from many other teachers of his time. Although they taught the children to sit still, to read, and to write, not all teachers really cared about the children or gave them special encouragement when they needed it.

But Christopher Dock treated the children as if they were his own. He taught them to read the Bible, and he tried to teach them to fear God and obey His Word out of love for Him. It was his habit to pray for the children each day after school was over. One evening when he did not come home, friends found him at school on his knees. He had died while praying for his students.

Study Exercises

1. List several things that made life in the middle colonies somewhat easier than life in the New England colonies.
2. List four ways the colonists kept and preserved food.
3. Why were most Pennsylvanians glad they or their parents had moved to America?
4. List several ways early Pennsylvania schools were different from your school.
5. How was Christopher Dock different from most teachers of his time?

Further Study

1. Why did most people have simple houses and clothing?
2. What were schoolhouses used for besides regular school classes?

24. Virginia and Maryland— Pioneers Moving South

Glossary Words

circuit rider   pioneer

frontier   populated

If you are like most people, you feel a little sorry to see a beautiful farm being sold in order to build houses there. Long before Pennsylvania was as *populated* as it is now, some people felt sorry to see so much forest cleared to make farms. They wanted to go farther into the forest, where they would not see so many neighbors' houses and where a dozen people would not be walking past their door every day.

Plenty of land lay to the west, but settlers in Pennsylvania found it hard to reach because the Appalachian Mountains blocked their way. Some of the settlers in Pennsylvania turned south into western Maryland and Virginia. Many settlers from eastern Maryland and Virginia were also moving west.

The people of the backwoods lived much more simply than richer people closer to the Atlantic coast. If they had money, people who lived near cities could buy clothing and furniture from England. Not the people of the backwoods. They carried with

Pioneers Move South

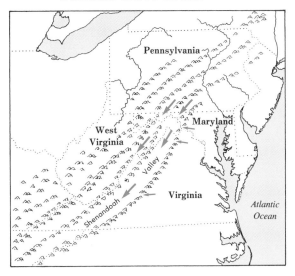

them a gun, a knife or two, an ax, a frying pan, and maybe a few other things they could not make. But nearly everything else—their houses, furniture, and clothing—they provided for themselves.

Their food was simple too. One food they often ate was called "hasty pudding" because it could be made in a hurry. It was simply cooked corn pudding.

Since the settlers needed money

A typical colonial cabin. This photograph was taken in more modern times, but early settlers' cabins looked much like this. Life changed slowly in these isolated clearings.

to buy a few things that they could not make for themselves, they needed to raise a crop to sell. Often this crop was tobacco.

Pioneers not only lived differently from other people, they also thought differently. Most of them were proud to be out on the edges of white people's settlements. They liked being able to live as they pleased, without having to obey any laws made by others. This got them into trouble sometimes when the government did make some laws that frontiersmen were supposed to obey. The Scriptures command everyone to "be subject unto the higher powers" (Romans 13:1).

But people on the *frontier* also knew how to work together. When a family built a house, neighbors would come together to help. A city dweller of the East might not know who lived just a few houses down the street. But a man on the frontier knew his neighbors for miles around because there were so few of them, and because he helped them and they helped him.

However, people on the frontier spent most of their time just getting food, clothing, and shelter. They suffered because they had almost no time to learn from books or read the Bible. Schools were hard to find. So were churches and preachers. A few ministers cared about the spiritual needs of people on the frontier. They traveled on horseback from country church to country church, preaching. They knew that everyone needs to hear the Gospel, even those who are very busy or who live far away from everyone else. These men were called *circuit riders*.

Circuit-riding preachers rode or walked from settlement to settlement in the sparsely populated wilderness. They traveled year round, through springtime beauty, winter barrenness, thunderstorms, and blizzards.

Study Exercises

1. (*a*) Why did some settlers want to go farther into the forest? (*b*) Why did the ones who moved from Pennsylvania go south instead of west?
2. (*a*) What did these pioneers take with them when they moved? (*b*) How did they get their houses, furniture, and clothing?
3. Name two reasons why people on the frontier knew their neighbors better than many people of the East did.
4. Why were schools, churches, and preachers hard to find on the frontier?
5. What was done to meet the frontier people's spiritual needs?

Further Study

1. Not everyone moved to the frontier. List some reasons why some people would have wanted to stay in the East.
2. Why were there fewer laws for the frontier people?

25. The South—Plantation Homes

Glossary Words

indigo   revolt

plantation   slavery

Have you ever wondered what life was like for people who lived on a southern plantation? Their mansions had broad porches with tall white pillars, and they were surrounded by large trees and well-kept gardens. Often a river ran close by, where boats could bring supplies and pick up farm products from the *plantation*. The owner's family had plenty of time, after their work was done, for music and dancing with well-dressed company.

But these people's life was not as pleasant as some people today might think. One big worry was the fear that their slaves would *revolt*. Plantation owners bought and sold slaves like animals, so how could they expect loyalty from the slaves? Besides, a

Most Southern plantation mansions were built near a river. This is Mount Vernon, the home of George Washington.

*Children of planta-
tion owners often had
special tutors to lead
them in their studies.
How was their schooling
different from the
schooling in the north-
ern colonies?*

life of sin is never as fun as it might appear. The Scriptures say, "The way of transgressors is hard" (Proverbs 13:15).

Little cottages for slaves stood near the big mansion. Perhaps you think of slaves as spending most of their time picking cotton. But in the early days of the South, cotton was not as important as it became later. Tobacco, rice, and *indigo* were important crops. In some areas, sugar cane was too. Besides working in the fields, slaves washed clothes, tended horses, and served as blacksmiths, cooks, and maids.

Schools for plantation owners' children were not the same as those for children in the North. Southerners lived too far apart for children from many families to attend the same school. Instead, the children were usually taught at home. As they grew older, some of them went to schools in Europe. Most slave children did not go to school at all.

Why did people in the South live so differently from people in New England? For one thing, the fertile land and long summers encouraged the people of the South to have large farms. For another, their religion was different. Most people in New England were Puritans who lived by strict rules, but many Southerners belonged to the Church of England, which allowed its members to live as they pleased. Reading the Bible and doing good deeds were not so important to plantation owners. Neither did *slavery* bother their consciences as much as it would have bothered most Puritans. The Scriptures command us to do what is right, not because of rules, but because we love God and our fellow men (Matthew 22:37–40).

Do not think that plantation owners and slaves were the only people who lived in the South. Many other people lived in towns or on small farms and did not own slaves. Still others lived back in the hills in simple little houses, as some people do today.

Study Exercises

1. The large farms of the South were called ——.
2. Why were southern plantations often built close to rivers?
3. (*a*) What crops did the slaves raise for their master? (*b*) What other work did they do?
4. (*a*) Why were the plantation owners' children taught at home? (*b*) What additional schooling did some of the children receive? (*c*) What was the reason that the masters did not provide schools for the slave children?
5. Give two ways in which the Southerners who belonged to the Church of England believed differently than the Puritans of New England.
6. Not all Southerners lived on plantations. Where did the others live?

Further Study

1. (*a*) Copy Luke 6:31. (*b*) Did the slave masters follow this command? (*c*) Whom were these plantation owners mainly concerned about?
2. Name one fear that worried the slave owners.
3. What do the Scriptures say about those who transgress (break) God's laws?

Chapter 4 Review

Reviewing What You Have Learned

A. *Write a glossary word for each definition.*

1. A large farm.
2. The area along the edge of a settled region.
3. Someone who pays a debt by working for a certain length of time.
4. A plant used to make blue dye.
5. An early one-page reader.
6. Filled with people.
7. The practice of owning people.
8. A settler in unclaimed territory.

B. *Choose the correct answer to complete each sentence.*

1. The French who settled along the St. Lawrence River ———.
   a. were strict Puritans
   b. owned their own land
   c. built their houses near the river on long, narrow farms

2. Some New Englanders began fishing because ———.
   a. they needed something for their indentured servants to do
   b. their land was not very good for farming
   c. they were producing too many animal products

3. Jonathan Edwards helped to start ———.
   a. the Great Awakening
   b. the early Pennsylvania schools
   c. the practice of using springhouses to keep food cool

4. Most Pennsylvanians were glad they or their parents had moved to America because ———.
   a. the Quakers had defeated the Indians
   b. they were able to offer their children a better life
   c. their children were not required to go to school

5. —— was one of the best-remembered teachers in early Pennsylvania.
   a. Christopher Dock
   b. George Whitefield
   c. William Penn

6. Some of the settlers decided to move farther into the forest because they ——.
   a. did not like to help their neighbors
   b. wanted to find an easier life
   c. wanted to live where there were fewer people and more trees

7. —— helped to meet the spiritual needs of the frontier people.
   a. The large number of churches
   b. Circuit riders
   c. Religious books

8. In the early days of the South, slaves ——.
   a. did most of the work on the plantation
   b. mainly raised cotton
   c. only raised crops

9. The southern plantation owners ——.
   a. had stricter views than the people of the North
   b. did not believe in slavery
   c. taught their children at home

Gaining Geographical Skills

1. Trace Map D in the map section. Label it "French and English Settlements in North America."

2. Color the French settlements one color and the English settlements another color.

3. Label the colonies that are labeled on the map in Lesson 21.

So Far This Year

Choose the correct answers. See how many you can give without looking back.

1. North America is in the (Northern, Southern) and (Eastern, Western) hemispheres.

2. Seasons in the (Southern, Eastern) Hemisphere are opposite from those in the Northern Hemisphere.

3. Temperatures are mild or moderate in most areas of (Canada, the United States).

4. Christopher Columbus discovered America while trying to find a new route to the (Near East, Far East).

5. The first lasting English settlement in North America was (Boston, Jamestown, New York).

6. The first lasting French settlement in North America was (Quebec, Ottawa, Montreal).

7. The (English, French) mainly set up trading posts, but the (English, French) established farms and towns.

8. The Dutch bought (Boston, Manhattan Island) from the Indians.

9. Life in the middle colonies was (easier, more difficult) than life in the New England colonies.

10. (Slaves, Indians) did much of the work on large southern plantations.

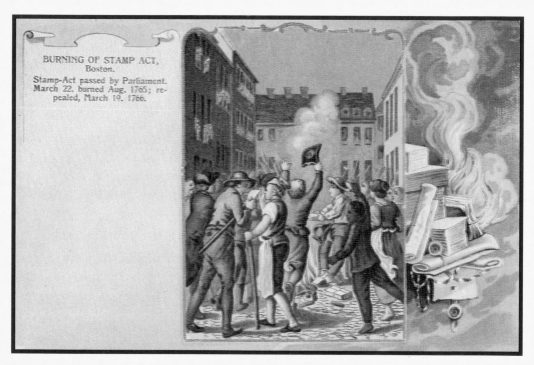

Some of the colonists did not want to be controlled and taxed by Great Britain. They burned the Stamp Act papers in the streets.

CHAPTER 5

THE STRUGGLE
TO GOVERN
NORTH AMERICA

26. How the French and Spanish Treated the Indians

Glossary Word

wigwam

We have already looked at ways English settlers treated the Indians. How did the French treat them?

The first French traders and trappers to venture into Indian country did not disturb the Indians very much. They did not clear land for farms but lived much as the Indians themselves did. They tried to make friends with the Indians because they wanted to trade with them.

The Indians brought their winter's catch of furs to trading posts and took metal, glass, and cloth goods home. They were happy for iron kettles because they lasted longer than their own clay or bark vessels. The knives they received in trade were sharper than their stone or bone tools. Guns from the white men were more powerful than bows and arrows.

However, dishonest traders began using liquor to cheat the Indians. They persuaded the Indians to trade furs for liquor rather than for the clothes and gunpowder they needed. Once the Indians were drunk, cheating them on the price of their furs was easy. The Scriptures say, "Woe unto him that giveth his neighbour drink" (Habakkuk 2:15).

Indian families suffered much misery because of "fire water," as they called it. Husbands who were usually kind to their wives became cruel when drink destroyed their good sense. Quiet, careful people became wild fighters. Some Indians who saw what drink was doing to their people pleaded with white men to stop the liquor trade. But the traders were making so much money from it that they never stopped.

Other Frenchmen who had contact with the Indians were Roman Catholic friars. To win the Indians, they lived in their *wigwams*, traveled with them, and taught them Catholic doctrines.

However, these friars found it very difficult to convert the Indians. Medicine men, who had been the main Indian leaders, tried to keep people from respecting the Catholic teachers. Many of the people scorned the friars and tormented other Indians who accepted their teachings. Sometimes they tortured and killed the

Living quarters for Indians who had joined the Catholic Church

Courtyard for non-Catholic Indians

Catholic Church and living quarters for priests

A restored French Catholic mission among the Huron Indians, known as Saint Marie.

friars themselves. The Indians who received baptism were mostly sick people, old people, and babies.

The Spanish sent out Catholic friars too. Far away in the hot, dry Southwest, Spanish soldiers and priests went into the deserts and mountains to start Spanish settlements where Texas, New Mexico, Arizona, and California are now. These settlements were called missions, but they were not like the missions we know. They included forts for the soldiers who kept order.

Instead of trying to make friends with the Indians as the French had, the Spanish simply moved in and took charge. They forced Indians to tend crops and herd cattle. They baptized Indians whether they liked it or not. This was not according to God's plan for His people. The Scriptures say, "For whosoever shall call upon the name of the Lord shall be saved" (Romans 10:13). No one can change another person's heart by forcing him to be baptized. Each person must come to God by his own choice.

The missions grew rich. They had large herds of cattle grazing around their beautiful buildings. Fields of wheat and orchards were irrigated from nearby streams.

But the Indians did not like being

A Catholic mission at Santa Barbara, California. The Spanish built many such missions in what is now the southwestern United States.

treated as slaves. Even though they had been baptized and had been told not to practice their Indian ceremonies, many Indians still practiced them secretly. Some Indians did not cooperate with the Catholics at all but attacked them from time to time.

Finally, in 1680, hundreds of Indians rose up in a great rebellion. They destroyed the missions, killed some of the Spaniards, and drove the rest out of the country. Soon hardly any Indians remained Catholic. They returned to their old way of life until the Spaniards returned years later.

Study Exercises

1. (a) Why did the Indians appreciate the first French traders and trappers? (b) How were the Indians cheated by some of the Frenchmen?
2. How did the French friars try to win the Indians to Catholic beliefs?
3. (a) Where did the Spanish establish outposts? (b) What two kinds of people did they send there?
4. Why were the Spanish able to baptize more Indians than the French?
5. How did the Indians show that they had not accepted the Catholic religion?

Further Study

1. Why did the French continue to sell liquor even after some of the Indians pleaded with them to stop?
2. The Catholic friars and priests did not teach everything that Jesus commanded. Read Matthew 28:18–20. Christ commands Christian missionaries to teach (a) ——— nations to observe (b) ——— the things He has commanded.

27. Indians and Settlers Break Their Friendship

Glossary Word

nonresistant

The settlers and Indians in Pennsylvania lived in peace for many years after William Penn founded the colony. The first settlers had tried to deal fairly with the Indians. The Indians remembered that William Penn had always paid them for the Indian land he wanted. One time he and the Indians had arranged that several men would walk for three days to mark off the amount of land he would receive. William stopped them after a day and a half.

But after William died, his son asked the Indians if he could have the rest of the land the Indians had promised his father. When the Indians agreed, Thomas hired three of the fastest runners he could find to "walk" the remaining day and a half. The Indians knew very well they were being cheated.

After the Indians had been cheated a number of times, they changed their minds about their old friends and began to fight the settlers. Some settlers, of course, were still fair-minded and friendly. But the Indians did not always know or care which white people were friendly and

which were not. When Indians burned cabins and scalped settlers, honest and gentle people like the Jacob Hochstetler family suffered along with their troublemaking neighbors.

William Penn's son had cheated the Indians; his grandson went a step further. He paid frontiersmen to kill Indians and take their scalps.

One event will illustrate how much some people hated all Indians. In Lancaster County, Pennsylvania, the number of Conestoga Indians had shrunk to fewer than fifty. They lived in peace with the white people, making brooms and weaving baskets. But some men from farther west heard how the Indians were accepted by their neighbors. This angered them because they knew that other Indians had killed white settlers. They thought all Indians should be treated as enemies. One day in 1763 they came to the tiny Indian village in Lancaster County and murdered every person they found.

Shocked, the people of the community took the remaining Indians and put them in the town jail for protection from the fierce white men. But

This sketch shows one way early settlers barred (locked) their doors. The latch could be easily lifted when the latchstring was outside. But when the latchstring was pulled inside, the door was locked.

the Paxton boys, as they were called, found out that the Indians were in the jail. They broke in and murdered every Indian there, including old people and children.

But usually the story of peace-loving people had a happy ending. You may have read the long poem "The Unbarred Door." It tells of a settler who left his door unbarred at night as a way of showing friendship to his Indian neighbors. One night after hearing that angry Indians were nearby, the man's wife persuaded him to bar the door. But then he could not sleep, so he finally got up and unbarred the door again. That night Indians did come, ready to kill. But before they attacked, they tried the door, just to see how the settler felt toward them. It opened. The Indians left the settler and his wife sleeping peacefully, and he never knew until years later how close he had come to death that night.

A Noble Pattern of Nonresistance

One night in the fall of 1757, the Jacob Hochstetler family was awakened by their barking dog. One of the sons, Jacob, opened the door to look out, but quickly closed it again when a bullet struck his leg. From the windows the family could see eight to ten Indians standing near their outdoor oven.

The Hochstetlers lived near Northkill Creek, about thirty miles north of Lancaster, Pennsylvania. Only the nearby Blue Mountains separated them from Indian lands.

Joseph and Christian, two other sons who lived at home, grabbed their guns. The Hochstetlers had plenty of bullets and gunpowder, and they might have been able to keep the Indians out. But their nonresistant Amish father would not let his sons shoot. "It is not right to kill others," he said firmly, "even to save ourselves." Jacob Hochstetler loved his family. He wanted to spare them from danger and death. But Jacob knew Jesus had taught His disciples to "love your enemies, bless them that curse you, [and] do good to them that hate you" (Matthew 5:44). Jacob would not allow his sons to return "evil for evil" (1 Peter 3:9).

The next hours were filled with horror. First the Indians set the house on fire. The Hochstetlers retreated to the cellar and sprinkled cider on the spots that began burning through the floor above them. Finally, they could stand the heat no longer. Looking out and seeing no Indians, they crawled out a window. But one young Indian was still in the orchard. He shouted, and the other Indians quickly returned. They killed Jacob's wife, his son Jacob, and his daughter. Then they marched Jacob and his sons Joseph and Christian over the mountains and into the wilderness.

According to an old story, Mrs. Hochstetler had once turned away a group of Indians who asked for food. If this is true, it could explain why the Indians were especially cruel to her. However, during this time the Indians and the French were at war against the English. Many innocent people on both sides were killed. The Indians, like the white men, did evils during war that they likely would not have done in times of peace.

The Indians separated the three captives, and during the next several years the Hochstetlers rarely if ever saw each other. The Indians adopted them as brothers and taught them to live as Indians. The boys quickly adjusted to their new life, but their father longed for his old home.

A number of years later Jacob managed to escape and find his way back home. The Indians returned his sons after the war, although by then Joseph and Christian hesitated to leave their Indian friends. They often visited the Indians in later years.

Jacob Hochstetler left an outstanding example of nonresistance. Today he has thousands of descendants among the Amish and Mennonites.

——————————————— Study Exercises ———————————————

1. (a) What is one thing William Penn did to show the Indians that he wanted to be fair? (b) How did Thomas Penn show that he was not like his father?
2. (a) How did the Indians respond to being cheated? (b) Why was this unfair to some of the settlers?
3. What does being nonresistant mean? (You may check the glossary if you need help.)
4. William Penn's grandson paid frontiersmen to —— the Indians.
5. Why did the frontiersmen kill the peaceful Indians in Lancaster County?
6. (a) How did the couple in the poem "The Unbarred Door" show their friendship toward the Indians? (b) How did the Indians respond to that friendship?

Further Study

1. This lesson shows us that both the settlers and the Indians were sometimes unfair. (a) Give two examples that show the settlers were not fair to the Indians. (b) Give one example that shows the Indians were not fair to the settlers.
2. This lesson also shows that some settlers and some Indians did respect each other. (a) Give two examples of settlers besides William Penn who were kind to the Indians. (b) Give one example of Indians who respected that kindness.

28. The French and Indian War

Glossary Word

empire

During the 1700s, two great *empires* were running an unfriendly race in the New World. Great Britain (England) claimed land from Georgia to New England. France claimed land farther north around the St. Lawrence River. Both empires also claimed huge areas besides these. In some places, Great Britain and France claimed the same land.

An important part of this land lay in the Ohio River Valley. Many fur-bearing animals lived in this valley, and the Ohio River itself served as a highway. Whoever controlled the river controlled the traffic on it. Both the British and the French knew that if the other nation controlled the river, their own free travel there would be cut off.

Before the French and Indian War   After the French and Indian War

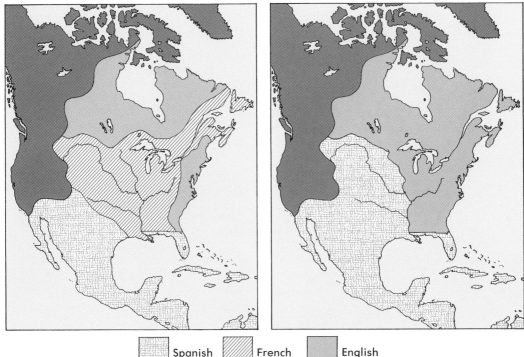

Spanish   French   English

In 1753 the British sent a young officer named George Washington to inform the French that they were building forts on land that belonged to Great Britain. But the French paid no attention to the warning. They built Fort Duquesne (doo KAYN) where two rivers join to form the Ohio River. Pittsburgh, Pennsylvania, stands there today.

In 1755 the British sent soldiers to capture Fort Duquesne. But before they reached the fort, Frenchmen and Indians shot at them from behind trees and bushes, and the British were badly defeated.

A battle fought at Quebec, Canada, in 1759 finally decided which side won the war. The fort at Quebec sat high on a cliff next to the St. Lawrence River. It was hard to at-tack, and the French felt secure. But one night the British found a way to sneak up the cliff. The next morning the French were shocked to find the British army standing just outside Quebec, ready to fight!

During the battle, both the British and the French commanders were badly wounded, and both of them died soon after. The British won the battle. It was the turning point of the war.

When the war ended, the French had lost a great area of land. In 1763 they agreed to give up the land that France had claimed in North America. New France would now belong to Great Britain.

Even before the war, the British and French had fought over Acadia, an area in Canada we now call Nova

The city of Quebec was built on a cliff overlooking the St. Lawrence River.

Scotia. Sometimes the British claimed it, sometimes the French. Finally, when the land fell into British hands, the British decided to scatter the Frenchmen who lived in Acadia so that in a war the Acadians would not help the French army. The French people living in Acadia were forced to leave their houses, their farm animals, and the land that had belonged to their forefathers. British ships took them to New York, to Pennsylvania, and to other places.

But after the French and Indian War was over, the British were more kind. They wanted the French people to be content with their new British rulers, so they allowed them to keep their old ways of doing things. The French were permitted to continue speaking French and worshiping in Catholic churches.

Suppose the French had won the war. Things would probably be different today. As it is now, we have a mostly English-speaking North America. A fairly small group of people, mostly in Quebec, speaks French. If the French had won, we might have a mostly French-speaking North America, with an English-speaking area along the eastern seacoast.

If the French had won, would they have allowed the British colonists the freedoms that the British allowed them? Would they have persecuted

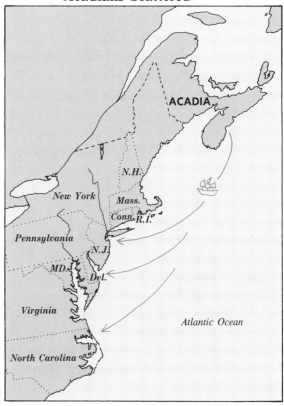

Acadians Scattered

people who believed differently than they did? We do not know. But it is fairly safe to think that North America would be mostly Roman Catholic, as Quebec is today. We do know it was God who allowed the British to win at this time, although we do not know all of His reasons.

What part did the Indians have in the French and Indian War? Many of them fought on the French side, for the French had won them with gifts and friendly talk. Besides, the Indians liked the French because they did not spoil Indian hunting grounds. Many Frenchmen trapped and hunted like the Indians. They did not cut down the forests to clear farmland as the English colonists did.

On the other hand, the British had powerful Indian friends too. The Iroquois had not forgotten Champlain and his guns. They still hated the French and any Indians friendly to them.

Both the French and the British told the Indians that if they won the war, they would give the Indians land for hunting. After the war, the British government made a law that settlers should not go west of the Appalachian Mountains, because the land there belonged to the Indians. But it was easier to make this law than to keep white settlers off Indian lands.

Study Exercises

1. Why did both the British and the French want to control the Ohio River?
2. (a) Who was sent to warn the French who were building Fort Duquesne? (b) What happened when the British tried to capture the fort?
3. Other battles were fought between the French and the British. (a) What finally determined who won the war? (b) What did the French agree to give Britain?
4. (a) How had the British treated the Frenchmen of Acadia? (b) How did the British treat the French after the French and Indian War?
5. If the French had won the war instead of the British, how might North America be different today?
6. Why did the Iroquois fight against the French and the other Indians?

Further Study

1. Why were the British kinder to the French after the war than they had been earlier?
2. (a) What did both the French and the British promise the Indians? (b) Why was it hard for them to keep their promise?

29. The Colonies Begin to Revolt

Glossary Words

ammunition	liberty	minutemen
boycott	massacre	repeal

The French and Indian War was over, but many people were complaining. Great Britain ruled the colonies from the other side of the Atlantic Ocean. And faraway Great Britain was making laws that the colonists thought were unfair.

For one thing, many colonists would have liked to push westward and settle in the Ohio River area. But Great Britain wanted no more trouble with the Indians. The British government decided that the colonists should stay on the east side of the Appalachian Mountains. The land west of the Appalachians would be for the Indians. But a number of colonists had been looking forward to making their homes and farms in the forests beyond the Appalachians. They were dissatisfied at the thought of having to give up their plans. Many of them moved to the forbidden area in spite of the law.

There were other problems. The British government thought that since British soldiers fought to protect the American colonists, it was only fair that the colonists should pay taxes to Great Britain. Many colonists did not agree. They argued, "If we have to pay taxes to a government, then we should be able to help make government decisions. It's all right for people in England to pay taxes, because they help to make the laws for England. But it's not fair for us to pay taxes to England, since England doesn't allow us to help decide what laws would be good for us."

Great Britain decided that a good way to force the colonists to pay taxes would be to have them buy stamps along with certain things they bought. Anybody who sold a calendar, a newspaper, or certain other goods had to place a stamp from the British government on it. Whoever bought a newspaper had to buy the stamp along with it. The money he paid for the stamp went to the British government. This tax law was known as the Stamp Act.

Some American colonists were so angry about having to pay taxes to Great Britain that they destroyed the office of a man who was appointed to

Settlers moved west to Ohio, even though the British government tried to save the West for the Indians.

sell stamps. Others came together and wrote a letter to the British government, asking that the tax law be changed. Most important, many Americans stopped buying goods that came from Great Britain. This act was called a *boycott*. English merchants began losing money.

When the British government saw how unhappy some Americans were over the Stamp Act, they decided to *repeal* the law. Americans would no longer have to buy stamps. But later the British made other laws that angered the American colonists all over again.

One evening in Boston, a crowd of boys began throwing snowballs at a British soldier. Other British soldiers hurried to the spot. But other angry

Americans came too. Finally the British soldiers began shooting, and several colonists were killed. News of this event spread through the colonies. People who already disliked the British were especially angry. They called this incident the Boston *Massacre*. Just then, however, the British government decided again to repeal the tax laws that had been made. But to show that they had a right to tax Americans, they continued collecting one small tax on tea.

Some colonists were disturbed because they knew why the British government was taxing tea. They did not mind paying a little extra money for tea. In fact, the tea that was taxed was cheaper than tea they could have gotten anywhere else. But the colonists did not like the idea of paying any taxes at all to Great Britain, for they had decided that all taxes from Great Britain were unfair.

One night, in the Boston Harbor, a group of colonists boarded a ship loaded with tea. The tea would soon be sold to storekeepers around Boston. To prevent this, the colonists broke open box after box of dried tea leaves and threw them into the harbor. Today this event is called the Boston Tea Party.

Some people who heard about the Boston Tea Party were delighted. But others, even those who did not like British taxes, shook their heads. They pointed out that it is wrong to destroy other people's property. They wished the Boston Tea Party had never happened.

Feelings grew worse between Great Britain and the colonies. One man, named Patrick Henry, felt so strongly that England was not respecting the colonies that he cried out, "Give me *liberty* or give me death!" Some of the American people decided among themselves that they would be ready to leave their homes and fight the British soldiers at any time. Because they could get ready to fight so quickly, they were called *minutemen*.

Then the British took action. In April of 1775, a British general decided to send soldiers to Concord, near Boston. The colonists there had collected guns and *ammunition*, and the general wanted to destroy their war supplies.

But Paul Revere, a man from Boston, heard of the British plans. One night one of Paul's friends watched to see if the British soldiers would march all the way to Concord by land or if they would take a shortcut by boat. When he knew, he climbed up into a church steeple and hung two lanterns in the window. Paul Revere's friends were waiting for the signal. When they saw two lanterns, they knew that the British would be traveling by sea. After receiving the message, Paul galloped off, waking minutemen as he went. This was the famous "midnight ride of Paul Revere."

The following day, the minutemen who fought the British soldiers at the little town of Lexington were soon scattered. But when the British arrived at Concord, the Americans fought again. A poet writing about this event years later said the Americans "fired the shot heard round the world." He did not mean that the battle itself was so important. Rather, it marked the day when Americans began fighting to win. The revolt had begun. Relations between the American colonies and Great Britain would never again be the same.

Both the British and the Americans were more concerned about themselves than about anyone else. The Scriptures say, "Look not every man on his own things, but every man also on the things of others" (Philippians 2:4).

--- Study Exercises ---

1. (a) Why did Great Britain make a law requiring the colonists to stay on the east side of the Appalachian Mountains? (b) Why were some of the colonists dissatisfied with this law?

2. (a) Why did the British government think the colonists should pay taxes to Great Britain? (b) Why did many colonists disagree?

3. (a) What was the Stamp Act? (b) Why was it repealed?

4. (a) Why did some colonists dislike paying tax on tea? (b) How did they prevent the British government from collecting this tax? (c) Why did some people wish the Boston Tea Party had never happened?

5. (a) Who were the minutemen? (b) How did the British plan to stop them?

Further Study

1. (a) How did the British show that they were mainly interested in themselves? (b) How did many colonists show that they also were mainly concerned about their own interests?

2. Read Matthew 22:15–22. The Jews also thought that they had unfair taxes. What did Jesus say about paying tribute (taxes) to Caesar?

30. The Revolutionary War

Glossary Words

Declaration of Independence   Second Continental Congress
retreat   surrender
revolutionary

By 1775, the American colonists and the British began to fight each other. Both sides had already lost lives. But some people still thought a war could be avoided. To discuss the matter, colony leaders came together at Philadelphia, Pennsylvania. This group of men was called the *Second Continental Congress*.

These men talked about the problems between England and the American colonies. Finally they decided that the thirteen colonies would be independent. They would rule themselves and not have England for a mother country anymore. They knew that England would not like this idea, but they decided to fight for independence.

The Second Continental Congress chose Thomas Jefferson, a man from Virginia, to write a paper clearly stating the reasons why the colonists wanted their independence. Jefferson wrote a long explanation called the *Declaration of Independence*. Then the men of the Second Continental Congress signed it. It is one of the most important papers written in the history of America. Today people can still see it, old and yellow but readable, sealed under glass in a

Independence Hall, where the Second Continental Congress met.

library in Washington, D.C.

The Declaration of Independence was signed on July 4, 1776. This was a very special day to the Americans. A few days later the colonists rang a big bell, now called the Liberty Bell, to celebrate becoming independent. Ever since then, Americans have celebrated the Fourth of July as Independence Day.

Hard times were ahead for the *revolutionary* government. England was the most powerful nation on earth, and British soldiers were well trained. The new American government was weak and had little money to buy guns, cannons, and ammunition for a war. Although many American soldiers knew how to use guns, they hardly knew how difficult army life could be. They had to be trained how to fight.

The revolutionary government chose George Washington, a man from Virginia, to be the commander of the American army. You have read how he had been sent in 1753 to tell the French to leave the Ohio River Valley. He had fought in a number of battles, and his men respected him for his bravery and his calm manner.

At first, the Revolutionary War went badly for the Americans. They could not stop the British from capturing New York City. George Washington and his men *retreated* farther

George Washington

and farther south, with the British coming after them. Finally they retreated across the Delaware River into Pennsylvania. The revolutionary government leaders fled from Philadelphia when they heard that British troops were getting close.

The war dragged on. The Americans won some battles, and the British won others. France decided to help America because they wanted to see the British defeated. In 1781 the French helped the Americans win an important battle. A British general named Cornwallis had made a serious mistake. He had led his army to Yorktown, Virginia, along the seacoast, where he thought British ships could bring him supplies. Instead, he found himself trapped. French ships cut off his way of escape by sea, and Washington's army surrounded him by land. The British **surrendered** there at Yorktown, in 1781. The British soldiers would go home, and Americans would govern their own country. In 1783, the British and the Americans signed a final peace treaty.

Did Canada also fight a revolutionary war against England? No. Although American leaders tried to persuade the French people in Canada to join them in their fight against England, the French Canadians refused.

However, Canada is also indepen-

United States After the Revolutionary War

British North America

Part of Mass. until 1820

Great Lakes

New York

VT
N.H.
Mass.
R.I.
Conn.

Pennsylvania

Northwest Territory

N.J.
MD.
Del.

Virginia

North Carolina

South Carolina

Georgia

Atlantic Ocean

Spanish Territory

Gulf of Mexico

dent today. England gave Canada her freedom one step at a time, in a peaceable way. You will read in a later lesson how Canada became a nation ninety years after the Americans declared their independence.

―――――――― Study Exercises ――――――――

1. What was the Second Continental Congress?
2. What did the Second Continental Congress decide?
3. (*a*) Why was the Declaration of Independence written? (*b*) When was it signed?
4. Who was chosen to command the American army?

5. (a) Which side won most battles during the first part of the war? (b) What major battle helped the Americans win the war?

6. How many years had passed between the signing of the Declaration of Independence and the signing of the final peace treaty?

7. How did the people of Canada gain their independence?

Further Study

1. Did everyone think that war between the British and the Americans was necessary?

2. Why did the Second Continental Congress choose George Washington to lead the American army?

3. Near the end of the war, which nation helped the Americans?

31. Those Who Would Not Fight

Glossary Words

Loyalist   Tory

During the Revolution, not everyone in the colonies wanted to fight England. About the same number wanted to remain loyal to England as the number wanting to break away. These people were called *Loyalists*, or *Tories*. Other people, such as most Mennonites and Quakers, had convictions against fighting.

One group of Seventh-day Baptists, who would not fight, lived in what is called the Ephrata Cloister, in Pennsylvania. Here they practiced humble, simple living, made books, farmed, and in other ways tried to serve the Lord. During the war the Cloister took in and nursed wounded soldiers, some from the British army, and some from the American army.

The American revolutionaries, called Patriots, sometimes mistreated Christians and Loyalists because they refused to fight. The Patriots took farm animals and even household furniture and sold them to help pay for the war. They also made the Christians and Loyalists pay fines. The Pennsylvania government made a law that all the white men in Pennsylvania must swear an oath (or promise) to be loyal to the Patriots instead of to the king of England. People who refused to make the promise could be forced to pay large fines or go to jail for three months, and they might even have their property taken away.

But a number of Christians did not promise loyalty. They believed in being loyal to their government, of course. But they (or their forefathers) had already promised their loyalty to the king of England. They were not sure that promising loyalty to the revolutionary government would be right.

A printer in Germantown named Christopher Sauer, who refused to take the oath, was chased out of bed at night by American soldiers and forced to walk to Valley Forge, where Washington's army was camped. Someone appealed to Washington for him, and a day later he was released. But he had been back in Germantown only a month when officers came again. They made a list of everything he had and arranged for an auction. Everything was sold, even his bed.

Later his house was sold too.

Near Easton, Pennsylvania, a dozen Mennonite men were arrested during the war. While they were in jail, the sheriff held auctions and sold all their household goods, including their stoves. At least one family had enough money to buy some of their own goods at the sale, but other families were left very poor. Children found themselves sleeping on the floor.

Several wives of the men in jail wrote to the Pennsylvania government, telling what had happened. The government helped the families with some money, although they were not repaid for nearly all they had lost. Perhaps Jesus would have said to them, as He did to people of His time, "Thou shalt be recompensed at the resurrection of the just" (Luke 14:14).

The British soldiers, too, caused the people difficulty. One Mennonite man owned a flour mill. When the British soldiers came, they broke up the machinery in his mill and took all his grain and flour.

But Christians took opportunities to show God's way of love and kindness. Once when a farmer's daughter was getting married, some of Washington's soldiers came looking for

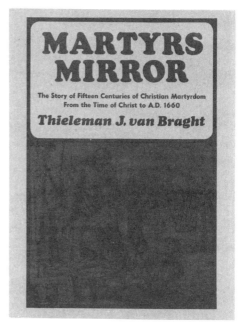

The Martyrs Mirror *is a large book that was written in Holland several centuries ago. It tells about Christians who were willing to suffer rather than fight back.*

Before the French and Indian War, the Mennonites had the Martyrs Mirror *translated and printed in their German language. They wanted to encourage their people to love their enemies, even in time of war. The* Martyrs Mirror *is now available in English.*

supplies. They were invited to sit down and eat with the other wedding guests. They had a good, friendly time, and afterwards the soldiers left without taking anything.

Study Exercises

1. Did all the colonists want to fight against England? Explain your answer.
2. How did Christians show love and kindness to both sides during the war?
3. (a) Why were some Christians put into jail? (b) In what other ways were they mistreated?
4. Besides the Americans, what other groups also caused trouble for these Christians?
5. (a) Did the nonresistant Christians hate those who caused them trouble? (b) How do you know?

Further Study

1. Read Romans 13:1, 2. The higher powers are earthly rulers. Whom did the nonresistant Christians consider to be the higher power over them?
2. (a) What promise did the Pennsylvania government want the men to make? (b) Why did this cause a problem for a number of Christians?
3. Some colonists would have refused to fight even if the king of England had asked them to. Why?

32. Making a New Government

Glossary Words

amendment	constitution	president
compromise	democracy	rights
Congress	House of Representatives	Senate

After the Revolutionary War, the thirteen American colonies were independent from Great Britain. But the colonies, now called states, had to decide how to rule themselves.

Setting up a good government was not easy. People said, "We don't want another king! He might oppress us the way King George did." And so, for a while, they tried having a weak central government. There was no king, not even a *president*. But this government had so little power that it could not even raise taxes. It had to ask the thirteen states for money, which they did not always give. Also, if any of the thirteen states had a disagreement, the central government had no authority to solve the problem.

More and more people saw that something needed to be done. They sent government leaders to Philadelphia in 1787 to discuss how to make their government better. The men at the meeting asked George Washington to be their chairman.

One of the men at the meeting was Benjamin Franklin. As a boy he had learned to enjoy reading, and as a man he proved that he had learned from his reading. He published an almanac, started the first free public library, experimented with electricity, invented bifocals, and helped the country in many ways. He was 81 years old by this time, and other men listened respectfully when he spoke.

The men began to talk about forming a new kind of government. They knew that they wanted a *democracy*. Still, they had many different ideas about the kind of democracy they should have. In their discussions they disagreed about many things.

One of the biggest arguments took place between men from large (heavily populated) states and those from small (less populated) states. They agreed that a good government should have men come from all over the country to help make laws. These men would represent the people back home by saying what laws their own people needed or did not need. But the question was, "Shall we send the same number of men to represent each state, or shall we send more representatives from large states than from small states?"

Of course, men from large states thought that more representatives should come from large states. They thought it was only fair that more men represent them in the government. But men from the smaller states argued, "If the government is made up of more men from large states, the large states might gain too much power. What if large states decide to make a law that hurts small states? What could small states do about it?"

After discussing the problem for a number of days, they finally agreed to *compromise*. Neither large states nor small states would get all they wanted. There would be a *Congress* made up of men who would represent the area they came from. Congress would be divided into two parts. In one part, called the *Senate*, two men

would represent each state, no matter how large or small it was. So small states would have as much power as large states. In the other part, called the *House of Representatives*, more men would represent large states than small states.

In this way both sides won. If the Senate passed a law that hurt large states, the House of Representatives could stop it. If the House of Representatives passed a law that hurt small states, the Senate could stop it.

After the men had agreed on enough points, they wrote a long paper describing how the new government was to work. Today we call this document the Constitution of the United States.

The *Constitution* keeps any one man from having too much power. You remember that to keep unwise laws from being passed, the two parts of Congress watch over each other. In the same way, the central government is made of three main parts that watch over each other. One part is

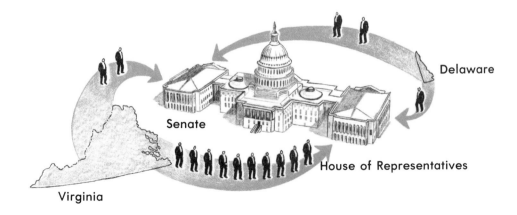

Senate

House of Representatives

Delaware

Virginia

The President lives in the White House.

Congress meets in the Capitol.

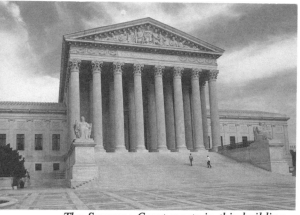

The Supreme Court meets in this building.

Congress, which makes laws. The second part is the president and his helpers, who make the laws work. The third part is the Supreme Court and other courts, which decide whether a law is being broken.

Congress or the president can keep the wrong kind of person from becoming a member of the Supreme Court. On the other hand, the Supreme Court or the president can sometimes stop Congress if it tries to pass poor laws. And Congress or the Supreme Court can stop the president if he does something wrong.

Once the makers of the Constitution were content that they had written a good document, one more important task remained. They had to persuade the people back home that the Constitution was a good plan. This was not always easy. People wanted to make sure the new government would not take away their newly found freedom.

Thomas Jefferson, who had been in France when the Constitution was written, later said he liked it. But he said it should also have a list of *rights* that people have in the United States. Other people thought so too. So ten *amendments* were added to the Constitution.

The First Amendment is perhaps the most important. It guarantees that people in the United States can worship freely. No religion may persecute any other religion. This amendment also guarantees that no one will be punished for publishing books, papers, or magazines. This means that the book you are reading is acceptable to the government and that no one will get into trouble for writing, printing, or reading it.

Once the Constitution included such a list of freedoms, the people began to accept it. By 1788, when enough states had voted to accept it, the Constitution became the basic law for the United States.

The makers of the Constitution may not have realized how good their document really was. Even though it was written in the days of horses and carriages, the Constitution works today in a time of jetliners and computers.

Does Canada have a constitution like this one? Yes. Although in some ways the Canadian government is different, its constitution provides the same freedoms that people in the United States enjoy.

Christians in the United States and Canada should thank God for the blessing of living under fair laws. They should also realize that if most people lose their respect for good laws, God might allow these freedoms to be taken away.

=============== Study Exercises ===============

1. (a) Why did the people of the United States want a weak central government at first? (b) Why did the government leaders decide that a new kind of government was needed?
2. (a) Who did the government leaders think should make laws in the new government they were planning? (b) Why did the states disagree about how many representatives would come from each state? (c) How was the disagreement settled?
3. What is the Constitution of the United States?
4. Name the three parts of the United States central government, and tell what each part does.
5. Why was a list of freedoms added to the Constitution?
6. What was needed before the Constitution could become the basic law of the United States?

7. In what way is Canada's constitution similar to the United States' constitution?

Further Study

1. Why did the government leaders take special care not to give too much power to one man or one group?
2. How do we know that the Constitution was a good plan for the new government?

33. Americans Move to Canada

Glossary Words

Conestoga wagon   descendant   emigrant

When the Revolutionary War was over and the Patriots had won, thousands of Loyalists living in the United States were unhappy. They had wanted England to continue ruling the colonies. Now that England had pulled out, they found themselves left in an unfriendly America. Many of them had lost their homes and all they owned. They wanted to leave.

The British government offered to take the Loyalists to Canada, where King George of England still ruled.

Americans Move to Canada

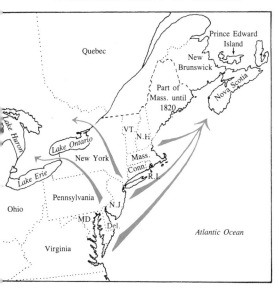

There they could have free land and a new start in life. Thousands of Loyalists boarded British ships and sailed to Nova Scotia. Some of them moved to nearby New Brunswick, Prince Edward Island, and Quebec. The government gave them tools and even food so that they could live until their first crops were harvested.

Many of the people had been doctors, craftsmen, and indoor workers. They were not used to cutting down trees and building rough cabins with logs. But they worked hard. In time, where there had been forests, sunlight fell on little fields that the men had cleared. Canada would be changing fast from now on. Life would be easier for these people's *descendants*. Descendants of the Loyalists still live in Canada today.

One later group that moved to Canada was Mennonites from Pennsylvania. They had heard that in Canada no one would try to make them serve in the army. Also, some of them felt overcrowded where they were. Being mostly farmers, they wished for more good land. Around 1800, they began to move to what is

Neighbors helping each other clear land. Imagine how long one man would have to work to do what this crew could do in one day.

It appears as though much good lumber was burned by the settlers in clearing land. But people needed food, and land had to be cleared in order to raise crops.

now Waterloo County, Ontario. A rich businessman there was selling hundreds of acres at good prices.

But then the news leaked out that the businessman did not really own the land. Though the Mennonites had paid him for it, they could not claim the land for their own. In order to have a lawful claim, they would have to buy it again. And in order to buy it again, they would need to buy a large tract of land with it—sixty thousand acres in all.

The Mennonites in Canada talked it over. They knew that God would not want them to use the law to force the cheating businessman into doing right. The Scriptures say, "Dearly beloved, avenge not yourselves, but rather give place unto wrath" (Romans 12:19). They also knew that they did not want to lose the homes for which they had worked so hard. But neither did they have the thousands of dollars it would take to buy the land. They decided that two men from Canada would go to Pennsylvania and ask their church brethren and sisters for help.

At first their friends in Pennsylvania did not know what to think, but at a meeting one of the old men said, "Truly we are in duty bound to assist those Canadian brethren in distress." Perhaps he was thinking of the verse, "Bear ye one another's burdens, and so fulfill the law of Christ" (Galatians 6:2). They decided to form a company. Every man who gave money to help his Canadian brethren would own part of the land in Canada. In only a few days they had collected twenty thousand dollars to pay for the land. The two Canadian men took the silver coins back to Canada in a wagon.

More Mennonite families began moving to Canada. The *emigrants* must have found it hard to say good-bye. They were leaving large farm-houses with acres of cleared fields. They would need to travel five hundred miles and could go only six or eight miles a day. Sometimes they had to float their boatlike *Conestoga wagons* across rivers. Reaching Canada, they found only deep forests that would have to be cut down.

At first, like others who had moved to Canada, they lived in simple log houses and used homemade furniture. But in a fairly short time they

A Conestoga wagon and a stagecoach near an inn.

had changed the wilderness of trees into attractive fields. Soon they were producing enough grain to supply a flour mill. They had started life over again in Canada, much as their grandparents or great-grandparents had done when they first came to America. In the area of this twice-bought land, the city of Kitchener, Ontario, stands today.

A gristmill, where farmers brought their grain to be ground. The miller's payment was often part of the meal or flour. Some mills also used the water power to saw lumber.

Study Exercises

1. Give three reasons why many Loyalists decided to move to Nova Scotia, New Brunswick, Prince Edward Island, and Quebec.
2. Give two reasons why some Mennonites decided to move to Ontario.
3. How did a businessman mistreat these Mennonites?
4. How were these Canadian Mennonites able to keep their land?
5. How were the Americans that moved to Canada similar to the colonists that you studied about in Lesson 24?

Gaining Geographical Skills

1. Trace Map D in the map section. Label it "North America After the Revolutionary War."
2. Label the thirteen original states.
3. Label these areas of Canada: Nova Scotia, New Brunswick, Prince Edward Island, Quebec, and Ontario.

Further Study

1. Why was the United States an unfriendly place for Loyalists to live during and after the Revolutionary War?
2. If the emigrants averaged seven miles each traveling day, about how many days would it have taken to travel from their old homes in Pennsylvania to their new homes in Canada?

Chapter 5 Review

Reviewing What You Have Learned

A. *Write a glossary word for each definition.*

1. A person who moves out of a country.
2. To do away with a law.
3. To stop dealing with someone.
4. A change in a law.
5. The highest officer in the United States government.
6. The part of Congress in which the states are represented according to their population.
7. The part of Congress in which each state is represented by two members.
8. Refusing to use force for protection.
9. To give up to an enemy in war.
10. Various nations or groups of people ruled by one government.
11. Freedom from the control of others.
12. A document stating why the American colonists wanted to be independent.

B. *Choose the correct answer to complete each sentence.*

1. Some Frenchmen mistreated the Indians by ——.
   a. using liquor to cheat them
   b. forcing them to work for the French
   c. requiring them to give up their land
2. William Penn's grandson ——.
   a. bought land from the Indians and took only half of what he had bought
   b. was nonresistant
   c. paid frontiersmen to kill Indians
3. When the white men and the Indians had conflicts, ——.
   a. only the Indians were unfair
   b. only the white men were unfair
   c. both the white men and the Indians were sometimes unfair

4. The French surrendered New France to Great Britain because
———.
   a. George Washington had captured Fort Duquesne
   b. the British had won the battle at Quebec
   c. the British had controlled the Ohio River before the French and Indian War

5. If the French instead of the British had won the French and Indian War, ———.
   a. most North Americans might be French-speaking Roman Catholics
   b. the British would not have forced the Acadians to leave their homes
   c. the Iroquois would have liked the French

6. The British government decided the colonists should buy stamps to help pay for ———.
   a. the land west of the Appalachian Mountains
   b. the protection the British soldiers gave the colonies
   c. the Boston Tea Party

7. The Second Continental Congress ———.
   a. was a group of British leaders
   b. decided that the thirteen colonies would fight to be independent
   c. chose Thomas Jefferson to command the American army

8. The battle at Yorktown helped ———.
   a. the Canadians gain their independence
   b. the Patriots decide to write the Declaration of Independence
   c. the Patriots win their war for independence

9. Some Christians were mistreated during the Revolutionary War because ———.
   a. they would not promise to be loyal to the Patriots
   b. nearly everyone else supported the revolutionary government
   c. they had treated the Patriots cruelly

10. The first government of the United States ———.
   a. was made up of three parts
   b. was described in a paper called the Constitution
   c. was too weak to raise taxes or settle disputes between states

11. Congress is responsible to ——.
    a. decide whether a law is being broken
    b. make laws
    c. make the laws work

12. Many Loyalists moved to Canada after the Revolutionary War because ——.
    a. King George of England had oppressed them
    b. it was easier to make a living in Canada
    c. they wanted to remain under British rule

13. One of the main reasons many Mennonites moved to Canada was that ——.
    a. they had heard that the Canadians would not try to make them fight in the army
    b. they did not really own their land in Pennsylvania
    c. they wanted to do something besides farming

C. *Write* true *or* false.

1. The Spanish sent Catholic priests and soldiers to start missions.

2. Thomas Penn was fair to the Indians, as his father had been.

3. The Indians hurt a few of the nonresistant Christians, even though the Christians had been kind to them.

4. The British and the French both wanted the Ohio River Valley because many fur-bearing animals lived there.

5. After the French and Indian War, the British allowed the French to keep their old way of doing things.

6. The British refused to allow the colonists the privilege of helping make laws.

7. The soldiers in the British army were called minutemen.

8. The small states were concerned that the large states would be too powerful if all the states had the same number of representatives in Congress.

9. Canada's constitution provides the same freedoms the United States' constitution does.

10. The Mennonites in Pennsylvania helped the Mennonites who had moved to Canada.

So Far This Year

Choose the correct answers. See how many you can give without looking back.

1. Temperatures are mild or moderate in most areas of (Canada, the United States).

2. Canada is (smaller, larger) than the United States, but it has (fewer, more) people.

3. Quebec was the first lasting (French, English, Spanish) settlement in North America.

4. The (English, French) mainly set up trading posts, but the (English, French) established farms and towns.

5. The Pilgrims, Quakers, and many other groups moved to America in search of (an easy life, freedom of worship, gold).

6. The French settled lands (north, south) of the English colonies.

7. Settlers who disliked populated areas moved to the (frontier, cities) in search of a simpler life with (fewer, more) laws.

8. (Slaves, Indians) did much of the work on large southern plantations.

9. Match.
   a. William Penn
   b. William Penn's grandson
   c. French fur traders
   d. Spanish soldiers and priests

   1. paid frontiersmen to kill Indians.
   2. paid Indians for land.
   3. forced Indians to work and be baptized.
   4. used liquor to cheat Indians.

10. The (English, French, Indians) won the French and Indian War and took control of New France.

THE COVERED WAGON

CHAPTER 6

THE SETTLED COUNTRY GROWS AND CHANGES

34. A Peaceful Revolution

Glossary Words

assembly line   Industrial Revolution   standard parts
card   loom   textile
cotton gin   spinning jenny

The *Industrial Revolution* was a change in the way things were manufactured. This caused great changes in the way people lived. During the Industrial Revolution, which began in the late 1700s, people began making machines to do work that had been done by hand. Today that kind of work is much easier for people than it was three hundred years ago—or even a hundred years ago.

During American colonial days, families not only sewed their own clothes but also made their own cloth. In an earlier lesson about New England, you learned what hard work it was to make wool cloth. The same was true for cotton. Cleaning cotton

The spinning wheel and loom

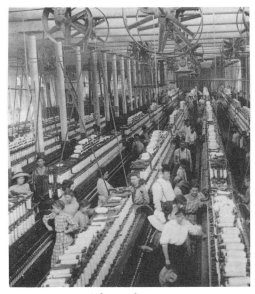

A large factory

Large factories took over the work of the spinning wheel and the loom. Notice that many of the workers in this factory were women or children.

took hours. The seeds had to be removed. Then the fluffy cotton bolls were *carded*—a process like combing—to straighten the fibers. The fibers were spun into thread on a spinning wheel, one thread at a time, and the thread was woven into cloth on a *loom*. During most of the 1700s, all these things were done by hand.

Around 1764, an Englishman named James Hargreaves invented what he called the *spinning jenny*. It could spin several threads at a time. Later, larger and better machines were built.

Up to this time, families had made yarn or cloth in their own cottages and had sold it to businessmen. But after *textile* machines were built, the businessmen decided it was easier to have all the people who spun thread come to a factory to work. This was a big change for people who had worked at home all their lives.

Was it a good change?

If you had talked to a young woman of that time, she might have said, "It is satisfying to know that I can now spin more thread than I could at home. This means that people can buy cloth more cheaply than before.

"But I must be away from my family for more than twelve hours every working day. I miss working closely with friends. The man I work for hardly knows me because he hires so many other workers. I cannot take a break whenever I wish because the machines keep right on going. I especially pity the children who must work in factories all day long. They should spend some of that time playing in the sunshine and doing errands for their parents. At the same time, some people have no work at all. Machines are doing what those people used to do."

The first spinning mills were built in England. The English factory owners wanted to keep Americans from finding out how to build spinning mills. But the secret of making spinning machines finally came to America. Samuel Slater, who brought the secret from England, knew that he dared not carry drawings of the machines, lest he be caught with them. So he memorized everything and carried the plans in his head! Samuel Slater built the first textile mill in Rhode Island in 1790.

But the spinning mills could spin cotton faster than farmers could produce it. Soon they began to run out of cotton. The problem was not that farmers could not grow enough cotton. The problem was getting the sticky seeds out of each cotton boll. Picking them out by hand took a long time.

A young man named Eli Whitney

heard how much farmers needed a machine to clean the cotton. Some people say a lady showed him how such a machine could be made. Maybe she was the real inventor. Anyway, by 1793 Eli Whitney had made a machine he called the *cotton gin*. Inside the machine, sawlike teeth pulled cotton between slats that were set close together, like teeth on a comb. Because they were thin, the cotton fibers could pass through. But the seeds, which were too thick to pass

through, stayed on the other side. Soon a cotton gin was made that could clean fifty times as much cotton as a man could clean by hand.

Up to this point, farmers did not plant much cotton because it took so long to clean the cotton. But the cotton gin made it profitable to plant huge fields of cotton. Workers would be needed to labor in the big fields. Although Eli Whitney probably did not realize it, his invention meant that Americans would want more

The blacks seem happy about Whitney's cotton gin. No more hours of picking out cotton seeds one by one! The gin soon changed the lifestyle of the entire South.

Standard parts made it possible to make products on assembly lines. Since each wheel is the same, it will fit on any of these Model T Fords.

slaves. The increase in slavery would lead to the biggest war ever fought on American soil.

Eli Whitney had an idea that was perhaps even more important than the cotton gin. Up to this time, when a craftsman made a gun, he made each part to fit that one gun and no others. If a part broke, the owner could not simply buy a spare part to replace the broken one. He needed to have a part made especially for that gun, for no other part would fit. Whitney decided that if all guns used exactly the same parts, craftsmen could make them much faster. When a gun broke, it could also be repaired much more quickly and easily. Soon people were making other things the same way.

Today, using **standard parts**, men and women work on **assembly lines**, making cars, shoes, typewriters, and many other things. As the product they are making comes slowly past on a belt or conveyor, each person adds his part—a windshield, a steering wheel, a headlight, or whatever he has been assigned to put in. He does this over and over, all day long. Every worker's job is fairly simple, but the assembly line can turn out some very complicated products.

Study Exercises

1. How did the Industrial Revolution change the way people lived?
2. (a) How did people make cloth during most of the 1700s? (b) Why could a spinning jenny make thread faster than a spinning wheel?
3. (a) What change brought by spinning mills did people think was good? (b) What changes did spinning mills bring that were not good?
4. (a) How did the plans for spinning mills come to America? (b) What problem did Americans face after they had spinning machines?
5. (a) What invention helped to increase the importance of the cotton crop in the South? (b) What evil did this invention help to increase?
6. How did Eli Whitney improve the way complicated products were made?

Further Study

1. Why did the English factory owners want to keep the Americans from finding out how to build spinning machines?
2. What helped lead to the biggest war ever fought in America?

35. *Explorers Map the Pacific Region*

Glossary Word

civilization

Around the time of the Revolutionary War, most white people still lived near the eastern edge of North America. *Civilization* was slowly creeping across the land from the Atlantic shore. While this was happening, a few explorers were interested in finding out what the West was like. Most of them worked for fur companies that wanted to claim the land and make friends with the Indians.

Captain James Cook, from England, tried to find a water passage across North America in 1778. Other explorers had looked for a waterway through North America, or else one to the north of it, which they called the Northwest Passage. Unlike other explorers, Captain Cook started on the

Western Explorations

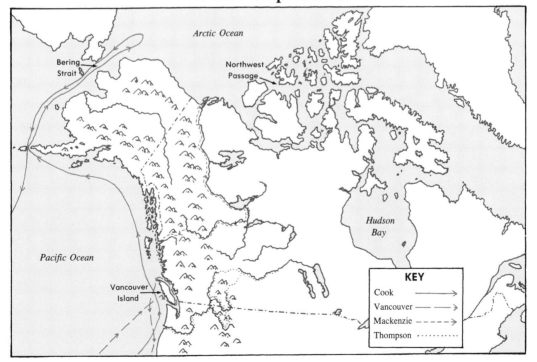

western side of North America instead of the eastern side.

As Captain Cook sailed northward along the coast, he explored bays and river channels, looking for a water passageway. But he and his men made no exciting discoveries. At last they sailed through the Bering Strait between what is Alaska and Russia today. Now they were in the icy Arctic Ocean. They spent nearly a month threading their way among the icebergs. Finally, when winter began to set in, Captain Cook left.

Captain Cook's voyage was not really a failure. He had named many new landmarks. Later explorers along the Pacific shore would know where they could find bays and the mouths of rivers.

But what about the Northwest Passage? If you examine a globe, you will see that in the far north of Canada, there are many islands. Through these islands there is a passage, but it is not used very much. In winter it is clogged with ice.

Captain Cook was killed in 1779, before he could explore the area again. But some years later, one of Cook's crewmen, George Vancouver, returned, commanding another English expedition. He added more details to explorers' maps of the western shore. By sailing around Vancouver Island, he proved that it is

an island. Today the island is named after him.

About ten years later (in 1789) an explorer named Sir Alexander Mackenzie tried to find a river from the middle of Canada out to the Pacific Ocean. He thought that a water route across even part of Canada would be better than nothing. Mackenzie did come upon a river that seemed promising. But after he had followed it west for several hundred miles, it turned north, taking him to the Arctic Ocean, instead of the Pacific.

Mackenzie turned back, calling the river he had discovered the River of Disappointment. But today we call it the Mackenzie River. This large river drains a huge area in western Canada. Even though it was a disappointment to Mackenzie, we know that God has a purpose in all of His creation. "O Lord, how manifold are thy works! in wisdom hast thou made them all: the earth is full of thy riches" (Psalm 104:24).

Mackenzie tried again, three years later. This time he and his crew paddled their canoes up the Peace River. In some places the waters were dangerously swift, with rocks and whirlpools always ready to wreck them. By following rivers and lakes and struggling along on foot where they could not ride, the men managed to reach the western side of the Rocky

Mountains. They finally left their canoes behind and followed an Indian trail across the country. After crossing the Coast Ranges, they came to a river again, and with borrowed Indian canoes they finished their journey to the Pacific. They were the first men to arrive on the western shore by coming from the east across the mountains.

Mackenzie was so pleased that he wrote a memory of his adventure on a big rock. Later someone found the rock, on which was written, "Alexander Mackenzie, from Canada, by land, the twenty-second of July, one thousand seven hundred and ninety-three."

Perhaps the most important river on the west coast of North America is the Columbia River. It flows through Canada for one part of its journey, and through the United States for the other part. Many of the first explorers knew about the Columbia. But the first man to explore it thoroughly was David Thompson, who arrived at the mouth of the river in 1811. There he found an American trading post that had been built just four months earlier.

The Americans welcomed Thompson and gave him supplies, but he was disappointed. He had wanted to claim the mouth of the Columbia for his own country, England. Many years later, David Thompson died a poor and forgotten man. But today people realize what a tremendous amount of useful information he helped to put on maps of North America.

David Thompson drew excellent maps. Hours of calculations and sightings went into charting rivers, mountains, and plains. Thompson is using a sextant, an instrument used to map newly explored regions.

=====   **Study Exercises**   =====

1. What was Captain James Cook trying to find?
2. What is the Northwest Passage?
3. Where did Vancouver Island get its name?
4. (a) What did Alexander Mackenzie try to find? (b) Which two rivers did he explore in his search?
5. (a) What is perhaps the most important river on the west coast of North America? (b) Who was the first white man to explore it thoroughly? (c) Why was he unable to claim it for England?

Gaining Geographical Skills

Use the map in this lesson and a globe to answer these questions.
1. Which explorer traveled the farthest north?
2. Which two explorers crossed the western mountain ranges?
3. Find North America on a globe. The Bering Strait divides North America from what other continent?

Further Study

1. Why was Mackenzie disappointed that the Mackenzie River emptied into the Arctic Ocean instead of the Pacific?
2. Many explorers were disappointed because they did not find what they were looking for. Why do we consider their explorations important anyway?

36. The United States Doubles in Size

Glossary Word

Louisiana Purchase

The western border of the United States has not always been the Pacific Ocean, as it is today. Until 1803, the United States extended only to the Mississippi River. How has the country grown since then?

About 1800, the United States was having trouble because the French owned New Orleans, the city at the mouth of the Mississippi. The Americans knew that the country controlling the mouth of a river controls the boat traffic on the river. That country decides whether boats can freely travel back and forth between the river and the ocean.

Americans living along the Mississippi were concerned. Many of them sent their goods down the Mississippi, around Florida, and up the Atlantic Coast to cities such as New York and Philadelphia. Would France cut off their trade? The United States was like a man who owns all of his farm except the driveway, which a neighbor owns. The neighbor decides when the driveway may be used, or perhaps that the farmer should pay for each time he uses it.

The president of the United States, Thomas Jefferson, thought that the French might be willing to sell New Orleans. He sent some of his men with an offer to buy it. To their surprise, the French were willing to sell not only New Orleans but a huge territory west of the Mississippi! France said that the United States could have over a half billion acres for just fifteen million dollars.

The men from the United States agreed to buy. But perhaps they gasped a little at what they were doing, for their purchase would make the United States twice as big as it had been before. This important agreement, signed in 1803, was called the *Louisiana Purchase.*

What kind of land did the United States now own? In 1804 Thomas Jefferson appointed two men, whose last names were Lewis and Clark, to lead an expedition through the Louisiana Territory. They were to return with a description of the country.

Lewis and Clark's journey lasted more than two years. They traveled up the Missouri River until it became so small that a man could straddle it. Along the way, they carefully wrote

Louisiana Purchase

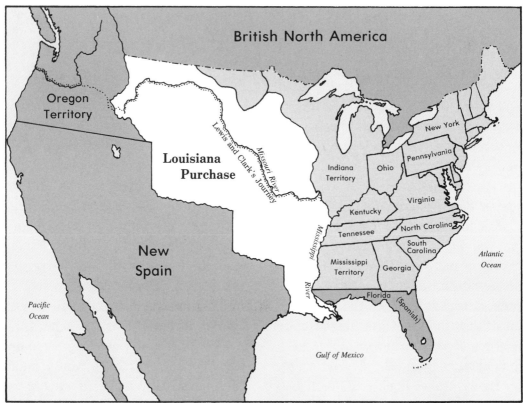

down many of the things they saw about the plants, the rivers, the animals, and the Indians. Traveling was not easy. One time when they could not find enough game animals to fill the cooking pot, they had to buy puppy stew from the Indians.

Although the Rocky Mountains marked the western edge of the Louisiana Territory, Jefferson's plan was that Lewis and Clark should travel all the way to the Pacific. A young Indian woman named Sacajawea (sak uh juh WEE uh), along with her French–Canadian husband, guided them across the Rocky Mountains. She helped them obtain food and horses from her Shoshone (shoh SHOH nee) Indian friends. When Lewis and Clark came to the Columbia River, they built canoes and floated down the river to the Pacific. After spending the winter near the ocean, Lewis and Clark headed back east. They returned with maps that showed how to travel to the Pacific. This opened the way for other explorers, traders, and farmers.

By the time Jefferson bought Louisiana, pioneers had found their way through the Appalachians and were settling the beautiful, rolling country that sloped gently toward the Mississippi. Ohio, Kentucky, and Tennessee were settled states by this time. Now the people were delighted to settle the vast new lands just across the Mississippi.

Some settlers from the East floated down the Ohio River on flatboats. A flatboat, much like a raft, was square at both ends because it did not need to go upstream. On it a family built a little shelter for themselves and loaded their furniture and animals. The current took them where they wanted to go. It was a pioneer's cheapest way to travel.

Most settlers who crossed the Mississippi did not travel too far before they found a new home. Farther west, large sections of the Louisiana Territory remained empty for a long time. In a later chapter you will read how those empty lands finally became home for many new settlers.

Lewis and Clark on their expedition to the West Coast. They explored areas that had never been seen by white men.

One of the easiest ways to travel west was by flatboat. All of a family's goods, including animals, were loaded on board for the trip down the river.

Mennonite and Amish People Move West

Most of the early Mennonites and Amish who came to America settled in eastern Pennsylvania. At first they found plenty of good, cheap land in Lancaster County and the surrounding areas. But by the end of the Revolutionary War, the Mennonites and Amish began looking for other places to settle. Some moved north to Canada. Others moved south to the wide, fertile valleys of western Maryland and Virginia. But many Mennonites and Amish who were looking for new lands turned west.

By 1800, Mennonites and Amish had started a number of settlements in western Pennsylvania. From there they moved steadily westward—to Ohio during the early 1800s; to Indiana, Illinois, and Iowa in the 1830s and 1840s; to Missouri in the 1860s; and to Nebraska and Kansas in the 1870s. By the 1880s, Mennonites were moving all the way to the western valleys of Oregon.

Study Exercises

1. How far west did the United States extend in 1800?

2. Why were the Americans concerned about France owning New Orleans?

3. (a) How did President Jefferson hope to solve the problems caused by France owning New Orleans? (b) How did the French respond to his offer? (c) What was the purchase called?

4. (a) What was the purpose of Lewis and Clark's trip? (b) Who helped them find a way to the Pacific Ocean? (c) What did they bring back that helped later explorers and settlers?

5. How did many of the settlers reach the western territories?

Gaining Geographical Skills

Trace Map B in the map section, and label it "Westward Expansion." Then do the following exercises.

1. Draw and label the Mississippi, the Ohio, and the Missouri rivers.

2. Label New Orleans at the mouth of the Mississippi.

3. Lightly color the Louisiana Purchase and label it. You will label additional areas in the next two lessons.

Further Study

1. Who first claimed for France the Mississippi River and all the lands that drained into it? (Lesson 15 might help you.)

2. Why was the Louisiana Territory more valuable to the Americans than it was to the French?

37. The United States Expands Again

Glossary Word

Mexican Cession

The United States was fast becoming a big, sprawling country. South of Georgia lay Florida, which the Spanish owned. Spain would have liked to keep Florida, but the Spanish saw that their foothold was too weak there. Sooner or later Florida was bound to become part of the young, growing United States. So Spain sold Florida to the United States in 1819.

The Spanish still owned huge territories in the deserts of the Southwest. The area of Texas, Arizona, New Mexico, and other states all belonged to Mexico, a province of Spain. In 1821 Mexico became an independent nation.

About this time the Mexican

United States Expands

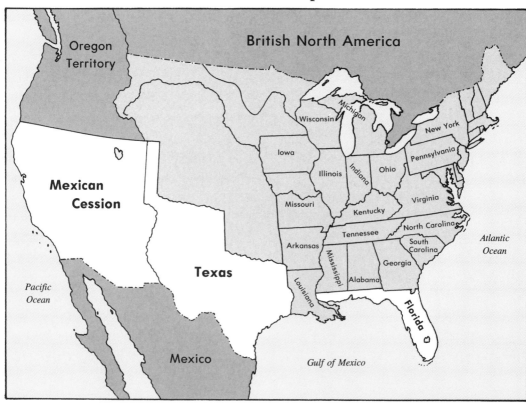

leaders made a decision they regretted afterwards. They allowed Americans to settle in Texas. Soon more Americans than Mexicans were living in Texas.

The Mexican government wanted the new settlers to become good citizens of Mexico, obey its laws, and belong to the Catholic Church. But the Americans wanted to live like Americans, not like Mexicans.

Mexico tried to stop more Americans from moving into Texas. This angered the Americans who were already living there. They did not want to be left by themselves in Mexican country. The Mexican government also made harsh new laws in an effort to control the pioneers in Texas.

In 1835 fighting broke out between Mexico and the Americans in Texas. The battle Americans remember best was fought over the Alamo (AL uh moh). The Alamo was a walled Catholic mission that the Americans used as a fort. Although there were fewer than two hundred Americans, they refused to give up, even when a Mexican army of three thousand soldiers attacked them. Every one of the Americans in the Alamo lost his life.

When other Americans in Texas heard of this, they were shocked. "Remember the Alamo!" became one

The Alamo is an old Catholic mission in Texas.

of their battle cries after that. Later they won an important battle, and the Mexican army left Texas.

The Texans would have liked to join the United States right away. But some Americans in the East did not want to accept Texas as a state. They did not like the fact that Texans owned slaves. Besides, Mexico threatened to declare war on the United States if they made Texas a state. When the Texans realized that they could not join the United States at that time, they decided to govern themselves for a while.

Nearly ten years later, in 1845, the United States did take Texas as a state. At the same time, the United States asked Mexico to sell California

Texas flew a "Lone Star" flag while it was an independent country. Later the other states allowed Texas to join the United States.

The early Texan settlers raised large herds of cattle. Cattle raising is still important in the Southwest.

and New Mexico. But Mexico did not want the United States to take any more of her land. Soon there was another war. During this war, United States soldiers fought against a military school in Mexico City where young Mexican army officers were being trained. Today Mexicans remember the young men who died there in the same way that Americans remember the Texans who died in the Alamo.

The United States won the Mexican War and took what is now California, New Mexico, Nevada, Utah, and parts of other states as her own. Many Americans were pleased with the *Mexican Cession*. Now their land stretched from one ocean to another.

But Mexico had lost almost half the land it had claimed. Even though the United States had paid for some of the land it had taken, Mexico had not wanted to sell it. For a long time afterward, the Mexicans did not like or trust the Americans.

Study Exercises

1. Why did Spain decide to sell Florida to the United States?
2. Why were the Mexicans sorry they had allowed Americans to settle in Texas?

3. Why were the Americans in Texas angry when Mexico tried to stop other Americans from coming?

4. (a) Why did the United States refuse to accept Texas as a state at first? (b) How long was Texas a self-governing country?

5. After the Americans had obtained the Mexican Cession, their land reached from one ocean to another. (a) Name the two oceans. (b) How did many Americans feel about having their country reach all the way across North America? (c) How did the Mexicans feel?

Gaining Geographical Skills

Fill in this information on the map you traced in Lesson 36.

1. Label the Florida Purchase, the Texas Annexation, and the Mexican Cession.

2. Lightly shade each of these sections in a different color.

Further Study

1. How had the Spanish settled the Southwest? (Lesson 26 might help you.)

2. What did the English and American settlers do differently from the Spanish that made their settlements more permanent?

38. *Two Nations Divide the Oregon Territory*

When Lewis and Clark had toured the West, Captain Lewis had told the Indians about Jesus and the Bible. Some time later, two Indians arrived in St. Louis on a special errand. Their tribes had sent them to ask someone to come to their country and teach them how to worship.

In response, several churches sent missionaries to the Oregon Territory. One couple they sent was Dr. Marcus Whitman and his wife Narcissa. The Whitmans lived on a farm and helped their Indian neighbors. At that time,

the Oregon Territory was a huge area containing what is now Oregon, Washington, and the southern half of British Columbia.

During the 1840s, thousands of settlers moved to the rich lands in Oregon, following the Oregon Trail through the wilderness. To reach Oregon, pioneers would start out from Missouri, cross the Great Plains in covered wagons pulled by oxen, pass through strange deserts, and struggle through the Rocky Mountains. The trip often took half a year.

Independence Rock and the Sweetwater River were landmarks for wagon trains moving west. Wagons formed circles at night for protection against Indian attack.

Whitman's mission in the Oregon Territory.

To help and protect each other, pioneers usually traveled in wagon trains with as many as a hundred wagons.

The story of John Sager is a touching one. He was a fourteen-year-old boy who started traveling to Oregon with his parents. Along the way, both of his parents became sick and died. John Sager's sadness made him all the more determined to reach Oregon. With his younger brothers and sisters, he pushed on. Later their horses were stolen, so they had to leave their covered wagon behind. They could not find enough to eat and their clothes became tattered. John's younger sister broke her leg and had

to ride on their skinny cow while John kept the swelling down with snowballs. They had so little food for their baby sister that toward the end, she appeared ready to die. Finally in Oregon, they stumbled up to the house of Dr. Marcus Whitman. The Whitmans, already very busy, somehow managed to take them in and later they adopted them as their own children. And the baby got better in spite of the hard trip.

The missionaries in the Oregon Territory were not always successful. Other white people had made it hard for the Indians to trust the missionaries. One time a man had threatened to give the Indians smallpox out of a bottle if they made trouble. The Indians never forgot that. When measles began to take people's lives, a story started going around among the Indians that Dr. Marcus Whitman had a measles bottle. The Indians massacred a number of white people, including Dr. Whitman and his wife. News of this event traveled far, and the flow of settlers into Oregon stopped for about twelve years.

Americans faced a serious problem in Oregon because England claimed it too. English explorers such as David Thompson and Alexander Mackenzie had gone through it. English traders had settled there. It was hard to say which country had more of a right to the Oregon Territory.

Some Americans wanted to fight to gain all the Oregon Territory. But in 1846 the United States and England agreed to divide it. They simply lengthened the line that was already dividing Canada and the United States, bringing it all the way out to the Pacific. It seemed sensible, however, not to divide Vancouver Island. So the dividing line dips around the southern end of the island.

The Division of the Oregon Territory

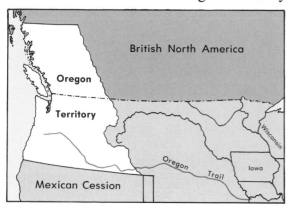

Study Exercises

1. (a) Why did the Indians ask the white men to come to the Oregon Territory? (b) Who responded to the Indians' request?
2. Why did thousands of settlers follow the missionaries to the Oregon Territory?
3. (a) How long did the trip to Oregon often take? (b) What made the trip difficult and dangerous?
4. List some of the heartaches and difficulties that John Sager's family faced.
5. Why did the Indians kill Dr. Whitman?

6. (*a*) Which two countries claimed the Oregon Territory? (*b*) How was the dispute settled?

Gaining Geographical Skills

1. Label the Oregon Territory on the map you traced in Lesson 36. Use another color to lightly shade the area.
2. Trace Map B in the map section. Label it "Trails to the West." Make a dotted line to show the Oregon Trail, and shade the Oregon area. In the next two lessons you will add other trails.

Further Study

1. List some reasons a trip from Missouri to Oregon would be much easier now than it was for John Sager.
2. Why was agreeing to divide the Oregon Territory a better way to settle the dispute than fighting another war?

39. *Mormons Settle Utah*

Glossary Words

basin   cult   polygamy

Barren desert stretched for miles and miles. Not only was the soil too dry for growing crops—in some places it was salty. Why would people make their homes in such a desolate place as Utah?

It all began during the early 1800s in the state of New York. A young man named Joseph Smith claimed he had seen a vision directing him to start a new church. Today we call this the Mormon Church. He gathered many followers and served as the first church president.

Many people did not like the false teachings of this new group. The Mormons taught that God's Word is found in the Book of Mormon as well as in the Bible. They believed that Joseph Smith was a prophet who could add to God's Word. The Scriptures warn against adding to what God has written. "If any man shall add unto these things, God shall add

Trails to the West

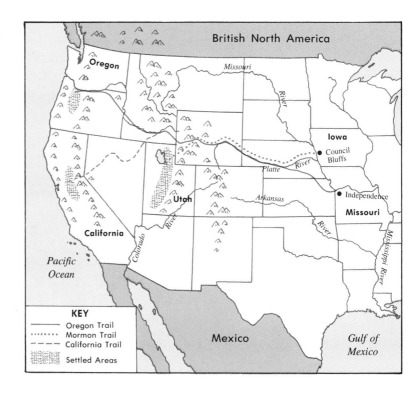

unto him the plagues that are written in this book'' (Revelation 22:18).

The Mormons also allowed *polygamy*, or the practice of having more than one wife. Jesus taught that a man shall "cleave to his wife: and they twain shall be one flesh" (Matthew 19:5). *Twain* means two, not three or more. Because of the Mormons' false beliefs, people opposed them wherever they went.

After Joseph Smith was shot and killed, a leader named Brigham Young took his place. The Mormons began looking for an area where they could live without being molested. Far away to the west, they chose a *basin* between the Rocky Mountains and the Sierra Nevada. Brigham Young led the first group of Mormons there to the Great Salt Lake in what is now Utah. The settlers lost no time in damming streams to irrigate their desert farmland. Their hard work changed the basin from a wasteland to fruitful farms.

Others followed the first settlers. As settlements grew, Mormon lead-ers asked some of the families to leave the old towns and move into new areas. The settlements spread into what is now southern Utah, Nevada, and Idaho.

In later years, the United States took control of the area. The Mormons were unhappy about this at first, but in 1890 they finally agreed to give up their practice of polygamy. Then Utah became a state.

The Mormons, however, still accept Joseph Smith and other leaders as prophets of God. They believe that the Book of Mormon and other writings are just as much God's Word as the Bible is. Most Christians consider Mormonism a *cult*.

The Mormons are known for their huge, costly temples. The first large temple was built in Salt Lake City in Utah. Since then, Mormon temples have been built in other places around the world. The Scriptures teach that God lives within true Christians (2 Corinthians 6:16) rather than in temples made by men (Acts 7:48).

The Mormons founded Salt Lake City near the Great Salt Lake, in what is now the state of Utah.

Study Exercises

1. How did the Mormon Church begin?
2. List three false teachings of the Mormon Church.
3. (a) Why did the Mormons go west? (b) Where did they settle?
4. The Mormon lands became a part of what country?
5. Why do most Christians consider Mormonism a cult?

Gaining Geographical Skills

1. Label Salt Lake City on the map you traced in Lesson 38.
2. Draw a solid line to show the Mormon Trail from Council Bluffs, Iowa, to Salt Lake City.

Further Study

1. Read Galatians 1:6–9. How should Christians respond to teachers who claim to have a gospel different from the one that the Bible teaches?
2. Read Revelation 22:18, 19. What two things does God warn against in this passage?

40. The Gold Rush

Glossary Words

bauxite	minerals	prospector
forty-niners	ore	stagecoach
ghost towns		

Gold! It makes some men rich and other men poor. That was what John Sutter learned in 1848 when gold was discovered on his property in California. Men swarmed onto his huge ranch. They set up camps, trampled his crops, and dug here and there. John Sutter's ranch was ruined.

Word of gold in California spread around the world. Eighty thousand men rushed to California during 1849 alone. They were called *forty-niners*. Many more moved into the state during the next ten years.

Some men came to California by ship. Others traveled across the Great Plains and the Rocky Mountains. The fastest way to travel over land was in a *stagecoach* pulled by four or six horses. Traveling from Missouri to California took just three weeks. But the ride was uncomfortable. The coach traveled day and night, stopping every ten or fifteen miles to change horses. The passengers had to sleep as best they could on the hard seats. Such travel could be dangerous too. Indians sometimes attacked stagecoaches. Robbers held up passengers, sometimes not only robbing but killing.

So many men poured into California that there was a severe shortage of food and shelter. Because gold was plentiful and other things were scarce, prices went sky-high. Eggs sold for as much as ten dollars a dozen and boots for as much as a hundred dollars a pair!

Towns sprang up quickly where only quiet hills had stood a short time before. People slept wherever they could find a place. Many ships that sailed into the San Francisco harbor were abandoned—left alone and uncared for—because all the sailors took off for the hills. They hoped to find a fortune for themselves. In 1850 about a thousand people lived on abandoned ships.

Mining towns were often dirty, noisy, and dangerous. Some rich miners lost their gold nuggets to robbers. Others were lured into card games and gambled their money away. Houses were often flimsy

Miners used several methods to find gold dust or gold nuggets. Some men panned for gold by filling a pan with muddy water and then slowly pouring the water out to see if any gold remained. Others looked for gold by digging in the ground or washing the soil away with water.

because the miners who built them did not plan to stay long. If a fire started, the houses burned fast.

At some mining towns, miners soon found all the gold worth digging for. Then everyone moved out, leaving their flimsy houses behind. Such empty towns are called *ghost towns*.

Not everyone became rich from digging gold. Many who could not find gold turned to farming in the sunny valleys of California. Others settled down as hotel owners, merchants, and tradesmen.

Ten years after gold was discovered in California, people began hearing rumors of gold in Colorado. This brought another flood of *prospectors*. Many of them became upset when they learned that the stories of gold in Colorado had been greatly exaggerated. Some hurried back to where they had come from. Others kept searching and made new discoveries of gold nearby.

Other Rocky Mountain states also received their share of visitors with gold fever. Idaho's climate was not as harsh as the climate in some other mining areas. Families brought their belongings and settled there for good.

Not long after, about 1857, people began hearing about gold in British Columbia. Soon miners from California and thousands of prospectors from other places were hurrying to the area. At that time, there were no easy roads—only narrow, dangerous trails. Finally the governor of British Columbia ordered that a wide, solid road be built so that miners could travel through the mountains more easily.

Not every miner in the country rushed west for gold. Some miners found copper far to the east in Newfoundland. Others discovered *bauxite* in Arkansas and iron *ore* in Minnesota. Men who worked with such *minerals* could earn a good living and produce metals more useful than gold.

The most important thing about the gold rush was not the gold. It was that many people went to live in the far West. If gold had been discovered in the East instead, people would have been content to remain there, and the West would have stayed empty for many more years. It is fascinating to notice where minerals are found in the earth and wonder why God made the world as He did! But God has given us even greater riches than gold. The Scriptures are

Many people settled in the West after the gold rush. These pioneers claimed a homestead in Idaho.

"more to be desired . . . than gold, yea, than much fine gold" (Psalm 19:10).

One big area still remained to be settled—the Great Plains. In later years, people would move in from east and west and fill the gap between.

Study Exercises

1. Who were the forty-niners?
2. What problems arose because of the housing shortage?
3. Read Ecclesiastes 5:10. This verse mentions silver, another valuable mineral. (*a*) Do you think the miners were satisfied with the gold they found? (*b*) Find something in this lesson to support your answer.
4. What improvement did the gold rush in British Columbia help bring?
5. What other minerals besides gold were discovered in North America?
6. How did the gold rushes help speed the settlement of the West?

Gaining Geographical Skills

On the map you traced in Lesson 38, draw a dashed line (– – –) to show the California Trail that the forty-niners used.

Further Study

1. What two main methods of travel did the forty-niners use to reach California?
2. What are ghost towns?
3. Why were jobs such as farming, owning a business, or working for someone else a better way to make a regular living than digging for gold?

41. Indians Lose Their Eastern Homes

Today many people east of the Mississippi hardly ever see an Indian. What became of the Indians in the eastern half of North America?

By the early 1800s, few Indians remained east of the Mississippi. Yet white people were not satisfied as long as the Indians owned land there. Either they forced the Indians out or the government made treaties with the Indian tribes so that the Indians would move west. The government often provided transportation and supplies for the Indians who were moving. The government also prom-ised to help the Indians, but it did not always keep the promises when the Indians needed help.

When the time came to move, some Indians were ready to pack their things and leave. They were tired of their white neighbors' ways. But other Indians hated to leave the eastern land they had always known and loved. They thought of the graves of their fathers, carelessly trampled by the white men. But like it or not, the Indians had to go. Sometimes soldiers were sent to round up the frightened people and start them on their march

Indian Lands West of the Mississippi

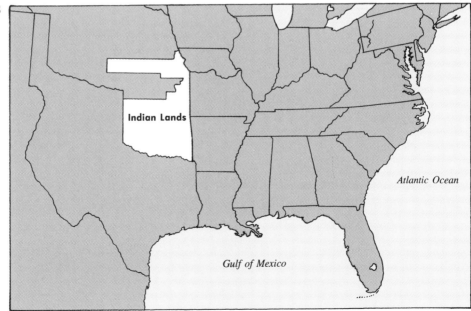

Indian Lands

Atlantic Ocean

Gulf of Mexico

to lands across the Mississippi.

The *migrating* Indians had a hard journey. Anyone who became sick had no time to lie down and rest. People who died were buried in lonely graves along the way. Whether it was hot and dusty or rainy and muddy, the Indians had to keep walking.

The people finally reached the plains beyond the Mississippi where they would make their new home. After they arrived, some of them lived poor, beggarly lives. Whiskey kept them sitting or lying around instead of working. But other Indians found the courage to build houses and plant fields. Hard as it was, they could make a new home and settle there.

They did not know that in the middle 1800s, white settlers would be moving in among them again. You will learn about this in a later lesson. The white men were like some Israelites who set their slaves free but later made them return to bondage (Jeremiah 34:8–11). God was angry with these Israelites for breaking their promise. And certainly God was also displeased with the oppression of American Indians, especially after the white men had made promises to them.

Study Exercises

1. In what two ways did white men get the Indians to move west?

2. (*a*) Why were some Indians ready to move west? (*b*) Why were others reluctant to go?

3. List several things that caused the Indians to suffer as they walked west.

4. After the Indians moved west, how did they adjust to their new home? Give two contrasting ways.

5. Would the Indians be permitted to keep these western lands for their own?

Further Study

1. Read Micah 2:1–3. (*a*) What were some Israelites taking away from the poor in Micah's time? (*b*) How were the white men who drove the Indians west like these sinful Israelites?

2. Read Ecclesiastes 5:4, 5. What is better than making a vow (promise) and not keeping it?

42. The Story of Hawaii

Captain Cook, whom you read about earlier, explored more than the northwestern shores of North America. In 1778 he discovered the Hawaiian Islands, where he was killed the next year. In spite of this, sea captains in later years made Hawaii a stopping place as they sailed across the Pacific. Some sailors chose to stay on these sunny islands, hoping to find a life of ease. Other seamen were forced to remain there by ship captains who did not want them for sailors anymore.

The first white people who actually planned to live in Hawaii were missionaries from New England. In the early 1800s, Hiram Bingham and other missionaries arrived in Hawaii. They saw that in spite of living on

Hawaii

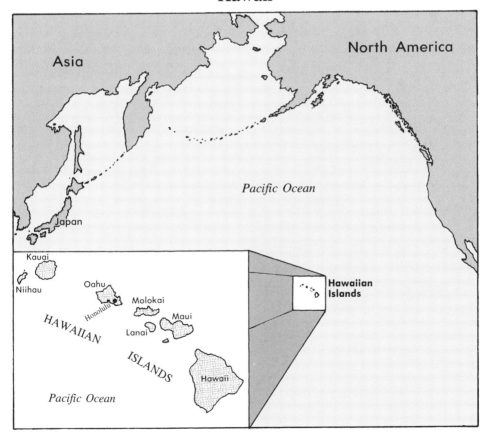

pleasant, sunny islands, the people were not happy. They stole from each other. They sacrificed human beings to idols. They sometimes quieted crying babies forever by burying them alive. Sinful sailors who stopped at the islands encouraged the people to do other wicked things.

Hiram Bingham and his fellow missionaries began holding services on Sundays. They opened schools because they wanted people to read the Bible. However, before they could teach the people to read Hawaiian, they had to decide how to write it. No one had written Hawaiian before. The missionaries chose a simple alphabet to show the people the sounds they used when they talked. Bingham and his fellow missionaries published the first books ever printed in the Hawaiian language.

The Hawaiian king insisted that he should be the first to be taught how to read. He encouraged his chiefs and friends to study also. When the people saw the king and the chiefs eagerly learning to read, they also began to attend classes. Children, parents, and grandparents went to school together. Some of the people who had just learned to read began to teach others.

Among the worst enemies that the missionaries faced were other English-speaking people. Sailors wanted to sell liquor to the people, and they wanted the people to join them in doing wrong things. They did not like it when the missionaries taught the people the Ten Commandments. Sometimes they tried to kill the missionaries, but the missionaries kept on teaching.

The missionaries began to see people's lives changing. The rulers of the islands began to make laws to help the people live decently, honor Sunday, and be faithful to their own husbands or wives. More and more people were leaving their idol worship—some to worship the true God, but others simply to be better accepted by the Americans and Europeans.

During the 1800s, people from many countries settled in Hawaii. But the United States influenced Hawaii the most. Hawaii became America's fiftieth state in 1959.

By the middle of the 1800s, Honolulu, the capital of Hawaii, was a growing settlement. Honolulu has become a large, modern city. Notice Diamond Head, an extinct volcano, in the background of both pictures.

Study Exercises

1. (a) —— discovered the Hawaiian Islands in (b) ——.
2. Look at the map in this lesson. Why were the Hawaiian Islands a good stopping place for ships crossing the Pacific Ocean?
3. How did Hawaiians live before white men moved to the islands?
4. Who were the first white people to move to Hawaii with plans to stay there?
5. (a) What skill did the missionaries teach the Hawaiians? (b) Who was the first to learn this skill?
6. What opposition did the missionaries face?
7. When did Hawaii become part of the United States?

Further Study

1. What did the missionaries need to do before they could teach the Hawaiians how to read?
2. What other missionaries that you studied in this chapter were hindered by white men?

43. How Canada Moved Toward Independence

Glossary Word

invade

After the American Revolution, Great Britain did not want to make the same mistakes again. She did not tax Canada as she had taxed the thirteen colonies. But Great Britain kept strong control of the Canadian government to keep the Canadians from rebelling against their mother country.

Around 1812, several European nations were at war with each other. The English tried to keep the United States from doing business with the nations that were fighting against England. This angered American businessmen, and they called for war on Great Britain. Some Americans also wanted to take Canada away from Great Britain and add it to the United States.

After United States declared war against Great Britain, American soldiers *invaded* Canada. A number of battles took place there. American soldiers burned British government buildings in what is now Toronto. British soldiers later arrived at Washington, D.C., and burned the Capitol Building and the White House in revenge. This war is called the War of 1812.

When the war ended, nothing the soldiers had fought over had changed. The United States had not captured Canada. Someone said that people had gained "nothing but peace." But people's attitudes had changed. Canadians had fought for their homes and their country. Now they felt more loyal to Canada than they had before. Although the United States never invaded Canada again, the Canadians had learned not to trust the Americans. This attitude would lead them, years later, to try to build a united Canada.

The British way of governing Canada worked, but not as well as it should have. The men that England placed in charge of Canada were not really interested in helping the Canadians. They cared more about pleasing themselves and England. The Canadians knew this. Some of them were so unhappy about their government that in 1837 they tried to start a revolt.

When the rulers of England heard this, they thought, "What can we do to avoid the kind of trouble we had in the thirteen colonies?" In 1838 they sent John Lambton to Canada to see

York, the capital of Ontario. York later became Toronto, one of Canada's largest cities.

what could be done. He sent some ideas back to England. One of his ideas was to give the Canadians more freedom to govern themselves. He said that if England allowed this, the Canadians would keep friendly ties with England.

The men ruling England were not sure they wanted to do this, but in 1846, they finally allowed Canadians to control many of their own affairs. Great Britain still held control over some things, but Canada had taken another big step toward independence.

Study Exercises

1. (a) How did the English anger American businessmen? (b) What else helped to start the War of 1812?
2. (a) What did the War of 1812 not change? (b) What did it change?
3. (a) How did the Canadians feel about the way the British were governing them? (b) Why did they feel this way?
4. How were feelings between England and Canada improved?

Further Study

1. Read James 4:1, 2. Why do men fight wars?

2. Like most worldly rulers, the leaders of Great Britain did not like to give up part of their control over Canada. In what way did Jesus command His disciples to be different from the rulers of this world? See Mark 10:42–45.

Chapter 6 Review

Reviewing What You Have Learned

A. *Write a glossary word for each definition.*

1. A line of workers putting things together in a factory.
2. A low area surrounded by higher land.
3. Valuable materials from the earth.
4. One who searches for valuable minerals.
5. Woven or knitted cloth.
6. An early spinning machine.
7. To move from one area and settle in another.
8. Parts that are made exactly alike.
9. A machine that removes seeds from cotton.
10. A mineral that contains aluminum.
11. A religion based on false teachings.
12. Changes that occurred when factories began making goods.

B. *Choose the correct answer to complete each sentence.*

1. Before the Industrial Revolution, ——.
   a. people did most of their work by hand
   b. life was easier
   c. children needed to work long hours in factories

2. Eli Whitney made manufacturing easier by ——.
   a. introducing the idea of using standard parts
   b. memorizing the plans for spinning mills and bringing them to America
   c. inventing the cotton gin

3. The water passageway through the northern islands of Canada is called the ——.
   a. Bering Strait
   b. Vancouver Passageway
   c. Northwest Passage

4. Before the United States bought the Louisiana Purchase, the United States extended only to ——.
   a. the Appalachian Mountains
   b. the Mississippi River
   c. the Missouri River

5. The United States bought Florida from ——.
   a. Mexico
   b. Spain
   c. France

6. Oregon Territory was claimed by both ——.
   a. the United States and Great Britain
   b. the United States and Mexico
   c. Great Britain and Canada

7. When the Mormons moved west, they settled in ——.
   a. Oregon Territory
   b. what is now California, Arizona, and New Mexico
   c. what is now Utah, Nevada, and Idaho

8. The gold rush helped the United States because ——.
   a. many people were able to enjoy life more
   b. it produced many ghost towns
   c. many people moved to the West

9. The eastern Indians moved west because ——.
   a. the white men were determined to move the Indians by treaties or by force
   b. all the eastern Indians were tired of the white men's ways
   c. the lands west of the Mississippi River were better hunting grounds

10. Hawaii became a part of the United States because ——.
    a. Captain Cook discovered the Hawaiian Islands
    b. the native Hawaiians tried to live according to the Ten Commandments
    c. the United States influenced Hawaii more than other countries did

11. The War of 1812 ———.
    a. helped the United States claim large areas of land
    b. helped the Canadians feel more loyal to their country
    c. began when the English invaded the United States
12. Relationships improved between England and Canada when ———.
    a. the English lowered the taxes that Canadians had to pay
    b. the English placed better governors in charge of Canada
    c. the English gave the Canadians more control of their own affairs

C. *Write* true *or* false.

1. The invention of the cotton gin helped increase slavery.
2. Alexander Mackenzie tried to find a river from the middle of Canada out to the Arctic Ocean.
3. Lewis and Clark explored the Louisiana Territory for the United States.
4. Mexico was eager to sell the Southwest to the United States.
5. Dr. Marcus Whitman was one of the first missionaries to go to Oregon Territory.
6. The Mormons believe that Joseph Smith was a prophet who could add to God's Word.
7. The forty-niners greatly increased the population of California.
8. The Indians found much better living conditions west of the Mississippi River.
9. The Hawaiian Islands are in the Pacific Ocean.
10. The Canadians fought for their independence.

So Far This Year

Choose the correct answers. See how many you can give without looking back.

1. North America is in the (Northern, Southern) and (Eastern, Western) hemispheres.

2. Match.

   a. Northeast Indians
   b. Southeast Indians
   c. Great Plains Indians
   d. Southwest Indians
   e. Intermountain and California Indians
   f. Northwest Coastal Indians
   g. Arctic peoples

   1. made large wooden houses, totem poles, and log canoes.
   2. included Inuit and Aleuts.
   3. included the best-known Indian tribe—the Iroquois.
   4. built pueblos and irrigated crops.
   5. were quick to learn white men's ways.
   6. lived in teepees and hunted buffalo.
   7. gathered seeds and nuts and made baskets.

3. (Christopher Columbus, Amerigo Vespucci) discovered America while trying to find a new route to the Far East.

4. Many settlers in (New England, Pennsylvania) turned to fishing because their hilly farms had poor soil.

5. (Slaves, Indians) did much of the work on large southern plantations.

6. The American colonists fought to be independent because they felt that the taxes and laws of (Great Britain, Pennsylvania, Virginia) were unfair.

7. During the Revolutionary War, some (minutemen, nonresistant Christians) were mistreated because they refused to fight.

8. The (Declaration of Independence, Constitution) describes how the United States government is to work.

9. The United States took a large area in the Southwest from (Great Britain, France, Mexico).

10. Choose three: The earliest settlers in the West included (Mennonites, Mormons, missionaries, manufacturers, miners).

Southern plantation owners benefited from the cheap labor of slaves. Did they love their neighbors as themselves?

1860

1861

1862

1863

1864

1865

CHAPTER 7

SLAVERY AND THE CIVIL WAR

44. Slavery and the Underground Railroad

Glossary Words

abolish   Underground Railroad

Slaves had lived in North America since early colonial days. George Washington himself had slaves. But as time went on, more and more people felt uncomfortable about owning other humans. A number of them said that when they died, their slaves could go free.

Giving up slavery was easier for people in the North than for people in the South. Because southern plantations were much larger than northern farms, the plantation owners could not possibly take care of them by themselves. They needed many helpers—helpers that did not cost too much.

People in the North began to point out some of the cruel things they saw in slavery. Sometimes slave families were separated. Children were bought by different owners. Some slaves were forced to work very hard all day long. They had only simple cottages to live in and received just enough food and clothing to keep them healthy enough to work. This did not seem right, especially when the plantation owner lived in a mansion.

But slave owners, who gained much money through having slaves, saw things differently. They said, "Most slave owners treat their slaves kindly. The slaves are much better off than they would be in Africa. They have enough to eat and wear. We take care of their health. Besides, the Bible does not directly say that slavery is wrong."

Slave owners pointed to verses such as 1 Peter 2:18, where servants are commanded to be subject to their masters even if the masters are cruel. But they overlooked verses such as Luke 6:31 (the Golden Rule). They also ignored Colossians 4:1, which says, "Masters, give unto your servants that which is just and equal; knowing that ye also have a Master in heaven." If a person obeys this verse, he will not treat his workers cruelly or make them work without wages. In other words, he will not own slaves!

People became upset when they read the book *Uncle Tom's Cabin*, published in 1852. It told about some of the terrible things some slaves suffered. Today people point out that the book says too much about slaves

$200 Reward.

RANAWAY from the subscriber, on the night of Thursday, the 30th of Sepember,

FIVE NEGRO SLAVES,

To-wit : one Negro man, his wife, and three children.

The man is a black negro, full height, very erect,his face a little thin. He is about forty years of age, and calls himself *Washington Reed,* and is known by the name of Washington. He is probably well dressed, possibly takes with him an ivory headed cane, and is of good address. Several of his teeth are gone.

*Mary,*his wife, is about thirty years of age, a bright mulatto woman, and quite stout and strong.

The oldest of the children is a boy, of the name of FIELDING, twelve years of age, a dark mulatto, with heavy eyelids. He probably wore a new cloth cap.

MATILDA, the second child, is a girl,six years of age,rather a dark mulatto,but a bright and smart looking child.

MALCOLM, the youngest, is a boy,four years old, a lighter mulatto than the last,and about equally as bright. He probably also wore a cloth cap. If examined,he will be found to have a swelling at the navel.

Washington and Mary have lived at or near St. Louis, with the subscriber, or about 15 years.

It is supposed that they are making their way to Chicago,and that a white man accompanies them, that they will travel chiefly at night, and most probably in a covered wagon.

A reward of $150 will be paid for their apprehension, so that I can get them, if taken within one hundred miles of St. Louis, and $200 if taken beyond that, and secured so that I can get them, and other reasonable additional charges, if delivered to the subscriber,or to THOMAS ALLEN, Esq., at St. Louis. Mo. The above negroes, for the last few years, have been in possession of Thomas Allen, Esq., of St. Louis.

WM. RUSSELL.

ST. LOUIS, Oct. 1, 1847.

Slave owners offered rewards for the capture and return of slaves who had run away. Can you think of reasons why this family might have fled from their master?

being mistreated, and too little about slaves being treated well. In this way, the book may have stirred people's emotions too much. It certainly helped readers to feel strongly one way or the other about slavery.

Some people thought they should fight slavery by helping slaves to escape. They would hide slaves from their owners and help them travel north. The slaves hoped to reach Canada, where they could be free. One man whose slave disappeared remarked that the slave must have gone off on an underground railroad. Of course the slaves did not travel underground, but the name *Underground Railroad* stuck.

Southerners began to fear that people who did not like their ways

White people helping slaves travel from one station to the next on the "Underground Railroad."
Slaves could be returned to their masters if they were caught before reaching Canada.

would pass laws to **abolish** slavery. If that happened, they would not be able to live as they always had. They talked about making the South a separate nation that was not part of the United States.

While the disagreement over slavery was becoming worse, a young man named Abraham Lincoln was growing up in Illinois. As a pioneer, he had split many fence rails, so people called him "the railsplitter." He was tall, awkward, and sad-faced. Yet he had a friendly, easy way about him that won him many friends. In 1860, he was elected president of the United States.

The Southerners knew that Lincoln hated slavery. They were afraid he would not be fair to the South. So, shortly after Lincoln's election, the southern states announced that they would no longer be a part of the United States. This was a serious decision that led to the worst war ever fought in North America.

How Did the Mennonites Feel About Slavery?

Most Mennonites who lived before the Civil War felt sorry for the black slaves. They believed it was wrong to own another person or force him to work without pay.

A few Mennonites, such as Jacob Miller of Washington County, Maryland, did own a slave. Jacob Miller also hired Negro slaves and paid their owners rather than the slaves themselves. It is not clear whether Jacob's church approved of this or not. But there is no record that Jacob treated these slaves cruelly. He set his slave free in his will.

Most Mennonite churches did not allow members to own slaves. Mennonites also spoke against hiring slaves from masters if the slaves themselves did not receive the money. They believed that Christ's way of love would not permit them to take advantage of another person.

Study Exercises

1. When did slavery begin in North America?
2. Why did the southern plantation owners want to keep their slaves?
3. List several things the people of the North pointed out about slavery to show how cruel it was.
4. What was the Underground Railroad?
5. (a) Why did some Southerners begin talking about making the South a separate nation? (b) What helped the southern states decide that they would no longer be a part of the United States?

Further Study

1. Why were Southerners more likely to find reasons that slavery should be permitted?
2. What book caused strong feelings against slavery?

45. *The War Between the States*

Glossary Words

assassinate	Emancipation Proclamation	Union
civil war	secede	

The United States was getting ready to fight another war. But this time the war would not be against a foreign country. Instead, the northern and the southern parts of the United States were preparing to fight each other. A war between different parts of the same country is called a *civil war*.

The Southerners wanted to *secede* from the United States and form a separate government. But the people of the North were determined to keep this from happening. They said the South was breaking the law, so they called Southerners Rebels. By 1861, soldiers from the South and from the North were fighting each other. The Southern army was fighting to free the South from the North; they called Northerners Yankees. The Northern army was fighting to save the *Union*—in other words, to keep the country together.

Both the Southern and the Northern people thought that in a few

The Civil War

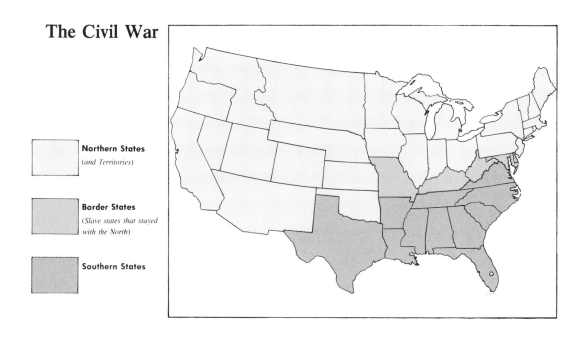

Northern States
(*and Territories*)

Border States
(*Slave states that stayed with the North*)

Southern States

weeks or months they would win the war. But battle after battle was fought, and the war lasted for a year, then two, three, and four.

The Civil War was especially sad. Soldiers helping the North had old friends and neighbors who were fighting for the South. Relatives marched off to help opposite sides in the war.

Not everyone chose to fight in the Civil War. The nonresistant Christians believed that all fighting is wrong. How could they go to war when Jesus had said "Love your enemies, bless them that curse you, [and] do good to them that hate you" (Matthew 5:44)? They would rather have suffered death themselves than kill another person. In the North, such people did not need to suffer much for their beliefs. They had to pay a fine, but they were not put in jail or forced into the army.

In the South, Christians had a much harder time staying out of the army. The South had fewer men than the North and needed soldiers badly. Officers put guns into men's hands and forced them onto the battlefield.

After one battle, an officer asked a Christian if he had shot. He replied, "I didn't see anything to shoot."

The officer said, "Didn't you see all those Yankees?"

The Christian replied, "All I saw was people. I don't shoot people."

Some Mennonites in the South hid to keep from being forced into the army. Others fled to the North. Fathers did not dare to stay with their families lest they be caught and punished. When one man's little child died, army officers came to the funeral, thinking he would probably be there. The man did come, but he had to change his appearance and stand along the outer edges of the crowd so that he would not be noticed.

The war caused the South a great deal of damage. Toward the end of the war, one Northern army purposely traveled through Georgia to burn barns, houses, and crops. They destroyed nearly everything in their path.

Because the South was mainly a farming region, it did not have many factories, so it could not manufacture many guns or much machinery. These things had to be shipped to the South from other countries. The North sent warships to the Southern ports and strangled the flow of goods in and out of the South. Not only war supplies, but clothes, medicine, and other goods became very scarce and expensive in the South.

The North had troubles too. Many people had a friend or loved one who had been killed or crippled in the war. In one of Abraham Lincoln's speeches near the end of the war, he said he believed that God was allowing the nation to be punished because of slavery. He quoted the Bible verse, "The judgments of the Lord are true and righteous altogether" (Psalm 19:9).

Northern people found out what real war was like when Robert E. Lee, the Southern commander, decided to invade the North. They were frightened. Would the Southern army attack cities and destroy property? A huge Northern army marched to stop the invasion.

The two big armies met in July, 1863, at the little town of Gettys-

burg, Pennsylvania. For three days, 165,000 men fought in and near the town. When the guns had stilled, about forty thousand men were dead or wounded. The Southern army had to retreat back to the South.

A special cemetery was set aside in memory of the soldiers who died in this battle. Abraham Lincoln came to a ceremony dedicating the new cemetery. There he gave his most famous speech, a short talk now called the Gettysburg Address. He said the United States government believes that all people are important, but that no one is more important

President Lincoln (third from left) reading the Emancipation Proclamation to his advisers.

than anyone else. This was his way of saying that it is wrong for a master to have slaves under him. He also said he hoped the nation would have "a new birth of freedom."

To help the North win the war, Lincoln had earlier made an announcement that all slaves of the South would be free. This was called the *Emancipation Proclamation*. This gave the Northern soldiers a new reason to keep on fighting. Also, it discouraged England from helping the South. English people saw clearly that if the North was fighting to free

Many former slaves attached themselves to the Union army after they were freed. They felt protected by the army, and also were fed by them.

The people of Richmond, Virginia, fled when Northern soldiers captured their city. Richmond was the capital of the South.

the slaves, the South was fighting to keep them. The English did not want to help slavery continue.

Finally General Lee saw that it was hopeless for the South to go on fighting. He met with the Northern commander, General Ulysses Grant, and surrendered his Southern army on April 9, 1865. The Northern soldiers were happy, but General Grant told them that he did not want them to fire their guns to celebrate winning the war. When he heard that the Southern soldiers were hungry, he sent food to them.

People everywhere were thankful that the war was over. Many people in the North considered Abraham Lincoln a hero. But five days after the war ended, an actor, John Wilkes Booth, shot Lincoln as he sat in a theater watching a play. Lincoln died the next morning.

All over the nation, people lowered American flags to half-mast. It was their way of showing their sorrow that the president had been *assassinated*. Lincoln had meant to treat the South kindly and fairly after the war, but now other government leaders would decide how to treat the South.

Study Exercises

1. (*a*) For what two reasons did the South fight in the Civil War? (*b*) For what two reasons did the North fight?

2. Why was the Civil War especially sad?

3. (*a*) How did the North treat the nonresistant Christians during the war? (*b*) Why did the nonresistant Christians in the South have a much harder time staying out of the army?

4. How did the North hurt the South by blocking the Southern ports?

5. Which battle helped the North to realize how destructive war can be?

6. (*a*) What was the Emancipation Proclamation? (*b*) How did it help the North win the war?

7. Was President Lincoln assassinated before or after the war was over?

Further Study

1. (*a*) When did Lincoln give the Gettysburg Address? (*b*) What did he mean when he said he hoped the nation would have "a new birth of freedom"?

2. Why was the death of President Lincoln a sad event for both the Northerners and the Southerners?

46. The South After the Civil War

Glossary Words

freedmen   sharecropper

Living in the South just after the Civil War must have been very difficult. Barns, houses, and railroads had to be rebuilt. Machines that no one had maintained during the war needed to be fixed. Slaves had run away, and the remaining slaves had been freed by the Emancipation Proclamation. The saddest fact of all was that many strong young men had been killed in the war and would not return.

Gone were the days when white ladies and gentlemen could spend much of their time visiting, dining, and playing games. Now many white women were doing their own washing, cooking, and sewing for the first time. Their husbands had their sleeves rolled up, working in the fields. Some of them had mistreated their slaves, but now they were suffering themselves.

The Scriptures say, "Go to now, ye rich men, weep and howl for your miseries that shall come upon you . . . Behold, the hire of the labourers who have reaped down your fields, which is of you kept back by fraud, crieth: and the cries of them

Many Southerners returned to ruined farms and homes after the war.

which have reaped are entered into the ears of the Lord of sabaoth" (James 5:1, 4).

Abraham Lincoln had said that after the war the North should act "with malice toward none, with charity for all." But many people in the North were bitter toward the South for killing their sons in the war. They wanted to punish the South. Congress passed harsh laws that made life difficult for Southerners. Plantation owners, especially, had to pay high taxes.

Many plantation owners found that they simply could not own a plantation anymore. They had too little money. Besides, they had too few helpers, since they no longer owned slaves. They had to sell most of the land from their plantations, a few acres here and a few acres there. This made many small farms.

By the early 1900s, the South could no longer be called a land of the very rich and the very poor. Some farmers had more land than others, it is true, but otherwise they were not much different from other people. Nearly everyone worked hard to make a living.

Even though times were hard in the South, the blacks were thankful for one thing—they were free! After the Civil War, for the first time, one could see groups of free black people, *freedmen*, walking along the roads. For once they could go wherever they wanted to, whenever they wanted to.

But the freed slaves needed to face real life. How would they buy food and clothing? Where would they live? They could not just walk away from their masters and go home, for they had no other homes. They did not own any land, and few of them had money.

Some freedmen decided to continue living on the plantation where they had lived and to work for the same man they had served before. But now that they were not slaves, the plantation owner paid them for their work. Many blacks became *sharecroppers*, whose pay was a share of the crop they helped to raise. Others rented land from a plantation owner and farmed it. Often they paid the rent with part of the crop they raised. Still other blacks chose to live in cities, and became masons, carpenters, mechanics, and other kinds of workers.

Handling their own money was new for the freedmen. Many of them did not know how to plan ahead so that their money would last from one payday to another. Some spent their earnings on fancy things and luxuries instead of on food and clothing. They lived in dirty, poorly kept cabins. But others saved their money and bought farms or trim little houses in town.

Because most blacks could not read, the government and some mission groups set up schools for them. The blacks came eagerly. At first, all ages studied in the same classroom. Fathers and sons sat learning from the same books. Of course, the young

After the Civil War, blacks of all ages attended school to learn how to read and write.

learned more easily than the old, and they continued to learn after a number of older ones had dropped out.

Many black families of the early 1900s were about as poor as their grandparents had been. But they had freedom, a treasure their grandparents had not had.

Study Exercises

1. List several reasons why life was difficult for most white Southerners after the Civil War.

2. Why did the people of the North pass harsh laws against the Southerners?

3. What happened to many of the large plantations?

4. What were the former slaves called?

5. (*a*) What were the blacks thankful for? (*b*) List several difficulties the blacks faced after the Civil War.

6. Why did blacks of all ages need to go to school?

Further Study

1. Lesson 25 mentioned several classes of people who lived in the South. Which Southerners were the least affected by the Emancipation Proclamation?

2. What is sharecropping?

Chapter 7 Review

Reviewing What You Have Learned

A. *Write a glossary word for each definition.*

1. A plan used to help slaves reach freedom.
2. The Northern states during the Civil War.
3. An announcement that freed the slaves.
4. People who have been freed from slavery.
5. To do away with.
6. To kill an important person.
7. To break away from a group.
8. Farm workers who earn part of the crops they raise.
9. A war between two groups of people in the same country.

B. *Choose the correct answer to complete each sentence.*

1. The Southerners decided to make the South a separate nation because ———.
    a. they strongly opposed slavery
    b. they wanted to help their slaves have a better life
    c. they were afraid Abraham Lincoln would try to abolish slavery
2. The Underground Railroad was ———.
    a. a secret railroad track that was built through a tunnel
    b. a plan some people used to secretly help slaves to freedom
    c. a secret trail the Southerners used when they wanted to separate slave families
3. During the Civil War, the Northerners fought ———.
    a. to free the North from the South
    b. to keep the country together
    c. to prove that they were opposed to nonresistance
4. The Civil War was especially sad because ———.
    a. many neighbors, relatives, and old friends fought on opposite sides
    b. the Northerners were unable to get the food, clothing, and other goods they needed from other countries
    c. nonresistant Christians in the South had to pay fines

5. The Emancipation Proclamation ——.
   a. was an announcement that set the slaves of the South free
   b. was given at Gettysburg, Pennsylvania
   c. encouraged England to help the South

6. After the Civil War, life was much more difficult for the ——.
   a. Western Indians
   b. black Northerners
   c. white Southerners

7. Many of the large plantations —— after the Civil War.
   a. were divided into small farms
   b. were bought by educated blacks
   c. continued to be worked by black slaves

So Far This Year

Choose the correct answers. See how many you can give without looking back.

1. Canada is (smaller, larger) than the United States, but it has (fewer, more) people.

2. Jamestown was the first lasting (Dutch, English, Spanish) settlement in North America.

3. Settlers who disliked populated areas moved to the (frontier, cities) in search of a simpler life with (fewer, more) laws.

4. Match.
   a. William Penn
   b. William Penn's grandson
   c. French fur traders
   d. Spanish soldiers and priests

   1. used liquor to cheat Indians.
   2. paid Indians for land.
   3. forced Indians to work and be baptized.
   4. paid frontiersmen to kill Indians.

5. Many Loyalists and Mennonites moved to (Canada, England, Georgia) after the Revolutionary War.

6. Most work was done by hand (before, during, after) the Industrial Revolution.

7. The United States bought (the Louisiana Territory, Florida) from France.

8. The United States and Great Britain divided the territory of (Oregon, Hawaii).

9. The colonists in (the United States, Canada) obtained their independence gradually and peacefully from Great Britain.

10. The (Civil War, Revolutionary War) started after the Southern states seceded from the United States.

1860

1862
Homestead Act offers
free land to settlers

1865

1867
Canada becomes a nation

1869
First transcontinental
railroad completed

1870

1874
Russian Mennonites
begin to settle on
Great Plains

1875

1880

1885
Canadian transcontinental
railroad completed

1885

1889
Unassigned Lands
opened to
homesteaders

1890

1893
Cherokee Outlet opened

1895

1900

1905

CHAPTER 8

SETTLEMENT OF
THE WEST

*Facing page: The white men crowded out Indians and buffalo
as they pushed westward and settled the Great Plains.*

47. *Homesteading on the Great Plains*

Glossary Words

dugout   sod   transcontinental
homestead   soddy

If you ever travel from east to west in the United States, you will notice that soon after you cross the Mississippi River, the trees seem to disappear. In the East, trees grow in practically every corner where they have not been cut down. But on the Great Plains, few trees grow unless they have been planted.

This difference between east and west was even more surprising to the first pioneers who traveled across the country. Trees had not yet been planted on the plains. Broad lands of tall grass stretched like an ocean before the pioneers. The bright blue sky seemed huge, the horizon far away. Some pioneers were frightened by the vastness and lonesomeness of it all. Others were delighted.

For years, settlers traveled across the Great Plains on their way to Oregon or California. Most of them never thought of stopping and settling on the plains, although some people settled in the states just west of the Mississippi. Farther west than that, it was drier and less inviting. A few families did set up ranches along the trail to Oregon and California, expecting to make their living by trading with wagon trains. But then from the mid-1860s through the 1880s, more people suddenly began to settle on the plains. What made the change?

The government was giving away land. Nearly any grown-up citizen of the United States could claim 160 acres of land. All he had to do was prove to the government that he could take care of those 160 acres, and then he would be allowed to call the land his own. His land was called his *homestead.*

One thing the government required was that each settler build a house on his homestead. The settlers usually wanted to plant crops as soon as possible, so they quickly put up the simplest kind of house they could build. Many of them built *dugouts.* First they dug a wide trench into the side of a bank. Next they closed off the front of it with a wall of blocks cut from the prairie *sod.* The settlers then put a roof across the trench and covered it with more sod. One

This family in Nebraska built their dugout into the side of a hill. The front and the roof were closed with blocks of sod. This photograph was taken in 1892.

window, one door, and a stovepipe through the roof finished the dugout. Those who could not afford a window or a door hung a buffalo robe or blanket in the doorway. Dugouts were cheap.

Most people lived in their dark little dugout only until they could build a better house on top of the ground. But even then the house was often made of sod blocks. This kind of house was called a *soddy*. A soddy was cool in summer and snug in winter, but its walls constantly shed crumbly dirt.

During the 1860s, two railroad companies began working to build the last stretch of railroad across the continent. One company started in Nebraska and headed west, and the other started in California and headed east. They worked at top speed, for the government rewarded them for every mile of track they laid. They pushed across prairies and mountains and through desolate, dry lands where no one lived. At last the two tracks met in Utah. The railroad company coming from the east had laid the most track, for it had crossed plains for much of the way. The railroad company coming from the west had crossed more mountains.

Soon other companies built *transcontinental* railroads. These railroad companies encouraged many people to settle on the prairies, because they knew this would give them more business. Families moving to the prairies received a free ride for themselves, their household goods, and their livestock. The railroads carried supplies to the new homes on the prairies and also took the settlers' crops to distant cities. Along the railroad tracks, new towns sprang up.

Men who traveled across the prairies went back east and told of the light, clear air. They talked about the prairie dogs, deer, wolves, buffalo, and Indians they had seen there. Most important, they told of the many acres of rich, black soil waiting to be farmed. More and more settlers moved westward to the beautiful flat country they had heard about.

Gradually the prairie changed. Where enormous herds of buffalo had

Laying railroad track across the prairie. After railroads were built, settlers found it easier to move west by train instead of by covered wagon. Do you think the Indians were happy to see railroads being built?

once grazed, barbed wire fences separated one farm from another. Crops of corn and wheat replaced the acres of wild prairie flowers. Today the Great Plains is still a broad, flat countryside, but many more trees, houses, and towns are found there. Few spots exist where you can look toward the horizon and wonder if any white man has ever walked on that land.

Many homesteader children attended one-room schools such as this. Compare this schoolroom with the colonial school illustrated in Lesson 23. Then compare both of them with your school.

Study Exercises

1. Why did people travel across the Great Plains for many years without thinking of settling there?
2. What made people eager to settle on the plains?
3. (*a*) What was one thing the government required of the plains settlers? (*b*) How did the settlers meet this requirement?
4. (*a*) How was the first transcontinental railroad built? (*b*) Why did the companies work at top speed?
5. How did the transcontinental railroads help the settlement of the Great Plains?

Further Study

1. Why did the government start giving land away?
2. The transcontinental railroads provided other benefits besides helping the prairie dwellers. (*a*) How did the transcontinental railroads help people who lived in California? (*b*) How did these railroads help people who lived in the East?

48. *The Great Plains Becomes a Breadbasket*

Glossary Words

      spring wheat   steppes   winter wheat

Farms on the rolling western plains are quite different from farms in the East. In the East, many farmers raise a variety of crops on small or medium-sized fields. But in the West, farmers raise only a few kinds of crops on fields with hundreds of acres each. It is interesting to learn how wheat-growing took a giant step forward in Kansas, Nebraska, and the Southwest during the 1870s.

About this time, many farmers living on the *steppes* of Russia were in trouble. As Christians, they did not believe they should serve in the armed forces. But the Russian government was planning to make them serve in the Russian army whether they wanted to or not.

In the United States, John Funk heard that the Mennonites in Russia wanted to leave. Deeply interested, he informed American Mennonites of what was happening to their Russian brethren and requested help for them. When leaders from the Russian colonies came to America to look for a place to settle, John Funk traveled with them and helped them. Soon groups of Russian Mennonites moved into Kansas and Nebraska.

The settlers on the Great Plains had tried raising different crops. To the north, wheat would grow well in the summertime. There farmers raised *spring wheat*; that is, they planted it in the spring and harvested it later the same year. In Kansas and Nebraska the climate was too warm for this kind of wheat to grow well.

The Russian Mennonites brought with them a type of wheat known as Turkey Red. It was a *winter wheat*, planted in the fall and harvested early the following summer. Because it grew earlier in the spring, it had fewer problems with insects and diseases. It did not easily wilt in the hot sunshine.

At first the millers did not like the new type of wheat because it was difficult to grind into flour. But farmers liked it because it grew so well on the plains, so millers changed their mill machinery to handle the hard grain. Housewives learned how to bake with winter wheat flour. They too liked it. For sixty years, practically all farmers in the area raised the Turkey Red wheat. So much wheat was raised in Kansas that it became known as the Breadbasket of America.

The Russian Mennonites were happy to find a peaceful refuge in America. Many settled in central Kansas. Large mills were built to handle their winter wheat.

Russian Mennonites Move to the American West

In the late 1700s, while many Mennonites were enjoying freedom in America, some Mennonites from Germany were finding freedom in Russia. Catherine II, the ruler of Russia, had given them a special invitation to move to the steppes of the Ukraine. She offered them large sections of land and promised that they would never be required to serve in the Russian army.

The Mennonites who moved to Russia prospered on their large farms. Then, in 1870, the Russian government announced that all young men in the country must serve in the army. The Mennonites were alarmed. Some of them were not as spiritual as their Anabaptist forefathers, but most of them still believed it is wrong for Christians to go to war. They asked the Russian government to continue granting them the privilege of not serving in the military. When the government refused to grant their request, they began making plans to move to North America.

Then the Russian officials became concerned. They did not want the Mennonites to leave, for they were some of the best farmers in the country. Finally the government agreed that instead of serving in the army, the young Mennonite men could serve their country by working in forests. After this agreement was reached, most of the Mennonites decided to stay in Russia. But some had already sold their farms and made arrangements to leave for the United States and Canada. About a third of the Mennonites in Russia migrated to North America between 1873 and 1880, bringing their Turkey Red wheat with them.

Study Exercises

1. How do farms in the West differ from farms in the East?
2. (a) Why did many Russian Mennonites decide to move to the United States? (b) Who helped them find a place to live?
3. (a) What kind of wheat did these farmers bring with them from Russia? (b) What were the advantages of this wheat?
4. What complaint did the millers have about the wheat?
5. How long was Turkey Red wheat raised by the farmers of Kansas and Nebraska?

Further Study

1. Why do western farmers have larger fields than eastern farmers have?
2. What helped make Kansas the Breadbasket of America?

49. Settlers Move Onto the Last Frontier

Glossary Words

reservation   populated

For years, wagon trains had rumbled through Indian territory without stopping. Though a few Indians attacked the travelers and stole horses, they generally did not mind too much as long as the white people moved on to California and Oregon. But when settlers began to make their homes on the Great Plains, most Indians felt threatened. Like any other people, they did not want to lose their way of life.

Many Indians of the plains depended on the buffalo for their living. White men often shot buffalo whether they needed meat or not. The Indians realized the buffalo would soon be gone. Also, the Indians needed empty, open spaces for hunting. White men's farms occupied more and more of those spaces.

The Indians began raiding and killing the new settlers. White men, however, were just as bad. They were determined to take the western lands. Sometimes white men started fights with Indians, and when the Indians fought back, the settlers asked the government to help them fight the Indians. Not even peaceful people (white or Indian) were safe from

White men killed large numbers of buffalo during the 1870s and early 1880s. Only a few buffalo were left on the plains by 1885. The Indians had depended on the buffalo for food.

bloody attacks.

The Indians finally had to surrender. Although they had won some battles, they were outnumbered by all the white settlers moving in. The Indian chiefs and fighters who had not been killed made peace.

The government set aside sections of land, usually of poorer quality, where the Indians could live. These areas are called *reservations*. Some reservations are small; a few of them, such as one for the Navajo Indians, are very large.

How could so many Indian tribes,

once scattered over the whole country, fit into the Indian reservations? North America had been sparsely *populated* and had never been full of Indians. So the Indians could be grouped together in a smaller space.

Also remember that by the time the Indians were placed on Indian reservations, many of them had died. White men's diseases and the effects of whiskey had cut down their number. Another reason the Indians could be placed in a smaller area was that they changed from hunting to farming and other occupations. This meant they could live off a smaller amount of land.

Canadians did not fight as many bloody battles with the Indians as Americans did. Like Indians in the United States, many Canadian Indians now live on land set aside for them, called reserves.

In 1888 and following years, some of the last big sections of land changed hands from Indians to white people. Land-hungry settlers had been urging the government to open a large Indian territory called Oklahoma. Newsmen also wrote glowing descriptions of the coveted lands. These descriptions made the lands sound almost like a garden of Eden. Some settlers even entered the lands but were removed by United States soldiers because they had no right to enter.

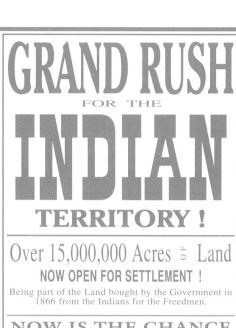

Railroad companies put out advertisements to bring settlers to land that the railroad companies owned. They hoped the settlers would create more business for the railroad. Do you think the advertisement is accurate in saying "The Indians are rejoicing to have the whites settle up this country"?

When the United States finally bought the lands from the Indians, thousands of white people were ready to settle in these Unassigned Lands. Fifty thousand settlers gathered at its edges, ready to enter at an appointed time. Within hours after the opening at noon on April 22, 1889, practically all the land was claimed. Some men entered the area before opening time to be sure they could stake a good claim. But soldiers were on the lookout for Sooners, as they were called. Not all Sooners were caught, but those who were caught lost their right to a claim.

Other runs for land followed. The biggest one was the great rush in 1893. The Cherokee Indians had agreed to give the Cherokee Outlet to the United States. This vast area was located in north-central Oklahoma. On September 16, 1893, the Outlet was opened to homesteaders. This time a hundred thousand people gathered, ready to dash for a claim. When pistol shots signaled the opening, the people rushed forward, some on horses, some on high-wheeled bicycles, others on wagons, or even on foot.

Within twenty-four hours, makeshift cities had sprung up. The families that scattered across the Outlet lived in wagons, tents, dugouts, and soddies until they had time to build regular houses. The farmers who settled these wide-open spaces found them a good place to graze cattle and raise grain.

Thousands of settlers rushed to claim land when the Cherokee Outlet was opened on September 16, 1893.

The Outlet was not settled in one day, as the Unassigned Lands had been. Few people lived in the western section until close to 1900. But settlers finally claimed all this huge land, which had once belonged to Indians. The frontier had disappeared.

This did not mean that the West was now as thickly settled as the East. But it did mean that one could no longer draw a line across the West and say, "Beyond this line white men have not settled."

Study Exercises

1. Give two reasons why the Indian way of life was threatened by white men.
2. (a) Why did the Indians finally have to give up trying to keep out white men? (b) What happened to the Indians?
3. Where were the last large sections of land that changed hands between white men and Indians?
4. (a) How many settlers gathered to claim the Unassigned Lands? (b) Who were the Sooners?
5. What type of farming did the Oklahoma settlers find profitable?

Further Study

1. How could all of the many North American Indian tribes fit onto the reservations?
2. How many years ago were the Unassigned Lands opened for white settlers?

50. Provinces Unite and Grow

Glossary Word

prime minister

As Canada grew and settlers moved west, many people wanted the separate Canadian colonies to join together and make one strong nation. One of these people was John A. Macdonald. He worked hard to unite all the colonies. When colony leaders met to talk over the matter, four colonies joined together, and formed a new country with four provinces: Nova Scotia, New Brunswick, Quebec, and Ontario. (Prince Edward Island and Newfoundland decided not to join at this time.) On July 1, 1867, for the first time, Canada was a nation. John A. Macdonald was chosen to be Canada's first *prime minister*.

Canada was soon growing. It expanded in much the same way as the United States. After the East had been settled for a while, people moved to the West. The Great Plains of Canada were filled in last.

It happened like this. The Canadians wanted British Columbia to join Canada, but the British Columbians were not sure about that. Some of them said, "The United States is closer to us than eastern Canada. Why not join the United States?"

Finally John Macdonald promised that if British Columbia joined Canada, the government would see that a railroad was built all the way from the East to British Columbia. The people of British Columbia agreed to this.

In the meantime, Canada bought

John A. Macdonald was Canada's first prime minister.

the huge area of land between the Hudson Bay and the Rocky Mountains. The land had belonged to the Hudson's Bay Company for many years. But as people moved into the area, it was only proper that the government, not a company, control the land.

In Manitoba, trouble arose when government surveyors came to divide the land into neat squares. French–Indian farmers already living there had long, narrow farms as farmers in Quebec had. They did not want the surveyors to cut across their property lines. Some of them fought, and the rebellion was put down by Canadian soldiers. But finally the Canadian government made laws that allowed these people to have land of their own.

Most of the territory that the railroad to British Columbia would run through was unsettled. Some Canadians hurried west to claim land along the planned railroad. They hoped to sell their land at a higher price after the railroad running nearby made it more valuable. But these people did not claim nearly all the land.

Railroad officials wanted more people to settle along the railroad because the settlers would buy and sell goods that the railroad carried. So the railroad companies advertised the plains and showed samples of grain that farms there could produce. The

After three years of work, this Manitoba farmer has turned his prairie land into a prosperous farm.

This was the first Canadian train to travel from the Atlantic Ocean to the Pacific Ocean in one trip.

government sent agents to advertise the Canadian land in Europe. Much of it was good land for grain, and best of all, it was free. Whole groups of people in Europe began to think of making the Canadian prairies their home.

Mennonites fearing persecution in Russia began settling in Manitoba in 1874, moving by whole villages at a time. The new settlers had to do many things quickly. They had to build barns and houses, dig wells, and break the tough sod to make fields. But the newcomers soon made themselves at home because Manitoba's prairies were much like the steppes they had left in Russia. In a short time their communities were prospering. By the end of the 1870s, 7,500 Mennonites had come.

Icelanders came to the prairies because there was not enough farmland in their own country. Swedes built a town in the area now called Saskatchewan. Mormons from the United States settled in what is now Alberta. Other Russians besides Mennonites flocked to the prairies.

Jews also moved to Canada, seeking relief from persecution in Russia and Europe. Many chose to live in cities, but a few tried life on the prairies. People from southern Europe came by the thousands. They had been poor and persecuted. Their farms had been tiny, and their soil had been overworked. Here they had freedom and 160 acres all their own.

Building the railroad to British Columbia took a long time. The

Canada in 1905

Rocky Mountains formed a mighty wall very difficult to work through. But when workmen finally finished it in the 1880s, it was the longest railroad in the world. The railroad and the settlements along it helped to add more provinces to Canada. By 1905, Canadian provinces stretched from the Atlantic Ocean to the Pacific Ocean. Prince Edward Island had joined the union in 1873. Newfoundland became the newest province in 1949.

─────────────── **Study Exercises** ───────────────

1. List the first four Canadian provinces.
2. Who was Canada's first prime minister?
3. (a) Why did the people of British Columbia consider joining the United States? (b) How did the Canadians persuade them to join Canada?
4. (a) Why did the railroad officials want more settlers along their railroad? (b) How much did the settlers have to pay for the land on the Canadian prairies?
5. List at least five groups of people who moved to the plains of Canada.

Gaining Geographical Skills

1. Trace Map C in the map section. Label it "Canada Expands Westward." Draw the route the railroad took from East to West.

2. Label the nine provinces that had joined Canada by 1905.

Further Study

1. List several ways the railroad helped Canada become a large country.

2. Why was it easy for the Mennonites from Russia to adjust to Manitoba?

Chapter 8 Review

Reviewing What You Have Learned

A. *Write a glossary word for each definition.*

1. Land given to settlers by the government.
2. A layer of soil held together by roots.
3. Large plains in Russia.
4. Filled with people.
5. An important leader in countries such as Canada.
6. A house made of sod.
7. A shelter dug into a hillside.
8. Land set aside for Indian use.
9. Wheat planted in the fall and harvested the next spring.
10. Reaching across a continent.

B. *Choose the correct answer to complete each sentence.*

1. People were eager to settle the Great Plains after ———.
   a. the government began giving land away
   b. they saw how green the plains were
   c. the government began building houses for them
2. The first transcontinental railroad was built ———.
   a. from North to South
   b. through the forests of the Great Plains
   c. by two railroad companies
3. The transcontinental railroads ———.
   a. helped the Indians
   b. caused many problems for the settlers on the plains
   c. encouraged people to settle the prairies
4. Turkey Red wheat helped settle the West because ———.
   a. it was a soft wheat that could be ground easily
   b. it was a hardy wheat that could be raised on the Great Plains
   c. it could be grown on small farms

5. The Indians who lived on the American Great Plains ———.
   a. killed buffalo for sport
   b. were forced onto reservations
   c. did not fight as many battles as the Canadian Indians did

6. Some of the last large sections of land that changed hands between the white men and the Indians were in ———.
   a. Oklahoma
   b. Oregon
   c. California

7. ——— were the first four Canadian provinces.
   a. Nova Scotia, New Brunswick, Manitoba, and Ontario
   b. Nova Scotia, New Brunswick, Ontario, and Quebec
   c. Nova Scotia, Newfoundland, Prince Edward Island, and British Columbia

8. The Canadian railroad ———.
   a. was built after the Canadian plains were settled
   b. was owned by a company that charged high prices for the land along the railroad
   c. encouraged British Columbia and other western territories to join Canada

So Far This Year

Choose the correct answers. See how many you can give without looking back.

1. Seasons in the (Southern, Eastern) Hemisphere are opposite from those in the Northern Hemisphere.

2. The first lasting French settlement in North America was (Ottawa, Quebec, Montreal).

3. The French settled lands (north, south) of the English colonies.

4. During the Revolutionary War, some (minutemen, nonresistant Christians) were mistreated because they refused to fight.

5. The (Declaration of Independence, Constitution) describes how the United States government is to work.

6. The United States took a large area in the (Southeast, Southwest) from Mexico.

7. Choose three: The earliest settlers in the West included (Mennonites, Mormons, missionaries, manufacturers, miners).

8. White men (asked, forced, did not want) the eastern Indians to move to western lands.

9. Before the Civil War, many Northerners began having strong feelings against (slavery, factory owners).

10. Before the Civil War, many (Northerners, Southerners) were afraid the (Northerners, Southerners) would make them give up their slaves.

11. After the Civil War, (Northerners, Southerners) had to adjust to life without slaves, and (black, Indian) people had to learn to provide for themselves.

12. Many settlers moved to the Great Plains after the government started giving away (land, food) and railroad companies built (local, transcontinental) railroads.

These farmers pull a wagonload of grain with a steam-powered tractor. By this time, steam engines had also been used to power trains and boats.

How Changes
of the 1800s
Affect Us

1790
1796 First smallpox vaccine
1800
1807 First successful steamboat
1810
1820
1825 Erie Canal opened
1830
1831 First successful reaper
1840
First telegraph *1844*
Sewing machine *1845*
1846 Surgery with ether demonstrated
1850
1860–1861 First nursing school opened Pony express
1860
1870
Telephone invented *1876*
Light bulb invented *1879*
1880

51. Doctors Make New Discoveries

52. Faster on Water, Faster on Land

53. Faster Communication

54. New Conveniences for the Home

55. Machinery Comes to the Farm

56. Conservation

51. Doctors Make New Discoveries

Glossary Words

antiseptic	pasteurize
immune	vaccination

While pioneers were spreading across the North American continent, doctors became pioneers too—but in a different way. They were exploring the causes of diseases and finding how to treat them. People were living longer than before. Up to this time, smallpox had killed many people. Even if a person with smallpox lived, he often had ugly scars for the rest of his life. The only good thing about smallpox was that you could not get it twice. A person who had the disease was *immune* to it afterwards.

A doctor in England, Edward Jenner, discovered that people who had suffered cowpox were also immune to smallpox. Cowpox was a much milder disease than smallpox. In 1796, Edward Jenner decided to perform a dangerous experiment. He took an eight-year-old boy and scratched his arm. Then he put cowpox germs into the scratches. He hoped that this treatment would make the boy immune not only to cowpox but also to smallpox. Later he scratched the boy's arm again, putting in germs of the dreaded smallpox. To his delight, the boy did not get sick. Dr. Jenner had given the first *vaccination.*

Doctors learned more about vaccinating people, and soon many people were being vaccinated for smallpox. Perhaps your parents or

Before the days of cars and modern hospitals, doctors visited sick people in their homes. Doctors were scarce, and many people died without receiving medical attention.

This mother has chosen to accept a newfangled idea, vaccination. The doctor is using a knife to vaccinate the child, since needles had not yet been developed.

grandparents carry a scar from the time they were vaccinated for this disease. Today no cases of smallpox are known in the world, and no one gets vaccinated for it anymore. But people still get vaccinated for many other diseases such as measles, mumps, diphtheria, whooping cough, tetanus, and polio.

Before the 1840s, surgery had always been very painful. There was no good way to put a patient to sleep. Because of the pain, patients could not hold still and had to be held down. An operation was almost as hard for

a kind-hearted doctor as for the patient.

But this changed when two Americans, a dentist and a doctor, experimented with a gas called ether. Patients who breathed it were safely put to sleep. Now doctors could perform long operations they had never dared to try before.

In 1860, a British woman named Florence Nightingale set up the first school for nurses in London, England. She trained nurses to check patients regularly. The nurses not only worked with the doctors but also spent time comforting and encouraging patients.

In those days, hardly anyone had been taught that germs cause sickness. A French scientist, Louis Pasteur, proved that they do, and he also taught people how to kill germs in food. Today milk and other foods are *pasteurized* to make them safe to eat or drink and to keep them from spoiling. Do you see how pasteurization got its name?

A British doctor named Joseph Lister was concerned because half the people who had surgery died from infections that developed afterwards. He began to try very hard to keep germs out of his operations. He learned to use *antiseptics* on his hands and instruments and on the bandages that covered the wounds. This was an important step toward safe surgery.

Doctors have also learned how to take care of newborn babies in better ways. Tiny babies get sick more easily than most people, and long ago many of them died. It is quite likely that someone living in your family would have died as a baby had it not been for the help doctors have learned to give.

Today not only doctors but anyone can learn much about how to be healthy. Long ago, butchers and storekeepers did not always worry if flies sat on the food they were selling or if they did not keep their meat cold enough. Now stores keep their food carefully covered and refrigerated if necessary. Years ago, people did not know for sure if the water in their wells was safe. Now we can test our drinking water for germs. In schools of the past, everyone drank from the same dipper. People avoid that today. At one time, no one knew much about vitamins. Now even cereal boxes tell you about vitamins.

This does not mean that our great-grandparents knew nothing about how to take care of themselves. Many people were careful to be clean, to eat good food, and to get enough sleep and exercise. But because of what they did not know, many people died of things they could have easily changed.

People years ago possibly took better care of their health in common-sense ways than people do today. Often people today are careless, eating too much, working too hard (or not hard enough), and getting too little exercise. They seem to think that if they get sick, the doctor will make them well again. But doctors are limited in what they can do. We must take proper care of our bodies and trust the Lord for what we and the doctors cannot do. He is the only one "who healeth all thy diseases" (Psalm 103:3).

Study Exercises

1. (a) Why did Edward Jenner infect a young boy with cowpox germs? (b) Why are smallpox vaccinations no longer given?
2. What discovery made surgery bearable for patients?

3. How did Florence Nightingale improve medical care?

4. How did pasteurization get its name?

5. What are antiseptics?

6. List several things people have learned that help them stay healthy.

Further Study

1. Why is vaccination often a good way to prevent a disease?

2. (*a*) Do the discoveries of modern doctors mean we do not need to be careful about our health? (*b*) Why?

52. *Faster on Water, Faster on Land*

Glossary Words

canal   lock   transportation

For many centuries, there was no fast way to travel. People walked, or if they were rich enough, they rode a donkey or horse. On water, they sailed if the wind blew; otherwise they rowed. These slow ways of traveling did not improve much as time went on. The first president of the United States could travel only as fast as King David had.

Not until the early 1800s did people learn to travel faster by water. At that time, people were more likely to travel by water than they are today. They especially liked water travel for hauling big loads long distances. Boats in water glide along much more easily than big wagons roll over rough roads. To make a boat go faster, men thought, "Why not put a

Paddle wheel steamboats were a familiar sight on America's large rivers. These steamers delivered passengers and goods up and down the Mississippi.

steam engine into it and make the engine row the boat or turn paddles?'' Several men tried it, but Robert Fulton was the first man to build a steamboat that was practical to use. It made its first journey up the Hudson River to Albany, New York, in 1807.

Steamboats could easily travel upstream. Because they did not need to wait for the wind, like sailboats, it was easier to make a schedule, planning exactly when they would arrive at towns along the way. People in those towns could now plan to ship their goods by steamboat, or they could plan a trip.

People who did not live near rivers began thinking, "Wouldn't it be wonderful if we could somehow float small boats across the countryside near to where we live? Then we could load things on boats instead of having to take them by wagon to the river." So with picks, shovels, and wheelbarrows, they began digging *canals* to bring the water where they wanted it. They planned for horses to walk along the canals, pulling the boats behind them.

People built canals nearly anywhere, even running them through tunnels and over bridges! Small hills did not stop them. On the sides of hills they built *locks* to help raise the boats to higher levels. One canal

Horses or mules could pull a much larger load in a canal boat than they could in a wagon.

system ran all the way from Philadelphia to Pittsburgh. What a job it must have been to cross all those hills!

Of course no one tried to run canals over mountains. Canal men took the canal boats out of the water and placed them on little railroad cars that were pulled by cables to the top of the mountain.

The Erie Canal was the first important canal in the United States. DeWitt Clinton, the governor of New York State, thought there should be a water route from New York City to Lake Erie. By looking at a map, could you guess where canal builders made the canal? Rather than running it straight from New York City across the countryside, they planned that

Early Canals

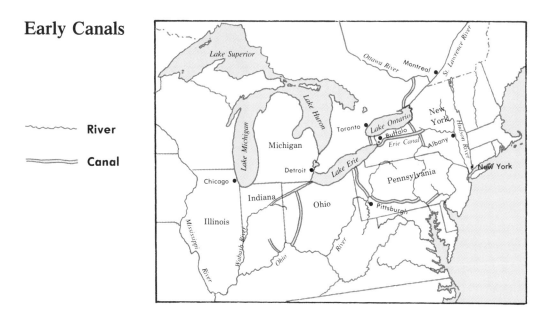

~~~~~~ **River**

══════ **Canal**

people would travel up the Hudson River to Albany and then travel by canal to Buffalo on Lake Erie. People laughed at Governor Clinton's idea. They called it "Clinton's Folly," and "Clinton's Big Ditch." But when the canal opened in 1825, people found that they could take a big load of goods from Buffalo to New York almost three times as fast as they could before. This made the goods cheaper.

People began to travel faster not only on water but also on land. Trains with steam engines started to take travelers on short journeys. But travel on a train was dirty and uncomfortable. When the windows were open, sparks from the steam engine blew into the passenger cars, damaging people's clothing. Bits of cinders

and ash settled on everyone. But people put up with these inconveniences because trains were fast.

People also liked trains for carrying freight. Trains could carry bigger loads than canal boats and could do it more cheaply. Besides, they could easily reach towns that no canals had ever reached. Soon hardly anyone was using canals. Railroads were running from one end of the country to the other.

Steam engines were used not only in trains but in some cars, such as the Stanley Steamer. But almost from the beginning of car making, another kind of engine proved better. The gasoline engine was lighter, smaller, and more powerful than a steam engine, and it did not take as much fuel. Nearly all cars run on gasoline or diesel fuel today.

By the early 1900s, people and products could travel much faster than they could in the year 1800. Milkmen could serve many customers in a day. Farmers could ship apples to faraway cities. People could go shopping in town and come back the same morning. They could get together from many miles around to work or to worship.

Today, even if we do not travel far, our lives are changed by fast *transportation*. Without it, mail from another state or province might take many weeks to reach us. We could not buy as many kinds of food in stores, and some kinds would be more expensive. Fresh food such as lettuce would be impossible for most people to get in winter.

Fast transportation does not make people better. It does not make life happier. But it does help to make life handier in some ways. Christians should use transportation to the glory of God, and especially to "go . . . into all the world, and preach the gospel to every creature" (Mark 16:15).

Study Exercises

1. In the early 1800s, why did people haul big loads by water instead of by land?
2. How were steamboats better than sailboats?
3. (a) Why did people begin building canals? (b) How did the boats cross small hills?
4. Which was the first important canal in the United States?
5. Give three reasons why people built railroads instead of more canals.
6. Give two ways fast transportation affects us, even if we do not travel far.

Further Study

1. Why was fast transportation even more important in large countries such as the United States and Canada than it was in the small countries of Europe?
2. Think of some ways fast transportation helps us. List some that are not mentioned in the lesson.

53. *Faster Communication*

Glossary Words

pony express   telegraph

If you have ever waited for a letter from across the country, it probably seemed that it took a long time to arrive. But it does not take as long as it did in the 1850s. In those days no mail went by airplane or even by truck. Stagecoaches and trains carried the mail. Stagecoaches took three weeks to go from Missouri to California. Railroads did not even

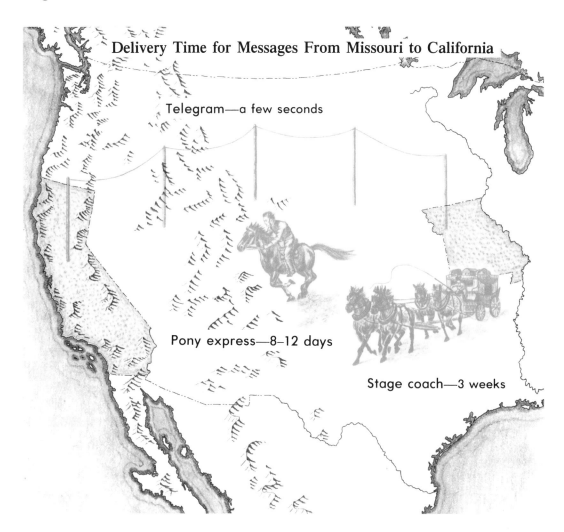

Delivery Time for Messages From Missouri to California

Telegram—a few seconds

Pony express—8–12 days

Stage coach—3 weeks

exist in that part of the country.

Then someone had the idea of sending mail from Missouri to California by *pony express*. The pony express worked like a relay race such as you may have played at recess. A pony would carry a rider and bags of mail for ten or fifteen miles. By that time the pony was worn out. At the next station along the way another pony would be waiting. The rider would jump off the tired pony, quickly put his mail bags on the fresh one, and away he would go again! The pony express could carry mail from Missouri to California in eight to twelve days. That was an exciting speed.

But then something even faster was invented—the *telegraph*. A telegraph sends messages in the form of short and long electrical signals called dots and dashes. These messages travel many miles through wires in the twinkling of an eye.

Samuel F. B. Morse developed the first successful telegraph in 1844. Like other inventors, he had trouble getting people to believe his invention would work. Finally he received enough money to set up a telegraph line between Washington, D.C., and Baltimore. When he was ready to demonstrate it, people gathered around him. Thirty-five miles away in Baltimore, Morse's helper waited for

A granddaughter of Samuel F. B. Morse shows the original telegraph instrument that was used to send the message "What Hath God Wrought."

a message. Morse tapped a message into the telegraph in dots and dashes. The person on the other end sent back the same message. As everyone watched, the telegraph tapped out the message Morse had sent. It was, "What hath God wrought!" It was a way of saying, "Look what God has done!"

By 1861, a message could be sent by telegraph from coast to coast. The pony express was no longer necessary. Then someone had an even greater idea. Why not lay a cable across the Atlantic Ocean from America to Europe? This was more difficult than running a cable across the United States. Storms tossed the ship that laid the cable. The cable snapped more than once. After several tries, a good telegraph cable linked Europe and America.

Newspapermen were glad for telegraph lines. They could quickly find out what was happening in distant places. Businessmen could make agreements with other businessmen by telegraph. For the first time, people could communicate faster than they would have by sending letters.

The next great step in communications came when Alexander Graham Bell invented the telephone. He had learned that sound could be sent through wires. This made him think that the sound of someone talking could also be sent through wires. Bell and his helper worked for months before they got the first words to come clearly over the telephone in 1876.

Telephones had some problems at first. The wires seemed to buzz and howl in people's ears, and they had to shout to be heard. Telephones were used only for short distances at first. The first telephone line across America was not complete until after 1900.

How different those days were from today, when we can call friends nearly anywhere in North America and in many foreign countries. Now people buy and sell things by telephone. They visit with friends thousands of miles away. They make calls from cars and airplanes. They make computers communicate with other computers through telephone lines.

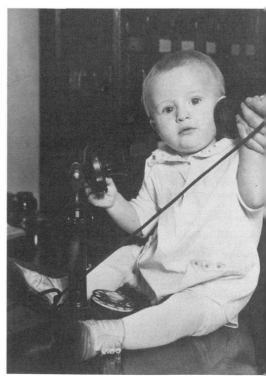

Early telephones had separate earpieces and mouthpieces. The rotary dial had been invented by the time this photograph was made.

Telephones can do much good if we use them right. They give Christians more opportunities to encourage one another. But it has never been easy for people to control their tongues, and now that our words can travel so easily, we need to be especially careful.

Study Exercises

1. (a) How long did it take a stagecoach to travel from Missouri to California? (b) How long did it take the pony express to carry mail that same distance?
2. (a) Who developed the first successful telegraph? (b) How does a telegraph send messages?
3. Why was the pony express no longer needed after 1861?
4. Why were newspapermen and businessmen glad for telegraph lines?
5. (a) Who invented the telephone? (b) What problems did telephones have at first?

Further Study

1. Have you ever received a letter or a telephone call from someone living far away from you? How did fast communication benefit you?
2. What was the first telegraph message sent from Washington, D.C., to Baltimore?
3. What made it difficult to lay a telegraph cable across the Atlantic Ocean?

54. New Conveniences for the Home

Even though the telephone had been invented in 1876, most people did not have telephones in their homes until later. Telephones had to be tested and improved for a while before people across the country accepted them. This was true for other inventions too.

By 1900, inventions had brought many changes into people's homes, especially in the kitchen. The open

The oven in this wood-burning cookstove is an improvement over earlier methods of baking.

fireplace with its big black cooking pot had disappeared. Instead, people used a cookstove. A cookstove did not waste as much wood or coal as a fireplace.

If the fire in the cookstove died out, the housewife no longer needed to borrow fire from a neighbor. She could simply reach into a drawer, get out a little wooden stick with a white or yellow phosphorus tip, and rub it against a rough surface. The match would catch fire, just like that! One big problem with those first matches, though, was that the phosphorus tip gave off poisonous fumes. People got sick from the fumes and even died. But then better matches were invented. Today we can use matches without worrying about poisonous fumes.

The old springhouse in the yard was no longer used much. Instead, a low wooden icebox in the kitchen kept food fresh. An iceman delivered huge blocks of ice to homes several times a week. A cold chunk was set in a special compartment in the upper part of the icebox.

Housewives still had to bring water into the kitchen in a bucket. But the old open well was gone. Instead of using a rope to lift a heavy bucketful of water from a deep hole, a

housewife needed only to pump a handle to fill her bucket.

Up to this time, people had preserved their food by drying, smoking, salting, or pickling it. Now they could keep food over wintertime with a new invention—canning! The jars were sealed with rubber rings under the lids. It was not until 1914 that someone invented the two-piece jar lids that are familiar to us.

The spinning wheel and the loom were gone. Families could buy cloth much more easily than they could make it. And now, many homes had another new invention—the sewing machine. Sewing by hand had always taken a long time, but for years no one could think of a way to make a machine that could sew. Elias Howe had finally thought of putting the eye of a needle in its point. This helped him solve the puzzle. To operate the sewing machine, the housewife pedaled a foot treadle. The machine could stitch a seam much faster than even a fast seamstress could.

By 1900, some families were starting to listen to phonograph records. The first records were not flat but were shaped like a short piece of pipe. The record player had to be cranked by hand. The songs sounded scratchy, but it was quite a new thing to hear recorded voices come out of a machine!

Another invention that began to change people's lives was the light bulb. Before light bulbs were invented, winter evenings seemed long and dark with light only from lamps and the fireplace. But in 1879, an inventor named Thomas Edison found a way to make light bulbs, which made a room seem as bright as day. People felt like staying up later in the evenings and getting more done. It was another step in changing from the old, slow-moving way of doing things to the faster pace of life we have today.

To live in a fast-moving world is good in some ways. But sometimes we wonder if people a hundred years ago had something good in their lives that we now miss. The days of long ago remind us that it is good to slow down sometimes, and to do with fewer things. No matter how many conveniences we have, we must always "seek . . . the kingdom of God" (Matthew 6:33).

Study Exercises

1. List the nine inventions that are mentioned in this lesson. After each invention, tell how it changed home life.
2. Why did families no longer have the spinning wheel and loom in their homes?

Further Study

1. List some ways you think living in a fast-moving world is good.
2. List some good things about life a hundred years ago that we miss.
3. Read Ecclesiastes 7:10. What is unwise to do when we think about how life was in the past?

55. *Machinery Comes to the Farm*

Glossary Words

combine	mechanical reaper	threshing machine
cradle	scythe	

Travelers and housewives were not the only ones helped by new inventions. Farmers changed their ways of working too. Early farmers had used wooden or iron plows. John Deere changed that by inventing the steel plow. Farmers liked the steel plow much better because the soil did not stick to it. Later, John Deere invented a plow that farmers could ride. That was a big improvement over walking behind the plow. Yet how surprised farmers of those days would have been if they had seen today's tractors plowing eight or ten furrows at a time!

Farmers in the West had very few trees to cut down for wood. Making board fences was out of the question. Someone invented barbed wire, from which fences could be made cheaply

and quickly. These new wire fences kept roaming buffalo and cattle from trampling farmers' crops. Cowboys, who had roamed the Great Plains along with their cattle, did not like to find fences blocking their way. Many of them cut the barbed wire. But farmers kept moving into the area and building more barbed wire fences. In the end, cattle owners and their cowboys learned that barbed wire could help them too. They bought large sections of land for their cattle and fenced them in.

The first farmers in America probably did not harvest grain much faster than the reapers did in the Book of Ruth. After the *scythe* was invented, farmers learned to place a wooden frame on it, called a *cradle*. The cradle caught the grain as it fell so that farmers could lay it in neat heaps. A cradle was heavy, but it saved time. Still, farmers needed a faster way to harvest grain. Often some of their crop rotted because the slow-moving scythes could not reap whole fields quickly enough.

Several men experimented with ways to reap grain faster. In the

1830s, Cyrus McCormick was the first man to put together a truly successful *mechanical reaper*. He found many eager buyers in the West, where fields were level and reapers worked especially well. Mechanical reapers made it possible for farmers to raise big fields of wheat without losing part of their crop.

When the noisy *threshing machine* was invented, farmers used it for the last step in their grain harvest. They fed bundles of grain stalks into its mouth. Clean grain poured out at one hole while the chaff and the straw blew out separately. Although threshing with a machine was warm, dusty work, it was faster than beating out the grain with sticks. Today, of course, farmers use *combines*, which reap the grain and thresh it in one operation.

Farmers tried steam tractors at one time, but they were too big and clumsy to do field work. After the invention of lighter, smaller kerosene engines, tractors were not so bulky. Tractors today have gasoline or diesel engines.

Because many eastern farms were

Cyrus McCormick's reaper helped grain farmers reap their crop more quickly.

small, most farmers could not afford all the new machinery. Sometimes a group of neighbors bought a machine together and shared it. Farmers in a neighborhood would take a threshing machine from farm to farm, all helping each other.

Study Exercises

1. Why did John Deere's steel plow work better than wooden or iron plows?
2. (a) Why did western farmers like barbed wire? (b) Why did cowboys dislike the barbed wire fences at first?
3. (a) How was the scythe improved? (b) Why did farmers still need a faster way to harvest grain?
4. (a) Who invented the mechanical reaper? (b) Why were many farmers in the West especially eager to buy them?
5. What did threshing machines do with the bundles of grain stalks?
6. Why are steam engines no longer used in tractors?
7. Why did eastern farmers often group together to buy machinery?

Further Study

1. Why was there a greater need for improved farm machinery after settlers began farming the large western areas of North America?
2. What two machines have been replaced by modern combines?

56. Conservation

Glossary Words

conserve   erosion   raw materials
crop rotation   import   topsoil
drought   natural resources

When you are careful to turn the faucet off after you wash your hands, you are *conserving* water. If water is scarce, you probably are more careful about conserving it. People in North America have learned to conserve various things so as not to run out of them.

People were not always so careful. When the first settlers came to North America, the forests seemed endless. If anyone had talked about running out of trees, people would have laughed. Indeed, they would have been happy not to have so many trees. They had to chop them down to clear fields for farming. They built houses with logs. They made chairs, stools, tables, and spoons of wood. They burned wood in their fireplaces.

Because people used wood so freely, vast forests soon disappeared. Today, when you look at the heavily populated countryside, it is hard to imagine the whole area covered with trees.

The same was true of farmland. For a long time, many farmers did not take care of their soil. They seemed to think, "What does it matter if our crops wear out the soil? Why should we take care of it? Isn't there more land in the West?" They seemed to have this idea even after hardly any more land was left in the West.

Miners made the same mistake. They were usually in a hurry and dug into the richest veins of coal and iron. They did not seem to worry about what their children and grandchildren would do when the supplies of minerals ran low.

But then people began to predict that sooner or later the United States would run out of its *natural resources*. In the early 1900s, President Theodore Roosevelt urged Americans to try harder to conserve their natural resources. The government passed laws setting aside national forests. People could not walk into those forests and dig wherever they wanted to or shoot any animals they pleased. The government made laws to protect wild animals such as the buffalo. People had shot so many of them that few were left.

Farmers too had to learn about

conserving their land. In the West, farmers had plowed up thousands of acres to plant grain. They had not thought much about protecting their soil from the wind. In later years, especially during the 1930s, severe *drought* came. The dusty soil began to blow around in great thick clouds. People had to hold damp cloths over their mouths in order to breathe. At some places the dust piled up like snowdrifts, nearly burying houses and barns. Worst of all, by losing *topsoil*, the farmers had lost the most valuable resource they had.

The process of soil being carried or worn away is called *erosion*. In some places water eroded the land. Farmers had worn out their soil and then moved off their farms. The soil was bare. When rain fell, there were not enough trees and plants to slow the water from rushing down slopes, and it took the soil with it. The water wore big gullies in the fields. Soil scientists say that carelessness and erosion have destroyed at least a hundred million acres of soil in the United States. That would make an ugly strip nearly sixty miles wide from the east coast of the United States to the west coast.

The dust storms of the 1930s blew valuable topsoil away.

Careless farming methods created washed-out gullies like this one.

Some farmers began keeping their soil covered with crops or grass. This kept the soil from being blown or washed away. When they planted crops on hills, they ran the rows across the slope instead of up and down. Each row worked like a little dam to keep water from rushing downhill. Other farmers planted rows of trees to slow down the winds that swept across the plains. Many farmers began to practice *crop rotation*, not growing the same crops year after year in the same soil.

Many of North America's natural resources have been lost forever. No one can replace all the minerals that have been wasted. The United States *imports* minerals and *raw materials* that it once could get from its own land. People are now practicing more conservation, hoping that North America will still have some natural resources and beautiful spaces for their children and grandchildren.

We know that someday "the earth also and the works that are therein shall be burned up" (2 Peter 3:10). Until then, however, we should carefully use the natural blessings of the earth to the glory of God.

Study Exercises

1. Why were the early North American settlers unconcerned about saving natural resources?
2. (*a*) Which president urged Americans to conserve their natural resources? (*b*) How did the government help protect some of the forests and wild animals?
3. What are two things that erode the land?
4. List four ways farmers slowed the erosion of their soil.
5. Where does the United States get the needed raw materials that it lacks?

Further Study

1. List some ways you can help conserve water, wood, and soil.
2. Why is wasting natural resources a form of selfishness?

Chapter 9 Review

Reviewing What You Have Learned

A. *Write a glossary word for each definition.*

1. A germ killer.
2. A method of fighting a dangerous disease by infecting a person with a mild disease.
3. To kill germs in a liquid by heating.
4. Not likely to catch a disease.
5. To bring goods into a country.
6. A device for sending messages by electric signals through wires.
7. A section of a canal used to raise and lower boats.
8. A mowing tool with a long curved blade.
9. To avoid waste by using something carefully.
10. A frame fastened on a scythe to catch grain.
11. A machine that cuts, threshes, and cleans grain.
12. The wearing away of the earth's surface.

B. *Choose the correct answer to complete each sentence.*

1. Edward Jenner ———.
   a. used antiseptics to put patients to sleep before operating on them
   b. performed a smallpox vaccination by using cowpox germs
   c. taught people how to pasteurize foods
2. People who lived in the early 1800s were more likely to haul big loads by ——— than they are today.
   a. rivers and canals
   b. roads
   c. railroads
3. People began building canals because ———.
   a. canal boats were faster than steamboats
   b. canals allowed boats to be floated to places that were not near rivers
   c. canals were easy to build

4. Railroads replaced canals because ——.
   a. trains had steam engines
   b. canals could not cross hills
   c. trains traveled faster than boats

5. The telegraph was more successful than the pony express because ——.
   a. the pony express took three weeks to deliver mail from Missouri to California
   b. people could talk to each other by using the telegraph lines
   c. the telegraph could send messages from coast to coast in a few seconds

6. The invention of —— encouraged people to stay up later in the evenings.
   a. matches
   b. hand water pumps
   c. light bulbs

7. Western farmers liked barbed wire because ——.
   a. it helped the cowboys herd cattle
   b. it allowed them to make fences cheaply and quickly to keep buffalo and cattle out of their fields
   c. it sped up their wheat harvesting

8. Western farmers especially liked the mechanical reaper because ——.
   a. it helped them harvest wheat from their big, level fields
   b. it could harvest and thresh the wheat in one operation
   c. it could separate the wheat from the chaff and straw

9. Many early North American settlers were ——.
   a. aware that some day all of the farmland would be in use
   b. unconcerned about saving natural resources
   c. already looking for ways to stop soil erosion

C. *Write* true *or* false.
   1. We can help our bodies stay healthy by taking proper care of them.
   2. Sailboats could travel upstream more easily than steamboats.
   3. Canal boats could haul freight better than trains.

4. Samuel F. B. Morse developed the first successful telegraph.

5. Early telephones were difficult to use.

6. Fireplaces waste less wood than cookstoves.

7. After farmers began using cradles on their scythes, they could easily harvest all their crops.

8. Most eastern farmers had a threshing machine of their own soon after the threshing machine was invented.

9. President Theodore Roosevelt urged Americans to conserve their natural resources.

10. Both water and wind can cause soil erosion.

So Far This Year

Choose the correct answers. See how many you can give without looking back.

1. Match.
   a. Northeast Indians
   b. Southeast Indians
   c. Great Plains Indians
   d. Southwest Indians
   e. Intermountain and California Indians
   f. Northwest Coastal Indians
   g. Arctic peoples

   1. made large wooden houses, totem poles, and log canoes.
   2. included Inuit and Aleuts.
   3. included the best-known Indian tribe—the Iroquois.
   4. built pueblos and irrigated crops.
   5. were quick to learn white men's ways.
   6. lived in teepees and hunted buffalo.
   7. gathered seeds and nuts and made baskets.

2. The (English, French) mainly set up trading posts, but the (English, French) established farms and towns.

3. Life in the New England colonies was (easier, more difficult) than life in the middle colonies.

4. The (English, French, Indians) won the French and Indian War and took control of New France.

5. The United States and Great Britain divided the territory of (Oregon, Hawaii).

6. The colonists in (the United States, Canada) obtained their independence gradually and peacefully from Great Britain.

7. The Emancipation Proclamation helped the North to win the Civil War by stating that the slaves would be (captured, freed).

8. Turkey Red (cotton, potatoes, wheat) was introduced on the Great Plains by Russian Mennonites.

9. In 1867, (two, four, seven) Canadian colonies joined to form the new country of Canada.

10. The invention of (tugboats, steamboats) made travel upstream easier.

Truckloads of agricultural products in Maine. The barrels in this photograph probably contain potatoes.

1910

World War I *1914–1918*

1920

1929
Great Depression begins

1930

World War II *1939–1945*

1940

1941
Japan attacks Pearl Harbor

1945
U.S. bombs Japan

1950

St. Lawrence Seaway opened to large ships

Alaska and Hawaii become states
1959

1960

First man in space *1961*

1963
President Kennedy assassinated

1969
First man on the moon

1970

1980

1990

2000

CHAPTER 10

NORTH AMERICA IN THE TWENTIETH CENTURY

57. *North America Enters a World War*

Glossary Words

allies	conscientious objector	epidemic
armistice	draft	Hutterite

World War I was more destructive than any war before it. Twenty-seven nations took part in it. Nearly ten million soldiers were killed, and over twenty-one million were wounded. Millions of other people were also killed or wounded. Property worth more than three hundred billion dollars was destroyed.

Why was World War I fought? That is a hard question to answer. It has been said that the nations rushed into war without really knowing why. We do know that during the years before the war, the nations of Europe each wanted to become more powerful and wealthy. Their leaders mistrusted each other more and more. They were

World War I

buying more weapons and training more soldiers to defend themselves. People in each nation were saying, "The country next door has made its army bigger. We must make our army bigger too so that they don't dare attack us."

Many nations had also made treaties with each other. Leaders of two nations would agree, "If an enemy country fights your country, we will help you. If enemies fight our country, you will help us." Nations that agree to work together like this are called *allies*. Little nations liked to have big nations on their side. Soon there were two groups of allied nations in Europe. England, France, Russia, and their friends were on one side. Germany and her friends were on the other.

In 1914, Austria and Hungary declared war on Serbia. Right away their allied countries rushed to help them. Soon most of the nations of Europe were at war.

Americans were shocked at the way Europeans had rushed into war. They wanted to stay out of it. But as time went on, it became hard for them not to take sides. Many Americans had friends in England or France or in countries allied with them. They did not want their friends to be defeated.

Canada entered the war along with Britain in 1914, but the United

It was hard for soldiers to say good-bye to their wives and children when they were leaving to join fighting overseas. No one knew who would come back and who would be killed.

States held back. The United States, however, did begin to ship arms to England. War came even closer when German submarines began sinking American ships. In 1917, after more than two hundred Americans had lost their lives on sinking ships, President Woodrow Wilson asked Congress to declare war.

This war was bloodier than earlier wars. Trucks had been invented, and armies could travel fast. Another invention was the tank, a heavy armor-plated machine resembling a bulldozer and armed with large guns. Pilots flew newly invented airplanes above the enemy to see what they were doing. At first, when they met enemy planes, the pilots waved. Later they carried guns and shot at each other. Soon pilots were shooting other planes down.

The United States government *drafted* most young American men into the armed forces. Only those with special permission from the government could stay at home. Some stayed home to raise food. Since the number of farmers decreased, the remaining farmers had to produce extra crops and meat. Other men were needed to work in factories. Women also took jobs in factories to replace the men who went to war.

Not all the men who were drafted in the United States and Canada were willing to join the armed forces. These men were called *conscientious objectors*, or C.O.s. Some of them simply did not like war or were afraid. But others were nonresistant; that is, they objected to fighting because they wanted to obey the teachings of Jesus. In both the United States and Canada, some government leaders tried to treat C.O.s fairly. In spite of this, a number of C.O.s suffered, especially in the United States. They were sent to military training camps where officers tried to force or trick them into wearing soldiers' uniforms. Some were sent to prison, and a few of

Some conscientious objectors suffered mistreatment in this military camp near Leavenworth, Kansas.

them were given only bread and water for a time. Two nonresistant *Hutterites* died from the poor treatment they received while in prison.

Feelings ran high. Sometimes neighborhoods grew angry at families who did not support the war. Mobs of men occasionally visited nonresistant people to threaten them and splash paint on their houses. Yet the nonresistant people showed their love to their neighbors, as well as to the enemy nations whom they would not fight.

Fighting stopped in Europe in 1918, when Germany signed an *armistice*. But the suffering continued. Loved family members were dead. People with arms and legs missing served as reminders of the horrors of war. At the close of the war, a serious *epidemic* spread around the world. American soldiers returning from Europe carried Spanish influenza home with them. More Americans died of the flu than had been killed in the war.

The winning nations wanted either to punish the losers or to forget about them. Although some people cared about those suffering in the defeated countries, most people wanted to rebuild their own lives and not worry about others. These attitudes caused serious trouble a few years later.

═══════════════ Study Exercises ═══════════════

1. List several things that happened in Europe before World War I, which eventually led to the war.
2. (*a*) When did Canada enter World War I? (*b*) When did the United States declare war?
3. List three inventions that made World War I worse than any war before it.
4. How did the United States get soldiers?
5. How were some nonresistant Christians mistreated during World War I?
6. After the war, what attitudes did the winning nations have that caused trouble again a few years later?

Further Study

1. (*a*) Why did government leaders say it was good to build up their armies before World War I? (*b*) Did their plan work?
2. After the war, what happened that killed more Americans than the war itself?

58. The Great Depression

Glossary Words

credit	interest	stock
depression	invest	stockholder

World War I was over. To many people, it seemed that pleasure and prosperity had come to stay. Workers were receiving good wages. They could buy new things such as electric washing machines and refrigerators, which they had not enjoyed when they were children.

People started buying on *credit*. If they did not have enough money for a refrigerator, the store allowed them to pay only part of the price and take the refrigerator home. The people agreed to pay the rest in small monthly payments later. But they had to pay extra money, called *interest*, for this favor.

People with extra money began to *invest* in manufacturing companies. Here is how investment works. Suppose your uncle wants to start a hat factory. He has enough money to build the factory but not enough to buy the hat-making machines he needs. So he asks your father and other men to lend him money (invest) to start his business. He says he hopes to sell enough hats to pay your father a small amount every year for the use of the money your father loaned him. This means that after a number of years, your uncle will have paid back more money than he borrowed.

Sometimes hundreds or even thousands of people invest money in a company. This makes each one a part owner of the company, though it may be only a very small part. Since these people have bought *stock* in the company, they are called *stockholders*. They hope the company makes money so some of that money will come into their own pockets. As long as they believe a company is doing well, they will keep their investment in it. If they see that a business is starting to lose money, they take their money out of it.

After World War I, people seemed so excited about investing their money that they forgot to use common sense. Suppose your uncle decided to double the size of his hat factory before he finished paying for his first factory. Other men might borrow money from the bank to invest in the hat factory. So many people might want to buy stock in your uncle's company that they would pay more for it than it was really worth.

Now just suppose that a few people began to get worried about the money they had invested. What if the business did not work out? What if people decided to stop wearing hats? If enough of these people withdrew money from your uncle's business, he might have to dismiss some of his workers because he could not afford to pay them.

Often when people see other people becoming fearful, they too become fearful. Seeing other people quickly take back their investments, they do the same. Soon many businesses across the country do not have enough money, and more and more workers are dismissed.

At a time like that, your uncle's business would really run into trouble. First, he hardly has enough money to keep his business going. Second, people who have no work have no money, so of course they do not buy hats. Your uncle sells fewer and fewer hats, so he has to tell more and more of his workers that he has no work for them.

This is the kind of thing that happened in 1929, when the Great *Depression* began. Because people had been buying so much, factories had been making more goods than

Many banks closed during the Great Depression. These people wait outside a bank hoping they will be able to get their money.

anyone had ordered. Then, as work and money became scarce, people bought less. Factories had many extra products that they could not sell. People who had bought furniture or cars on credit were in trouble too. They had planned to pay with money that they earned later, but now that money would not be coming.

Farmers also suffered. Many had borrowed money to buy farms. When the depression began, the farmers got very low prices for their farm products. They did not earn as much money as they had expected, so they could not pay back their loans. Many farmers had to give up their farms.

Many men had been used to working hard to support their families, but

Government projects provided jobs for some men. Such projects often benefited the whole community in some way. These men are paving a road.

Some families received free food delivered to their door.

now they spent days and weeks looking for jobs. Although they hated to beg for food, people had to stand in breadlines where free food was given out. A few people set up apple crates on street corners and sold apples one by one to make a little money.

Some men left home and simply walked around on the roads, finding odd jobs and asking for meals here and there. People called them tramps. In our time the government gives money to people who have no jobs. They do not need to walk around looking for food. That is why people in the country hardly ever see tramps today.

During the Great Depression,

some people made clothes, towels, rugs, and other things from cotton feed sacks. Some with hardly enough food learned what it means to pray, "Give us this day our daily bread." They were thankful for simple meals such as cooked cornmeal.

Could such a depression ever happen again? Many people have asked that question. Perhaps hard times will come again, and if so, they will teach us all some good lessons. We might be surprised how simply we can live and eat and dress if we have no other choice. Those who trust in the Lord can learn to be content whether they have much or little.

Study Exercises

1. How do people buy things on credit?
2. Why do businessmen ask people to invest money in their companies?
3. What happens if too many stockholders withdraw their money from a company?
4. What happened to many farmers who had borrowed money to buy farms?
5. How did men who had lost their jobs try to support their families?
6. How does the way people live change during a depression?

Further Study

1. What kind of living did many people enjoy before the Great Depression?
2. Proverbs 22:7 says "the borrower is servant to the lender." After World War I, some people had carelessly borrowed money or bought things on credit. Besides providing for their daily needs, what additional burden did these people face during the depression?

59. North America Enters World War II

Glossary Words

atomic bomb   race
concentration camp   ration

People hoped that World War I would be the war to end all wars. After World War I, the leaders of many nations signed an agreement saying that they did not believe war was the answer to their problems.

But in some ways World War I just got the world ready for a bigger war. England, France, and their allies in Europe had tried to punish Germany for her part in the war by making Germany pay a huge sum of money. The German people felt bad about the way their country was being treated. Besides, not only the United States but the whole world was suffering a depression. Germany was hit hard. Millions of Germans were starving. Her people felt bitter and angry. They determined to make their country great and strong again.

In 1933, a strong leader in Germany, named Adolf Hitler, came to power. He told his fellow Germans that they belonged to a special *race*. He believed that Germany should rule other countries. So Germany began taking over other countries. At first the other nations dreaded war so

Hitler (front left) with other German officials.

much that they did not fight. But in 1939, when Hitler demanded that Poland surrender, Poland refused. Other countries saw that Hitler wanted to conquer not only Poland but their own countries as well. They went to help Poland. Once again, England, France, and their allies found themselves fighting Germany and her new ally, Italy. World War II had begun.

North Americans began hearing that the Germans were persecuting

Jews. But they did not hear all of the horrors. Millions of Jews were herded into *concentration camps*. They were worked like slaves, starved, and beaten to death. Many were killed in gas chambers. People have estimated that by the time the war was over, six million Jews had died.

Once again, the United States stayed out of the war longer than Canada. But the United States lent much war material to the fighting countries. Factories that had been making peacetime goods started to make war equipment. One car factory started to make army tanks. Huge new factories were built. Men who did not have jobs during the depression could now find work. Strangely, the war helped the Great Depression to end.

On the other side of the world, Japan was making herself strong. Like Germany, Japan wanted more land and began seizing it from other countries along the Pacific Ocean.

On December 7, 1941, Japanese fighter planes attacked Pearl Harbor in Hawaii, sinking ships and destroying most of the American planes there. President Franklin Roosevelt asked the United States Congress to declare war on Japan, Germany, and Italy.

Again, men were drafted. Some were sent to Europe to fight the Germans and Italians. Others were sent to the Pacific Ocean to fight the

World War II

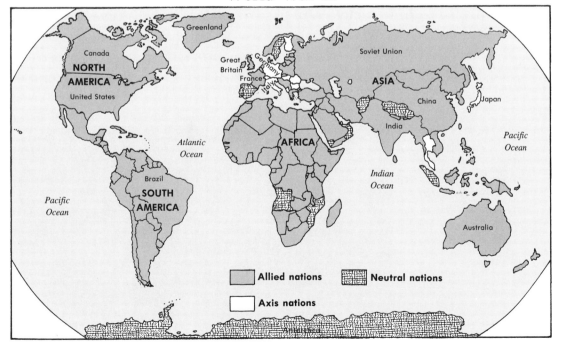

Japanese. Many women began doing the jobs men had left. They helped to weld and rivet ships and airplanes. Even prisoners were taken to factories to work.

Because of the war, some goods such as rubber and gasoline were in very short supply. The government *rationed* these things, allowing each person to buy a certain amount and no more. The government also rationed foods such as sugar, coffee, butter, and meat.

Although they were fighting a major war, the governments of the United States and Canada did not force men to serve in the armed forces if they had a conscience against it. The conscientious objectors were sent to work camps, where they were given useful jobs that were not related to war. In Canada, these camps were called Alternate Service Work camps. In the United States they were called Civilian Public Service (CPS) camps.

Many conscientious objectors worked in hospitals. Some worked in fire towers or fought forest fires. Others built roads and planted trees. A few young men allowed doctors to expose them to germs. When they got sick, the doctors could learn more about the disease with which they were experimenting.

Germany was defeated in 1945. But Japan was still fighting on the islands of the Pacific. The war there might have lasted much longer except for a terrible new weapon that America developed.

That August, an American plane dropped a bomb on the Japanese city of Hiroshima. The bomb exploded with a blinding flash, killing nearly 100,000 people instantly. It was an *atomic bomb*, the most powerful weapon the world had ever known. In the weeks that followed, thousands more people became sick and died because of the radiation (harmful

These people are waiting in line to exchange their ration coupons for shoes. Once the coupons were used, they could not buy any more shoes until they were given more coupons.

rays) the bomb had given off. After the United States dropped a second atomic bomb on another Japanese city, Japan surrendered.

World War II was over, but many questions had to be faced. What would happen to the people in the war-crushed nations? Who would pay to clean up and rebuild the war-torn cities? The United States and Canada did not have to rebuild their own cities because no battles had been fought there. So they spent billions of dollars to help the nations in Europe. Today the defeated nations are prospering again.

World War II destroyed more property and lives than any other war in history. These men in Europe are starting to clean up the ruins of their city.

Study Exercises

1. (a) Why did the German people feel bitter and angry after World War I? (b) What did Adolf Hitler believe the Germans should do?

2. (a) Why did the other nations in Europe not fight when Germany started to take over countries? (b) When did the other countries in Europe begin fighting?

3. What race of people did the Germans especially mistreat?

4. (a) How did the United States help the fighting nations before Congress declared war? (b) What finally caused the United States to enter the war?

5. What did conscientious objectors do during the war?

6. What terrible weapon helped to end World War II?

Further Study

1. Why were goods rationed during World War II?

2. Find out the population of a city near you. (An encyclopedia article about your state may help you.) How does the population of that city compare with the number of people who were killed instantly by the first atomic bomb?

60. Communism and the Cold War

Glossary Words

Cold War   communism

After World War II, North Americans were glad to become peacetime people again. Factories that had made war equipment began to make cars, trucks, and many handy appliances and household articles. Thousands of young men came home from the armed forces and soon were married. So many babies were born during the next few years that people still talk about the "baby boom."

The nations wanted to prevent more wars if they could. So they decided to form a group of nations that would get together and talk problems over. They thought that if the nations discussed their problems, they would find a way to keep from fighting over them. A few months after World War II ended in 1945, Canada, the United States, and most other nations formed a group, called the United Nations, or the U.N.

But many problems soon turned up that the United Nations could not solve. Peace after World War II was not as peaceful as people had hoped. The Soviet Union, the world's largest country, had become a Communist country in 1917. Something similar happened in 1949 when China, the nation with the largest population, also became a Communist country. *Communism* continued to grow until it spread to about a third of the countries of the world. Many North Americans became worried as more and more countries were controlled by Communists.

What frightens people about communism?

1. Communist countries are not free. People in those countries are not permitted to say everything they believe, nor are they permitted to print books the government does not like.

2. Communists believe that faith in God is bad for the people. They persecute Christians, especially those who teach others to be Christians.

3. Communists have tried to make the whole world Communist. They have used armed forces to make a country accept a Communist government.

Because North Americans did not want to be overrun by Communists, they wanted a strong army, navy, and air force. You recall that before the

The United Nations headquarters in New York City. Many countries send representatives here to try to solve problems between nations. Although some agreements have been reached, many problems remain.

tried to influence those on the other side to see things their way. Because little actual fighting took place between the Communists and the non-Communists, this struggle between them was called the *Cold War*.

Sometimes, though, the Cold War turned hot. In 1950, North Korea, a Communist country, invaded South Korea in an attempt to make it a Communist country too. The United States and her allies fought to keep this from happening. This was called the Korean War.

Several years later, war began between North Vietnam and South Vietnam. The United States sent more and more soldiers to keep South Vietnam from becoming a Communist country. But many Americans opposed the war. After fighting several years, the American armed forces left South Vietnam to take care of itself. But then North Vietnam attacked strongly again, and the government of South Vietnam collapsed. Today North Vietnam and South Vietnam are one Communist country, called Vietnam. For the United States, this amounted to losing a war for the first time in history.

Since then the United States and the Soviet Union have built a larger supply of powerful weapons than ever before. From time to time they have met with each other to try to cut

world wars, nations built up their military might. This happened again as tensions grew between the United States and the Soviet Union. Both countries worked hard at building the largest supply of bombs, missiles, and other war equipment. They both had other nations on their side, and both

During the Cold War, Communist countries built fences along their borders to keep their citizens from leaving. This wire barrier was later replaced by a concrete wall, known as the Berlin Wall.

down the number of missiles, bombs, and other war materials that they have.

Canada does not have such powerful armed forces as the United States. So Canadians are better liked and trusted in some parts of the world than citizens of the United States are. This has proven helpful to Canadian missionaries.

What do Christians believe about all this? Christians too are concerned about communism. They know that Christians have often suffered under Communist rule, but they also know that communism cannot stop people from being Christians, even in Communist countries. In recent years, many Communist leaders and governments have fallen, but the Word of God is as powerful as ever!

Christians are concerned too about

the weapons of destruction that the nations of the world have collected. They realize that this buildup results from distrust and ill will among nations. But Christians know that God has not called them to tell government leaders what to do, nor do they expect the nations of the world to obey the Sermon on the Mount and other peaceful teachings of Jesus. However, God does want Christians to spread the Gospel. If people's lives are changed, they will not go to war.

Study Exercises

1. Why was the United Nations formed?
2. Give three reasons why most North Americans have feared communism.
3. (a) What was the "Cold War"? (b) List two times when the Cold War turned hot.
4. Which two countries were the leaders in the buildup of weapons?
5. Why do some countries accept Canadian missionaries more readily than American missionaries?
6. How does God want Christians to help our troubled world?

Further Study

1. How far did communism spread?
2. Read Romans 8:28 and John 16:33. Why are Christians less concerned than many people of the world about the weapons that nations have collected?

61. *North America Faces Recent Challenges*

Glossary Word

inflation

Since World War II most North Americans have been prospering. They have been able to buy things that their parents were never able to buy. But since World War II they have also faced a problem with **inflation**. During times of inflation, money loses its value. People need to pay more and more for things, because their money is no longer worth as much as it had been. Someone has said that before inflation starts, a housewife goes to the store with her money in her purse and comes home with her groceries in a shopping bag. But during a time of inflation, she goes to the store with her money in a shopping bag and comes home with her groceries in her purse!

The situation in North America has never been that bad. But such things have happened in other countries. One visitor to China during its civil war paid $750,000 for a handkerchief. Another person carried seventeen pounds of money just to pay his bills. One of the worst things about inflation is that the money which people have saved is almost worthless when they want to use it. Imagine

saving money all your life, only to find in the end that all it will buy is a handkerchief. That is why North Americans are concerned about inflation, even though they are the most prosperous people in the world. The Scriptures tell us to trust in the living God rather than in uncertain riches (1 Timothy 6:17).

What important events have taken place in North America since World War II? In 1959, Alaska became the forty-ninth state. Although it has few people, Alaska is by far the largest state. The same year, sunny Hawaii joined the union, and flag makers put the fiftieth star on the American flag.

Also in 1959, Canada's St. Lawrence Seaway was opened to large ships. This allowed them to sail all the way from the Atlantic to ports along the Great Lakes. A few years later, the Trans-Canada Highway was completed. (*Trans* means "across.") People could now drive on a highway all the way across Canada.

In 1961, the first American took a short trip into outer space. And in 1969, the first men walked on the moon. Several years later, the space

A sale bill showing what some items cost in 1938. How much have prices increased since then?

Man first walked on the moon in 1969.

Ships can sail up the St. Lawrence Seaway to the Great Lakes.

shuttle was developed. It can be sent into outer space and then return to earth like an airplane.

Many North Americans felt proud at moments like these. But there were other times when people did not feel so proud. In 1963, John F. Kennedy, president of the United States, was shot and killed as he rode through Dallas, Texas. Several other important government men were killed during the next twenty years, and a few,

including President Ronald Reagan, were wounded. These incidents jolted many Americans and made them feel less sure of their future.

In 1974, President Richard Nixon had to resign from being president because it was found that he had told lies. Several of his assistants were sent to prison because they also had helped to deceive the American people. This affair was called the Watergate scandal.

These are just a few of the ups and downs North Americans have experienced. Yet, in spite of problems in North America, Christians who live there should remember that God put them there for good reasons and that they have much to be thankful for. North America is not a bad place to live. People are still free to worship and serve God as they believe they should.

North America is a fairly safe place to live, compared to many other places on earth. Most people obey the laws. Christians in free countries such as the United States and Canada should be thankful for the many opportunities they have to serve the Lord. The Bible teaches us to pray that we may lead "a quiet and peaceable life in all godliness and honesty" (1 Timothy 2:2). Since God has answered that prayer for most people in North America, we ought to thank Him.

Study Exercises

1. What happens during times of inflation?
2. List at least four important events that have taken place in the United States since World War II.
3. Name two important achievements that have helped the Canadian transportation system.
4. List some things North American Christians should thank God for.

Further Study

1. Find Alaska on a globe or a world map. Why do you think this largest state has very few people?
2. Why is the St. Lawrence Seaway important for trade?

Chapter 10 Review

Reviewing What You Have Learned

A. *Write a glossary word for each definition.*

1. A group of people with the same ancestors.
2. To put out money to gain a profit.
3. Trust given to someone for future payment.
4. An agreement to stop fighting.
5. Nations that help each other.
6. A system of government in which the state owns and controls goods and property.
7. An unusual rise in prices.
8. To control the amount one can buy.
9. A struggle between nations without actual fighting.
10. To require persons to join the armed forces.
11. A time when people and businesses are not making much money.
12. A prison camp for the enemies of a country.
13. A widespread outbreak of disease.
14. Part ownership of a company.
15. A person who believes it is wrong to fight in a war.

B. *Choose the correct answer to complete each sentence.*

1. World War I was ———.
   a. more destructive than any war before it
   b. started by the United States and Russia
   c. fought before trucks and airplanes had been invented

2. Problems began developing again after World War I because ———.
   a. the government had put all the C.O.s into prison
   b. Germany had refused to sign the armistice
   c. the winning nations of the war had punished the losers

3. During the Great Depression, many people ———.
   a. began buying things on credit
   b. lost their jobs and had to live simply
   c. invested money in big companies

4. Many farmers who had borrowed money to buy farms before the Great Depression ——.
   a. had to give up their farms because they could not pay their debts
   b. were able to sell apples for a high price
   c. started giving away food in breadlines

5. Adolf Hitler believed ——.
   a. the Jews were God's special people
   b. Germany should rule other countries
   c. war should be avoided if possible

6. The United States entered World War II after Japan ——.
   a. began lending war materials to the fighting nations
   b. was hit by two atomic bombs
   c. attacked Pearl Harbor

7. Most North Americans have feared communism because ——.
   a. everyone in Communist countries is required to attend the state church
   b. the Communists do not like large countries
   c. people in Communist countries are not free

8. Christians do not worry about communism as much as some people because ——.
   a. they know communism cannot stop people from being Christians
   b. Communist governments usually allow Christians to preach freely
   c. Communist countries do not have many weapons

9. After World War II, the ——.
   a. United States and the Soviet Union both built large supplies of powerful weapons
   b. United Nations kept any more wars from beginning
   c. Cold War helped keep good relations between most countries of the world

10. North American Christians should be especially thankful that ——.
    a. Americans have learned to travel in space
    b. they have freedom of worship
    c. no American president since Abraham Lincoln has been shot

So Far This Year

Choose the correct answers. See how many you can give without looking back.

1. North America is in the (Northern, Southern) and (Eastern, Western) hemispheres.

2. Christopher Columbus discovered America while trying to find a new route to the (Near East, Far East).

3. Many settlers in (New England, Pennsylvania) turned to fishing because their hilly farms had poor soil.

4. The American colonists fought to be independent because they felt that the taxes and laws of (Great Britain, Pennsylvania, Virginia) were unfair.

5. Most work was done by hand (before, during, after) the Industrial Revolution.

6. The (Civil War, Revolutionary War) started after the Southern states seceded from the United States.

7. Many settlers moved to the Great Plains after the government started giving away (land, food) and railroad companies built (local, transcontinental) railroads.

8. (Kansas, Oklahoma, Texas) was the last big section of Indian land to be taken by white settlers.

9. Match.
   a. Edward Jenner
   b. Louis Pasteur
   c. Samuel Morse
   d. Cyrus McCormick
   e. Theodore Roosevelt

   1. developed the telegraph.
   2. urged Americans to conserve.
   3. discovered smallpox vaccination.
   4. invented the mechanical reaper.
   5. learned how to kill germs in food.

10. World War II ended soon after (Canada, England, the United States) dropped atomic bombs on two Japanese cities.

CHAPTER 11

MODERN LIFE IN NORTH AMERICA

Facing page: Large cities have grown up in North America where the Indians once hunted. People, goods, and news travel quickly to distant parts of the continent and the world. But modern man still faces problems caused by selfishness, greed, and other sins.

62. *Faster and Easier*

Glossary Words

computer chip   robot   satellite

People sometimes talk about how surprised someone such as George Washington would be if he were to see North America today. Really, many of the surprising changes have taken place only in the past few years. If your great-grandparents had fallen asleep when they were children and awakened today, they too would be amazed.

Think of the wonders of transportation. Until only about a hundred years ago, no one had ever flown an airplane—not even as high as the birds. But after the Wright brothers flew the first simple airplane in 1903, airplane builders learned quickly.

Today a jumbo jet can carry about five hundred people above the clouds and fly at six hundred miles per hour. Each day, thousands of people fly from one end of North America to the other. Planes have been developed that can carry passengers at over 1,200 miles per hour, almost twice the speed of sound.

Not everyone in North America travels in airplanes, but almost everyone has traveled in cars. Not too long ago (in the early 1900s) this method of transportation was new and strange. During those days several men invented cars, but they were expensive. Henry Ford improved the way of

The first successful airplane flight made by Wilbur and Orville Wright, at Kitty Hawk, North Carolina.

Modern jetliners can carry hundreds of passengers for thousands of miles.

Henry Ford giving his uncle a ride in a 1912 Model T Ford. Model T Fords were the first cars many people could afford to buy.

making cars on assembly lines and sold them for a cheaper price. Many people liked Ford's Model T because it was the first car they could afford. Soon other companies were making cheaper cars too, and most North Americans bought cars. Today, people use cars every day and would hardly know how to live without them.

Does modern transportation cause any problems? Yes, traffic jams and car accidents are examples. Another serious problem is air pollution. The millions of cars on the roads each give off poisonous exhaust fumes. In cities, air polluted with so many fumes can cause health problems. Laws now require car manufacturers to make cars that do not give off as many bad fumes. Some cities use electric buses because they do not smoke. They have an arm that runs along electric wires above them.

Modern communication is even faster than modern travel. When you talk long-distance on the telephone, your voice reaches a friend a thousand miles away as quickly as it reaches someone sitting in the room with you. People can make telephone calls from cars and airplanes. Businessmen can send copies of letters over the telephone. Computers can "talk" to other computers on the telephone.

Radio and television are other ways in which communication has become faster. Television programs can travel by cable or by signals from tower to tower across the land. Or they can be sent to a *satellite* more than 22,000 miles above the earth. The satellite sends the signals down again to another part of the earth, thousands of miles away.

People learn much from television. But the effects of television show that some inventions can do much more harm than good. The makers of TV shows try hard to make them exciting, because that is what people want to see. Actors dress indecently and use bad words. They pretend to hurt and kill each other. TV watchers get used to seeing crime and hearing foul language. Christians avoid much evil by refusing to have television or radio in their homes.

Modern conveniences have helped to speed up many of our tasks. Some cameras not only snap a picture; they also develop it. In the kitchen, instant coffee and instant soups make snacking quick and easy. A microwave oven can bake a potato in four to seven minutes instead of an hour.

Your grandmother may remember taking very wrinkled clothes off the line. It took much ironing to make shirts, trousers, and dresses look neat. Permanent press clothes have changed that. They need little ironing, and they do not become wrinkled so easily.

Probably one of the most important inventions in the past fifty years is the computer. The first computers were clumsy, room-size machines. But then the *computer chip* was developed. Inventors crammed thousands of electronic circuits into a chip that can be held with a tweezers. Today people carry around computers no bigger than a briefcase.

Computer chips have made other things possible—such as inexpensive watches that tell the exact time. Without chips, there would be no calculators. The first calculators were expensive, but now people can buy them for less than ten dollars.

Computers serve as the "brains" of *robots*. Robots can do some jobs better than people. For example, robots can paint cars without wearing masks for protection against the fumes. Robots never become careless.

Computer-controlled robots do many jobs in modern factories. This robot is welding the frame of a new General Motors car.

And they do not need to be paid wages. Computers help people keep track of enormous amounts of information—much more than anyone would have tried to keep record of before. The scanner that reads the code on the package of cheese you buy does more than ring up the price. The computer keeps track of how many packages of cheese were bought and how many the store has left. It keeps information on thousands of store items.

Probably more and more people will own computers in their homes. This book was written on a computer. As each word was typed, it appeared on a screen. The writer could erase or rearrange words—even sentences or paragraphs—just by pushing a few buttons.

Are modern inventions good or bad? That is like asking if knives are good or bad. It depends on the way we use them. If we can use inventions to do good work, they might be right to use. But if we see that using them will get us into trouble, we should not have them.

Even if people today have three times as many things as people had long ago, that does not mean they are three times as happy. Jesus said, "A man's life consisteth not in the abundance of the things which he possesseth" (Luke 12:15). But then, having fewer things does not always make people happy either. People are happy when they have learned to be content and thank God for whatever they have.

Study Exercises

1. (*a*) When did the first airplane flight take place? (*b*) How many years ago was that?
2. (*a*) How did Henry Ford help to make cars affordable? (*b*) What problems do cars cause?

3. When you use a telephone, how quickly can your voice reach a friend a thousand miles away ?

4. Give an example of how modern communication has done much harm.

5. List several things that use computer chips besides regular computers.

6. What determines whether an invention is good or bad?

Further Study

1. How have people tried to reduce air pollution?

2. How big were the first computers?

3. Have you ever read anything that was written on a computer?

63. Rich and Free in a Poor World

Glossary Words

immigrant   Iron Curtain   melting pot

Most of the world's poor countries are in Africa, Asia, and South America. Europe and North America have many rich countries. More rich people live in the United States than in any other country of the world.

What do we mean by "rich"? Most people do not think they are rich compared to others. And yet they have enough to eat and even enough to feed a pet or two. Most North Americans and Europeans have enough money to buy nearly anything they need or want. To many people in the world, that is very, very rich!

The United States and Canada are not only rich but free. In many countries, people have not been permitted to worship as they believed God wanted them to worship. Newspapers could say only what the government allowed them to say. In eastern Europe, people who lived in Communist countries were kept from leaving the country. The border they could not cross was called the *Iron Curtain*.

North America does not need to keep people from leaving. More people want to get into North America than can get in. In the past, *immigrants* seemed to pour into the United States. Many crossed the Atlantic Ocean to New York City by ship. After the Statue of Liberty was built, immigrants coming into New York Harbor were excited to see the statue holding her torch high. The statue was a symbol of freedom to all who came.

Millions of immigrants have come to North America. The Statue of Liberty was erected as a symbol of welcome.

After various wars in Europe, many people found their cities wrecked and their countryside torn up. Their homes were gone. Often their freedom was gone too. They fled across the ocean to North America, where they could live in peace and freedom again.

But at the same time, some Americans were starting to frown over how many immigrants were coming. They were saying, "We want our country to be a *melting pot* where people from many countries learn to be Americans. If too many foreign people come at once, they might stick together in a group and keep their foreign ways. They might not support America. They might want to live off the government and not help pay taxes. Then what will happen to our government and our freedom?"

The governments of the United States and Canada have made laws to reduce the flow of people into their countries. Today people still come to North America, but not too many may come at one time. The governments try to keep out people who might commit crimes or take welfare money from the government.

These laws please many North Americans. But others feel bad. They say, "Should we be selfish and keep our rich country all to ourselves? After all, we were immigrants too, or else our ancestors were. See how very poor some people are in other countries. Shouldn't we allow more of them to come to our country so that they can get a new start?" These are hard questions for lawmakers to answer.

Christians should respect the laws of the country in which they live. They do not need to decide whether the government is doing enough to help the world's poor people.

But Christians do need to help others. Perhaps they cannot help other people as much as they would like. But they can show they care in many ways. Not wasting food, taking care of our clothes, and spending our money wisely are things we can do so that we have more to give to others.

When children your age have money, they face temptations to buy things they do not need. So if your parents give you very little spending money and watch what you spend it on, be glad! They are teaching you saving habits that will help you "to give to him that needeth" (Ephesians 4:28).

This arch on the border of the United States and Canada symbolizes the openness and peace between the two countries.

The inscription "Children of a Common Mother" refers to the many things Americans and Canadians have in common. Both countries were once ruled by England, and both have the same language, and similar laws, customs, and ideas.

Study Exercises

1. (a) Which continents have most of the world's poor countries? (b) Which continents have many rich countries?

2. In what way are most North Americans rich, even if they do not think they are rich?

3. What often caused large groups of Europeans to move to North America?

4. (a) Why did some North Americans begin worrying about the many immigrants coming to their country? (b) How did the United States and Canada limit the number of immigrants?

5. Why do some North Americans feel that more immigrants should be allowed to come to their countries?

6. Why should Christians learn to use money wisely?

Further Study

1. Why was the border between the Communist countries in Europe and the free countries in Europe called the Iron Curtain?

2. (a) Why have Communists needed to keep people from leaving their countries? (b) What kind of country would you rather live in: one that has to keep people from leaving, or one that limits the number of people entering?

64. How Society Has Changed

Glossary Words

drugs   society

In the 1800s, most American people believed in God, tried to obey the Ten Commandments, and went to church. This does not mean that all of them were true Christians, but they respected God and His Word. A visitor to America in the 1830s said, "America is great because she is good. If America ever ceases to be good, she will cease being great."

Since then, North American *society* has made many changes. Have these changes helped people to be good? A few have, but most have not. We will look at some of those changes.

Homes have changed in several important ways. One of the most important changes is that men and women no longer work at separate tasks as they had in the past. Fathers used to earn the living for the family, and mothers were "keepers at home" as the Bible teaches (Titus 2:5). Today more than half the married women in North America work outside their home. Some are businesswomen, nurses, factory workers, lawyers— even fire fighters.

This creates problems. Mothers who work away from home have less time for their children than those who stay at home. They must leave their little children with baby sitters. Older children come home from school to an empty house because their parents have not arrived home from work yet. Because they must unlock the door for themselves, they are called "latch-key children."

Women who earn their own money sometimes feel that they do not need to depend so much on their husbands. Married people no longer feel that remaining faithful to each other is very important. If marriage does not make them as happy as they had hoped, they get a divorce. Many people no longer think of divorce as wrong, even though in God's sight it always will be.

Many churches too have changed. They are no longer strict about sin. They no longer forbid divorce and remarriage. They do not require their members to dress modestly, to keep the Lord's Day, to attend church services regularly, and to avoid pleasure seeking. Some preachers still teach against sin but allow their members to live as they choose.

Churches are forgetting about

preparing people for heaven. They want to make this earth as much like heaven as possible. Instead of changing wicked people's hearts, they are asking the government to pass laws to change people's behavior.

When people do not care much about obeying the Bible, they cause problems for themselves and the people around them. For example, one problem today is that people steal little things out of stores. Such people are called shoplifters. Because of shoplifting, stores across North America lose many thousands of dollars every year. The stores must raise their prices to make up for what is stolen. Honest customers have to pay a higher price for every item they buy. But the people who really lose are the shoplifters themselves.

Another problem is the rising abuse of *drugs*. Doctors sometimes use strong drugs as pain relievers or for other reasons. But if they are taken in high doses, these drugs can become habit forming. This means that the user becomes addicted to them; he has such a strong desire for drugs that he will do almost anything to get them. He may even rob or kill people to get the drugs, or to get money to buy them.

Strong, habit-forming drugs are locked away so that not everyone can get them. The law forbids people to use these drugs without good reasons. People who take them just to get a good feeling harm their bodies. They lose their ability to think well, and they are not able to stop taking the drugs without getting very sick.

Christian families enjoy living together.

Many parents are concerned about the changes in society that are not good. They send their children to schools where they can have Christian teachers and textbooks.

People who are addicted to drugs can stop using them, but it is very, very difficult.

A young man called Ben, his father, and his grandfather show how society has slowly changed. Ben's grandfather used to say, "I believe the Bible—every word of it!" He read it every day and went to church every Sunday and every Wednesday evening. He loved revival meetings. He liked preachers who spoke firmly against sin and kept their churches holy. Was he looking for the Lord to come again? "Yes, I am!" he would say. "I might still be living when He comes!"

Ben's father likes to go to church too on Sundays, but he skips it when the roads are snowy or he has stayed up too late on Saturday evening. He thinks it is good to obey the Ten Commandments. But if you ask him a question about the Bible, he says, "I think my minister could answer that question." If you mention that the Lord is coming soon, he says, "He might. We'll have to wait and see, I guess."

Ben goes to church on Easter, but he skipped last Easter. A few times he has read a little in the Bible to see what it is about. But he would rather read an article called "Stand Up for

Yourself," or a book called *I'm Somebody*. Ben's father is worried because Ben's friends are using drugs that make them do strange things. Ben admits that he has tried drugs a few times. If you remind him that the Lord is coming soon, he smiles and says, "Uh-huh." And that is all he will say.

Some people still serve the Lord with all their hearts, regardless of the bad things others do. Christian fathers and mothers still love each other and will continue to all their lives. Even though people have said that marriage will soon go out of date, that has not happened. God has made sure of it!

Also, more and more parents are teaching their children to serve the Lord in Christian school settings. They have found Christian textbooks and teachers for their children. That is why you are studying this book now.

Study Exercises

1. (*a*) Who used to earn the living for families? (*b*) How has this changed in many homes?
2. (*a*) How are young children affected by a working mother? (*b*) What problem may older children face?
3. What other problem have working wives brought to homes?
4. List several ways many churches have changed.
5. List some problems that come when people do not care about following the Bible.
6. (*a*) Can people serve the Lord even when most other people are not obeying the Bible? (*b*) Read 1 Peter 1:24, 25. How long will God's Word be true?

Further Study

1. Read Titus 2:4, 5, where God gives some commands to young women. Write the phrase that tells where wives are to work.
2. Read Romans 7:1-3. How long does marriage bind a husband and a wife together?

65. What About the Future?

Glossary Word

slums

In 1939, a number of Americans tried to guess what the world would be like in the future. They made pictures and models of cities, houses, and farms as they hoped the world would be. We are living many years later, in what was the future for them. Did they guess right? In some ways, they did. Some other guesses they made were far wrong.

What did they think cities would be like by today? They guessed that highways with many lanes would run into the cities. That was right. But they also guessed that cars would travel 100 miles per hour, guided by control towers. There would be no accidents or traffic jams. If you have traveled on city freeways lately, you know it is not that way!

The people looking into the future said very little about *slums* or poor people. They made models of beautiful cities with extremely tall skyscrapers. Today there are more skyscrapers than there were at that time, but there still are slums.

The people talked about a future world where everyone would work together in peace. They did not know that World War II was just around the corner. They also did not guess that thirty years later men would walk on the moon. Neither did they know that people would carry small calculators in their pockets.

All this goes to show that people can only guess about the future. They will be partly right and partly wrong. Perhaps some new invention will change our lives in ways we have not guessed yet.

Only God knows just what the future will be like. But He has told us a little about it, and what He tells us is not just guesses. It will take place! Some of the things that God said would come to pass have already happened.

What did Jesus say about the future when He lived on earth? "Ye shall hear of wars and rumors of wars" (Matthew 24:6). Do you hear of wars going on today? Do you hear of places where it sounds like there might be a war soon? Such things are taking place all the time.

"There shall be famines, and pestilences, and earthquakes" (Matthew 24:7). Almanacs and encyclopedias can tell you about such troubles that the earth has had in recent years.

"Ye shall be hated of all men for my name's sake" (Matthew 10:22). Christians have been persecuted in many Communist countries and other places.

In spite of all this, Jesus said, "Be not terrified" (Luke 21:9). Even though many troubles will come, God will take care of His people. He even gives some of them freedom, money, and a comfortable life. He gives them the opportunity to share the Gospel with others. That is what we enjoy, and we ought to thank Him.

Jesus also said, "And when these things begin to come to pass, then look up, and lift up your heads; for your redemption draweth nigh" (Luke 21:28). The Lord will come and bring an end to all the guessing about the future. For His people, that will be better than anyone could ever guess it would be.

Study Exercises

1. Name one guess made in 1939 that was correct.
2. List several guesses that were not correct.
3. List several things that have happened that the people of 1939 had not guessed would happen.
4. How can we know some things that will happen in the future?
5. What makes it possible for Christians to live in a troubled world without being terrified?

Further Study

1. Do you hear of wars being fought today? Find out where current wars and trouble spots are. Your parents or teacher may be able to help you. Even during times of apparent peace, the Bible gives us this warning: "When they shall say, Peace and safety; then sudden destruction cometh upon them" (1 Thessalonians 5:3).
2. Read Revelation 22:1–7. Why did God inspire John to write the Book of Revelation?

Chapter 11 Review

Reviewing What You Have Learned

A. *Write a glossary word for each definition.*

1. An object that revolves around the earth.
2. A community of people with similar ideas.
3. Poor, crowded areas in cities.
4. A person moving into a new country.
5. A machine that can do some jobs automatically.
6. A place where a variety of people learn the same way of life.
7. A tiny square of material used to run modern electronic equipment.
8. Guarded border in Europe during the Cold War.

B. *Choose the correct answer to complete each sentence.*

1. The first airplane flight was taken in ——.
   a. 1953
   b. 1803
   c. 1903
2. One of the most important developments of the past fifty years is ——.
   a. permanent press clothes
   b. the computer chip
   c. the robot
3. —— determines whether the invention is good or bad.
   a. The way an invention is used
   b. The way an invention satisfies us
   c. The amount of time and money an invention saves
4. —— have more rich countries than the other continents of the world.
   a. Africa and Asia
   b. Australia and South America
   c. Europe and North America

5. Many Europeans moved to North America because ——.
   a. they were eager to find freedom and peace
   b. they wanted to see the Statue of Liberty
   c. they were rich and could afford long trips

6. Some North Americans wanted to limit the number of immigrants coming to their countries because ——.
   a. they realized that their ancestors had also been immigrants
   b. they were afraid the foreigners would bring harm to their countries
   c. they did not want people from Communist countries to come

7. The large number of married women who work away from home has ——.
   a. had little influence on North American society
   b. strengthened many families
   c. brought problems to many homes

8. God's Word ——.
   a. will be true as long as people believe and obey it
   b. will be true until churches stop teaching it
   c. will always be true, even if only a few people obey it

9. Men in the past ——.
   a. correctly guessed that men would walk on the moon
   b. knew that we would live in a peaceful world
   c. have proved by their guesses that only God knows what will happen in the future

10. Christians can look forward to the future because ——.
    a. they know God will take care of them
    b. God has told them exactly what will happen in the future
    c. they know God will not allow them to have troubles

So Far This Year

Choose the correct answers. See how many you can give without looking back.

1. Temperatures are mild or moderate in most areas of (Canada, the United States).

2. The (English, French) mainly set up trading posts, but the (English, French) established farms and towns.

3. The Dutch bought (Boston, Manhattan Island) from the Indians.

4. The French settled lands (north, south) of the English colonies.

5. Match.
   - a. William Penn
   - b. William Penn's grandson
   - c. French fur traders
   - d. Spanish soldiers and priests.

   1. paid frontiersmen to kill Indians.
   2. used liquor to cheat Indians.
   3. forced Indians to work and be baptized.
   4. paid Indians for land.

6. The United States bought (the Louisiana Territory, Florida) from France.

7. Before the Civil War, many Northerners began having strong feelings against (slavery, factory owners).

8. In 1867, (two, four, seven) Canadian colonies joined to form the new country of Canada.

9. The building of a (canal, highway, railroad) across the Canadian prairie helped to bring additional provinces into Canada.

10. (Stagecoaches, Trains, Pony express riders) eventually replaced canal boats.

11. The United States entered World War II after (Germany, Japan, Russia) bombed Pearl Harbor in Hawaii.

12. The struggle between Communist countries and non-Communist countries was called (the Cold War, communism, inflation).

13. North American Christians should be especially thankful for their (space program, freedom of religion, St. Lawrence Seaway).

14. During the past century, many North Americans have (turned away from the Bible, encouraged mothers to stay at home).

15. Only —— knows exactly what will happen in the future.

Farms like these in Iowa help feed the people of North America and the world.

CHAPTER 12

REGIONS OF UNITED STATES

Regions of United States

New England States

Middle Atlantic States

Southern States

Midwestern States

Rocky Mountain States

Pacific Coast States

Southwestern States

Maine

VT. N.H. Mass. Conn. R.I.

N.J. Del.

New York

Pennsylvania

MD.

Virginia

West Virginia

North Carolina

South Carolina

Georgia

Florida

Ohio

Kentucky

Tennessee

Alabama

Mississippi

Michigan

Indiana

Illinois

Wisconsin

Minnesota

Missouri

Arkansas

Louisiana

Iowa

North Dakota

South Dakota

Nebraska

Kansas

Oklahoma

Texas

Montana

Wyoming

Colorado

New Mexico

Idaho

Utah

Arizona

Washington

Oregon

Nevada

California

66. The New England States

Glossary Words

growing season   newsprint   softwood
manufacturing   pulp   tourist

Many people like the New England countryside with its hilly pastures and stone fences, neat little villages, and white churches. Forests and long mountains are usually nearby, and old lighthouses stand along the seashore. God's handiwork is especially beautiful in autumn, when leaves in the forests change colors.

The farther south in New England you go, the more crowded and busy it becomes. Rhode Island, Massachusetts, and Connecticut are among the most densely populated states in the country. Boston, Massachusetts, is New England's biggest city and busiest port. New York City is not in the New England States, but it is close by. Thousands of people from Connecticut travel there to work every day.

In New England, the most important industry is *manufacturing.* What is there about New England that makes people want to build factories there?

Years ago people saw that the rushing streams of New England were well-suited for turning water wheels to run mills. In time, textile mills employed many people. So did

The New England States

other kinds of factories. Today factories run on electricity rather than water power, but New England's streams still help run the factories by

Factories in Lawrence, Massachusetts

turning generators that produce electricity.

A second reason factories are built in New England is that New England has many people. "Many hands make work light," we say. In New England, the many hands get a lot of work done in the factories.

Thirdly, manufacturing is easier than farming in much of New England. Many of the hillsides are steep, much of the soil is poor. Farmers have to haul stones out of their fields year after year. And the *growing season* is short.

Factories in New England mostly produce machinery. The metal they use might have to come from far away, and factory owners may have to pay high prices for it. A factory that makes small items such as tweezers would not need to pay much for the little bit of metal it takes to make a tweezers. The factory can sell the tweezers for much more money than it paid for the metal.

Such things as typewriters, guns, and silverware are also made in New England. But some large items are also made there, such as helicopters, jet engines, and submarines.

Most of Maine is covered with

softwood trees—pines, spruces, and other evergreens. These trees are made into lumber, Christmas trees, and hundreds of millions of toothpicks. But most important, the wood from Maine's trees can be ground or cooked into soft *pulp*. Paper mills use the pulp to make paper, especially the kind used for printing newspapers, called *newsprint*. Although the other New England states also have forests, all five states combined produce much less paper than Maine.

Some New England factories make things from leather. In Maine, more people work in factories that make shoes and other leather products than in any other kind of factory.

Another important industry in New England is the *tourist* trade. During winter, people come to enjoy the snow. And during summer, many people come to cool New England from the hot cities farther south. They admire the Green Mountains of Vermont and the White Mountains of Maine and New Hampshire. They visit historical spots such as Plymouth, where the Pilgrims had their first Thanksgiving. At Boston, they walk

A village in Vermont, among the beautiful hills and mountains of New England. Farming is difficult because of poor soil and hilly fields.

Gathering sap from maple trees in Vermont. The sap is taken to the sugarhouse, where it is boiled until it thickens into maple syrup.

Tubes and pipelines are often used instead of buckets. The sap from each tree runs into a tube, which connects to pipelines that run directly into storage tanks in the sugarhouse.

A lighthouse in Maine. Such lighthouses help ships find their way around rocky points on the coast.

on old, narrow, winding streets. Tourist guides and owners of motels, campgrounds, and stores are glad to see the visitors come because of the money they spend in New England.

New England has some good farmland, but in northern New England, farmers find it hard to grow things like sweet corn, beans, and tomatoes.

So they raise root crops such as potatoes and also raise animals. Cattle eat grass and hay, which grows well even in the northern part of New England. New England produces much meat, milk, and eggs.

Apples are a hardy fruit, and New England produces many of them. Potatoes grow well in northern Maine.

Cranberry bogs in Massachusetts produce more cranberries than anywhere else in the country. And Vermont, with all its sugar maple trees, is well known for maple sugar and syrup.

Fishing is not nearly as important in New England as other industries are. Nevertheless, Maine and Massachusetts are leading fishing states. Maine sells more lobsters than any other state. The rugged coastline of New England is not straight. Its many bays, inlets, and coves make good protecting harbors for fishing boats and for other kinds of ships as well.

Study Exercises

1. Name the biggest city of New England.
2. Why are streams and rivers important to New England?
3. (a) What is the main product of New England factories? (b) Name some kinds of it.
4. What is the most important product manufactured from Maine's trees?
5. In Maine, what kind of factories hire the most people?
6. Name three industries of New England besides manufacturing.

Gaining Geographical Skills

1. Trace Map E in the map section, and label it "The New England States."
2. Draw symbols for the Green Mountains and White Mountains, and label them.
3. Label each state and its capital city.

Further Study

1. (a) What do tourists like about New England? (b) Why are some New England people glad when tourists come?
2. Why is New England not an important farming region?

67. The Middle Atlantic States

Glossary Words

Fall Line   perishable   truck farmers

The Middle Atlantic region is one of the most important areas in the United States. About forty million people live there. Many cities and towns sprinkle this area. Here we find the biggest seaports of the east coast. Much manufacturing is done in these busy towns and cities.

The Middle Atlantic States

There is much more to the Middle Atlantic region than bustling cities. New York is not only a big city but also a big state. Some New Yorkers live hundreds of miles away from New York City. The other Middle Atlantic States—Pennsylvania, New Jersey, Delaware, and Maryland—also have many square miles of quiet countryside. But since most of the people live or work in the big cities, we will look at the cities first.

The biggest and most interesting city in this region is New York City. In fact, it is the largest city in the United States. More than seven million people live there; that is more people than live in most states. Little cities near New York City have been swallowed up as New York keeps spreading out, so that you cannot tell where one city stops and another begins. New York City has nearly a thousand public schools, nearly two hundred public libraries, and over one hundred hospitals. It has nine underwater tunnels and over two hundred miles of subway track.

New York City fills five small counties, like a giant that has to sleep on several beds shoved together. The

New York City is the most heavily populated city in the United States.

five counties are called boroughs, and their names are Manhattan, Bronx, Brooklyn, Queens, and Staten Island. Manhattan is the oldest part of the city and has the most skyscrapers.

Why did New York City grow so big? One important reason is that it has a fine harbor. Another is that people can travel easily from New York to the West and to Canada through valleys in the Appalachian Mountains.

The city of Philadelphia, Pennsylvania, is not as large as New York City. But with a million and a half people, it is still large. It grew partly because of its long waterfront along the Delaware River where ships can dock, safe from ocean storms.

Philadelphia has a number of special historical spots. One of them is Independence Hall, where the Declaration of Independence was signed. Not far from it, visitors can see the big Liberty Bell.

Like New York City, Philadelphia has grown and swallowed up nearby towns. Germantown, for example, is now a neighborhood in Philadelphia.

Washington, D.C., is quite an unusual city. It does not have many factory smokestacks or busy docks loading ships. Its business is governing the country. The president lives in Washington, in the White House. The Capitol building, where Congress meets, is also in Washington, as well as other government buildings, many of them built of marble.

Many people enjoy living in cities. But when cities are big, their problems are big too. How can everyone find a house to live in? Where will all the garbage be taken? What about the smoke from thousands of chimneys and exhaust fumes from thousands of cars?

In poor sections of the cities live many untrained people who have no jobs. They cannot type, weld, paint signs, or build furniture. Cities give them money to help them live. In New York City, about one out of every four or five people receives money from the government. Cities can hardly afford this, along with everything else they must pay for.

Now let us think how people of the Middle Atlantic region earn their living. By far the most common way is manufacturing. New York manufacturers make practically everything.

Large government buildings have been built in the Washington, D.C., area.

Cities in the Middle Atlantic states have spread out over the surrounding countryside. These houses will be part of a new suburb near Washington, D.C.

Pennsylvania has a number of steel-making cities. Delaware and New Jersey have big chemical companies. And of course each state produces many more products than just these—anything from shoes, paint, and candy to cars and small airplanes.

Farmers in the Middle Atlantic States produce millions of dollars' worth of goods every year. Much milk from farms goes to the people in the cities nearby. Milk is a *perishable* product. It should be produced near

the people who buy it so that they can use it before it spoils.

Truck farmers, who raise fruits and vegetables, also do a good business near the cities. So many truck farmers live in New Jersey that it is called the Garden State.

In the Middle Atlantic States, God created three main regions that run north and south. Along the coast lies the flat lowland, which is called the Atlantic Coastal Plain. If you run your finger on the map along the line

Farming is important in the Middle Atlantic States. This dairy farm is in the Piedmont region.

Fall Line. There the land rises suddenly to the west, and hills begin. Near the Fall Line, many rivers have rapids or waterfalls. Sailors learned long ago that they had to stop at the Fall Line and unload because they could go no farther. Here cities sprang up.

West of the Fall Line lies the Piedmont, which contains some of the best farmland in the Middle Atlantic States. It is hilly, but not too hilly for cities and farms.

Beyond the Piedmont rise the Appalachian Mountains. To people traveling west in the early days, the Appalachians stood like long walls, one behind the other, with hardly any way around them. Today railroads and highways tunnel through them or curve and climb among them.

of big cities—Trenton, Philadelphia, Wilmington, Baltimore, and Washington, D.C.—the land east of your finger is the Coastal Plain.

Where you run your finger is the

Study Exercises

1. What is the largest city in the United States?
2. What city governs the United States?
3. What is the main industry in the Middle Atlantic States?
4. Why is New Jersey called the Garden State?
5. What is the Piedmont?
6. What occupation thrives in the Piedmont?

Gaining Geographical Skills

1. Trace Map F in the map section, and label it "The Middle Atlantic States."

2. Lightly shade the Coastal Plain yellow, the Piedmont green, and the Appalachian Mountains brown.

3. Label each state and its capital city. Also label New York City, Philadelphia, and Washington, D.C.

Further Study

1. (*a*) What is the Fall Line? (*b*) What was in the rivers that stopped the sailors but helped cities to grow?

2. What are some problems that cities face?

68. *The Southern States*

Glossary Words

bituminous coal	coke	hardwood
boll weevil	concentrate	levee
citrus fruit	delta	

What comes to people's minds when they think of the South? Cotton fields? Orange trees? Warm winters? Yes, these things are found there if you go far enough south. The Deep South also has trees hanging with Spanish moss, large swamps, cypress forests, and beautiful mansions with tall white pillars.

But the "South" extends as far north as Virginia. In fact, many people include Maryland and Delaware in the South. So, what is true of the Deep South might not be true of the border states close to more northern regions.

The South lies closer to the equator than the other regions you

The Southern States

have studied so far, so southern people enjoy a mild climate. Although winters bring ice and snow to much of the South, the places farthest south get little or no snow—just rain.

Flowers in the South bloom early in the springtime—azaleas, laurels, rhododendrons, and many others. Many people in the North, attracted by the southern climate, are moving to the sunbelt to stay. House builders are busy in the South, especially in Florida, the Sunshine State.

In recent years, manufacturing has increased in the South. Factory owners today like to build their factories close to the cotton, petroleum, and other raw materials they get from the South. They also find ready workers, since many people in the South are glad for the jobs that factories provide.

Some southern factories produce chemicals and chemical products, such as drugs, soap, fertilizer, paint, and plastic. Many of these items are made from petroleum. A number of chemical factories get their petroleum from the oil wells near the Gulf of Mexico. Did you know that some plastics are made from petroleum?

Textile mills in the South take the cotton bales that come from southern farms, and they produce thread, yarn, and cloth. Other factories refine or package the rice, sugar, peanuts, and other foods grown in the South.

Cypress trees in Florida. Notice the Spanish moss hanging from the branches. Many other kinds of trees thrive in the warm climate of the South.

A number of southern states mine soft coal, also called **bituminous** (bi TOO muh nus) **coal**. Soft coal is good for burning in factories and power plants. Much of it is also made into a fuel called *coke*, which is burned in steel mills.

Over half of the South is covered

with forests. Some of the trees are *hardwoods*, such as oak. Hardwoods make beautiful furniture, floors, and cabinets. Other trees are softwoods, such as pine. Turpentine comes from southern pines. Much paper and lumber also come from the South.

Farms are not the same all over the South. Virginia and West Virginia raise beautiful crops of apples. But apple trees do not produce well in the warmer states farther south. South Carolina and Georgia are known for their peach orchards, and Florida for its orange groves.

Although tobacco grows in some northern states, most of the tobacco is raised in the South. It is produced in each of the Southern States except Mississippi, Louisiana, and Arkansas. The market for tobacco is not as good as it once was. Many people have stopped using tobacco because they are concerned about the harm it does to their health. Christians avoid tobacco because their bodies are the temple of the Holy Ghost (1 Corinthians 3:16, 17). A number of Southern farmers have changed to other crops to make a living.

Oranges and other citrus fruits grow in Florida.

Truck farmers and orchard owners do well in the Southern States. Southern truck farmers ship their crops north to people hungry for fresh produce. Important crops in the South include sweet potatoes from Louisiana and Georgia, pecans and peanuts from Georgia and Alabama, and watermelons from Georgia.

Soybeans are raised in most of the Southern States. But they are especially important in Mississippi, Arkansas, and Alabama.

Cotton grows well in Tennessee, Mississippi, and Alabama. Southern farmers used to raise so much cotton that they called it King Cotton. Many of them raised almost nothing else. But then an enemy attacked— an insect from Mexico. The *boll weevil* lays eggs in cotton bolls, destroying crops. It spread through the South in the early 1900s, and farmers who planted only cotton suffered huge losses.

Southern farmers saw that they had to plant crops other than cotton. To their surprise, they prospered better when they raised several crops than when they had raised only one. If anything bad happened to one crop, they could usually depend on others. Besides, raising several different kinds of crops was good for the soil. In one town in Alabama, the people have set up a monument to the boll

Large amounts of cotton are still grown in the South, even though cotton is no longer "king." Large machines do the work that was once done by slaves.

weevil because of the lesson it taught them.

Some parts of the South are moist as well as warm. Sugar cane and rice grow well there. Much sugar cane is raised in Florida and Louisiana. Arkansas and Louisiana produce much rice. Florida has numerous orange groves. Most of the oranges are made into juice *concentrate*. Other *citrus fruits* such as tangerines and grapefruits also grow in Florida.

The Tennessee River Valley includes parts of seven states. At one time trees covered the area's many hills and mountains. But farmers and miners cut down too many of the trees on the hills, and with no tree roots to hold the soil in place, rains washed it away. Farms were ruined. Rivers flooded whenever it rained hard. The United States government formed the TVA (Tennessee Valley Authority) to solve these problems. The TVA planted trees where forests had been cut down. It built dams to control flooding and generate electricity. Today the TVA sells inexpensive electricity to thousands of people in the South.

The same regions you studied in the Middle Atlantic States—the Atlantic Coastal Plain, the Piedmont, and the Appalachians—extend through much of the South. Beyond the Appalachians, to the west, the hills become fewer. Finally the land flattens and slopes gently toward the Mississippi River.

Beyond the Mississippi, the land gradually begins to slope up again. In Arkansas and southern Missouri is an area of hills and mountains. The best-known of these are the beautiful Ozark Mountains.

The Mississippi is the largest river in the United States, and a very busy water highway. Up and down the river, towboats push strings of barges—large, flat boats that hold

A tugboat pushing barges on the Mississippi River.

many tons of cargo. *Levees* (LEV eez), earthen walls strengthened with metal and asphalt, help to keep the river from flooding cities and villages when it rises. A severe flood can destroy much property and take many lives.

The muddy Mississippi carries fertile soil with it. When it reaches the Gulf of Mexico, the current slows and the soil settles to the bottom. This soil builds up, forming many islands at the mouth of the river. These islands, with forking streams flowing among them, are called a *delta*.

Many ships sail to the busy port of New Orleans, even though it lies a hundred miles up the Mississippi from the Gulf of Mexico. In the past, Spain and France each controlled New Orleans for a time. This explains the Spanish-looking buildings and the French customs found there.

Study Exercises

1. Match these words to the definitions given below.

   bituminous   boll weevil   citrus fruit   levees
   coke   concentrate   barges   delta

   a. Oranges, tangerines, lemons, limes, and grapefruit.
   b. A soft grade of coal used for burning in factories.
   c. A fuel made from coal and used in steel mills.
   d. Banks of earth, metal, and asphalt set up along a river to prevent flooding.
   e. An area of land built up with soil carried there by a river.
   f. Large, flat boats that must be pushed by other boats.
   g. A condensed form of something such as juice.
   h. An insect that destroys cotton crops by laying eggs in the cotton bolls.
2. Why is the climate mild in the South?
3. What are several crops grown in the South? (Name at least three.)
4. What are some chemical products made in southern factories?
5. What products come from southern forests?
6. What two groups of mountains are in the Southern States?

Gaining Geographical Skills

1. Trace Map G in the map section, and label it "The Southern States."

2. Label each state and its capital city.

3. Label the Mississippi River and the Tennessee River.

4. Print in each state the names of crops mentioned in this lesson that are raised there.

Further Study

1. (a) What caused problems in the Tennessee River Valley? (b) What has the Tennessee Valley Authority done to correct those problems?

2. What good did the boll weevil do for the farmers of the South?

3. (a) What mixture of culture is found in New Orleans? (b) Why?

69. The Midwestern States

Glossary Words

pollution   precipitation   trade

The Midwest is a pleasant place to live. Nearly sixty million people call it home. It lies just far enough from the equator to have cold winters and hot summers. The countryside is fairly flat. Most of it is good farmland. God blessed the Midwest with rich, black soil that is not too rocky or too dry for crops and animals. In this prosperous region are large cities where much trading and manufacturing is done.

We will look at the most important manufacturing states first. To help yourself remember them, point to Ohio on the map and then run your finger through Indiana, Illinois, Wisconsin, and Michigan. Do you see that four of these states touch Lake Michigan? Here, clustered close to the Great Lakes, are most of the important trading and manufacturing cities of the Midwest. Now find Cleveland, Toledo, Detroit, Gary, Chicago, and Milwaukee. Do you see how they can *trade* with each other by water?

These cities trade with the whole world. Waterways now connect all the

The Midwestern States

Great Lakes to the ocean. Four of the Great Lakes border the Midwestern States: Lake Erie, Lake Huron, Lake Michigan, and Lake Superior.

Other cities not bordering the Great Lakes can send their goods down rivers to the Mississippi River and on to New Orleans. The Ohio River is busy with barges and has several good-sized cities such as Cincinnati, Ohio. The Missouri River is another important trade route of the Midwest. St. Louis, located where the Missouri River empties into the Mississippi, has grown into a large city.

Chicago is another city that has grown fast because of the traffic that goes through it. Much land traffic as well as water traffic travels through Chicago because it lies along the shortest route around the tip of Lake Michigan. Highways and railroads meet here, making Chicago the busiest crossroad in the country and the largest city in the Midwestern states.

Chicago's thousands of factories keep many workers busy. Over half the people of Illinois live in the Chicago area. But there are several other important cities of the Midwest besides Chicago.

Cleveland is the biggest city in Ohio, and one of the busiest ports on the Great Lakes. Detroit is called the Automobile Capital of the World because more cars and trucks are

Trains like these have helped make Chicago the busiest transportation center in the United States. Ships, airplanes, and trucks also carry goods to and from Chicago.

made there than in any other city.

The backbone of most industries like the automobile industry is steel. Much iron ore is mined in Minnesota and is shipped across the lakes to the steel-making cities such as Chicago, Detroit, Cleveland, and Buffalo. Gary, a city close to Chicago, is a giant steel-making center. These cities also have coal nearby, which is needed to heat the iron ore and turn it into steel.

Midwestern cities face the same problems you have studied in other cities. *Pollution* in the air creates problems. There are slums. Many black people believe that they could live better if white businessmen gave them jobs and if they could live in decent houses. Riots have started because of the ill feelings between black and white people.

Midwestern farmers produce the country's main food supply. Food processing plants nearby turn tons of corn into corn syrup and cornstarch. Train car loads of wheat are ground into flour. Some dairy plants make milk into butter and cheese, especially in Wisconsin and Minnesota. And Chicago has long been known as a meat-packing city.

Notice that corn, wheat, and animal products were especially mentioned above. The Midwest is so well known for these products that we say it contains a corn belt, wheat belt, and dairy belt.

Wisconsin and its neighbors lie in the dairy belt. In the cool climate here, farmers raise grass and hay for cattle. Some farmers in the dairy belt face a problem that farmers in the East do not have. They are far away from many big cities. They would

A tractor is ready for tires as it reaches the end of the assembly line in a Wisconsin factory. The Midwest has many important manufacturing cities.

have to pay too much to ship their milk to the cities, so they sell their milk to nearby food plants that make butter and cheese. These products do not spoil as quickly as milk, and they can be shipped long distances more easily.

Iowa lies in the heart of the corn belt and raises more corn than any other state. Neighboring states are also leading corn producers. Some of the corn goes to mills to make our food. But most of it feeds hogs and cattle. So if we eat meat we get food from corn even though we do not eat the corn.

Toward the western edge of the corn belt, the land gradually becomes drier because of less *precipitation*. This area is called the Great Plains. Here God created a level or rolling

Large fields of corn and other crops are grown in the Midwestern states. Much of the grain is shipped down the Mississippi River on barges or loaded onto ships on the Great Lakes.

land with hardly any trees except those that were planted. Because of the drier climate, farmers find raising corn more difficult. The farther west you go in the Great Plains, the more wheat fields you see. By far the most important wheat-producing state in the United States is Kansas. People often call Kansas the Breadbasket of America.

Farmers in different parts of the wheat belt raise different kinds of wheat. In the southern part, they plant winter wheat in the fall. The wheat gets a head start before cold weather comes. During winter, the wheat does not grow, but it helps to hold the soil in place. When warm weather comes again, the winter wheat finishes growing. In the northern part

of the wheat belt, where the winters are too bitterly cold for winter wheat to do well, farmers plant spring wheat and harvest it later the same year. Many big flour mills in the Midwest grind the wheat into flour.

Some parts of the Great Plains are too dry even for wheat. In the past, farmers learned that they should not plow up the land. The wheat they planted did not serve as well as prairie grass in keeping the soil from blowing away. So today these parts of the Great Plains have huge ranches where cattle and sheep roam.

In studying regions, we must be careful when we say, "Kansas is a wheat state, Iowa is a corn state, and Wisconsin is a dairy state." Remember, most other states also produce corn, wheat, and dairy products. Also, Midwestern states produce many other things besides what they are famous for. Oats, soybeans, sunflowers, sugar beets, vegetables, and other farm products come from the Midwest. Besides, we have not considered the many oil wells of the Midwest, the gold mines of South Dakota, or the forests of the northernmost states of the Midwest. Learning all there is to know about the Midwest would take a long time.

Study Exercises

1. Name the Midwestern cities that fit these descriptions.
    a. The busiest crossroad in the country.
    b. The biggest city in Ohio.
    c. The Automobile Capital of the World.
    d. A giant steelmaking center.
2. Name the state that leads in production of each of these items:
    (a) corn, (b) wheat, (c) milk.
3. What happens if the soil is plowed in very dry areas?

Gaining Geographical Skills

1. Trace Map H in the map section, and label it "The Midwestern States."
2. Label each state and its capital city.
3. Label the Ohio and Missouri rivers, and the four Great Lakes that border the Midwestern States.
4. Label the six great trading and manufacturing cities named in the second paragraph of the lesson.

Further Study

1. How can the cities in the Midwest trade with other parts of the world?
2. What is the difference between winter wheat and spring wheat?

70. The Southwestern States

Glossary Words

reservoir   vegetation

Names such as Oklahoma, Texas, New Mexico, and Arizona make some people think of lonely ranches, dusty roads, and hot deserts. But other people enjoy the blue skies, sunshine, and clear air of the Southwest. They know that even deserts can be colorful. People have named New Mexico the Land of Enchantment.

The Southwest becomes hot in the summer, but in the winter the warm climate attracts visitors from farther north. Many people move to the Southwest because the dry air is good for their health. Of course the Southwest is not all desert. Near the Gulf of Mexico, Texas is so damp that farmers can raise rice. In other parts of the Southwest where the *vegetation* is not so lush, farmers raise wheat and graze cattle. Even the parts that could be called desert are usually different from the desert that we picture in our minds. Instead of drifting sand dunes, there are cactuses and shrubs, broken stones, and bare rocks. In some parts, there are mountains.

The Southwestern States have a different flavor because of the Indians and Spanish-speaking people who live there. One out of every five or six persons is Spanish-speaking. Many of

The Southwestern States

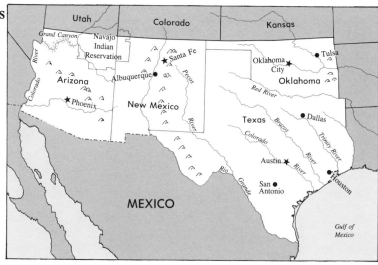

Cattle grazing on a large ranch in Texas.

them have come from nearby Mexico. Their different customs and foods help make this part of the United States interesting.

Many Indians still live in the Southwest. At one time most of Oklahoma was an Indian reservation. In fact, the name *Oklahoma* means "red people" in Indian language. Arizona and New Mexico still have the biggest Indian reservation in the United States— as big as West Vir-

ginia. However, not all the Indians live on reservations.

How do Southwestern people earn their living? Remember three C's: Cattle, Cotton, and Citrus fruits.

The most important of these is cattle. (Sheep and goats also are widely raised in the Southwest.) Because of the warm climate, ranchers can let their cattle out on pasture the year round. But ranchers face a major problem—in dry areas grass does not

Cattle are fattened in feedlots such as these in Texas before they go to market.

grow well. Ranches must be large to provide food for the animals. The average ranch in the Southwest covers over three thousand acres!

The Southwestern States produce much cotton. Texas farmers grow cotton in areas that are almost too dry for it. But they are too dry for the cotton boll weevil too, and that makes cotton worth growing.

The third *C* stands for citrus fruits. Although Southwestern States do not produce as many oranges as Florida and California, they are still important suppliers.

Mining has helped make the South-

west important. Remember two other *C*'s: Copper and Crude oil (petroleum). Much of the nation's copper comes from Arizona. But even more important to the Southwest is oil. Texas produces more than any other state. New Mexico and Oklahoma also count oil as their most important mineral. In Oklahoma, oil wells have even been drilled on the front lawn of the capitol building.

As a traveler goes through the Southwest, here and there across the country he can see pumps in lonely fields, slowly rocking, drawing oil out of the ground. The oil then runs through a pipeline to a collecting tank.

Oil well drillers also get natural gas from their wells. Natural gas heats homes and schools, cooks food, and dries laundry. Factories use large amounts of it. Underground pipelines carry oil and natural gas across the country. People in New York City can get natural gas that came through a pipeline all the way from Texas.

The Southwest offers a number of unusual sights, such as strange, flat-topped mountains and tall saguaro (suh GWAHR oh) cactuses with spiny arms. People often visit the Grand Canyon in Arizona. The Grand Canyon is two hundred fifty miles long, and a mile deep in some places. It is lined with steep red rock walls, boulders, and cliffs. Along its bottom

Desert covers much of the Southwest. Different kinds of cactuses grow there, such as the tall saguaro cactus in the center of this photo.

The Grand Canyon is a beautiful display of God's handiwork.

rushes the Colorado River. The Southwest reminds visitors that God can make a place beautiful even if it is quite different from what they are used to.

One problem with living in the Southwestern States is a shortage of water. Farmers know that some of the desert soil is actually quite fertile. All it needs is water. But the few rivers cannot supply enough water to irrigate large areas. Besides, the growing cities need water too.

To help this need, the people of the Southwest have built dams. Dams store water in huge lakes called *reservoirs*. The water can be used during dry seasons. The dams also slow rivers down during flood time, helping to keep them from carrying away good topsoil. The water falling at dams turns large generators that make electricity. The Hoover Dam on the western border of Arizona is 725 feet high, as tall as a skyscraper. The water it holds back makes a lake 115 miles long. This is enough water to irrigate a million acres.

Hoover Dam, built across a narrow canyon, backs up a large reservoir of water.

Study Exercises

1. Why are there so many Spanish-speaking people in the Southwest?
2. In what states is the biggest Indian reservation of the United States?
3. What animals are widely raised in the Southwest?
4. Name five things beginning with C that are important products of the Southwest.

Gaining Geographical Skills

1. Trace Map I in the map section, and label it "The Southwestern States."
2. Draw and label the Colorado River. Color a narrow yellow margin on both sides of the river to represent the Grand Canyon.
3. Label the Navajo Indian Reservation.
4. Label each state and its capital city.

Further Study

1. (a) How is the dryness of the Southwest an advantage? (b) How is it a disadvantage?
2. Why do the ranches need to be so large?

71. *The Rocky Mountain States*

Glossary Words

arid	fallow	rain shadow
continental divide	pass	sagebrush
dry farming		

How would you like a desert filled with salt instead of sand? How would you like to live in a house heated by water from a hot spring? Or to travel from a hot valley to a nearby mountain where you can throw snowballs? Such things are found in the Rocky Mountain States.

Do not think that the Rocky Mountains States are completely full of rocky mountains. A map shows that the mountains only run through them like broken chains laid across a floor. But crossing the mountains is still difficult. Highways must go through *passes* in the mountains or through tunnels. Roads that go up over the mountain passes must weave back and forth; otherwise they would be too steep for cars to climb.

West of the first tall mountains are other mountain ranges, and still others. Between them may be clear, blue lakes and beautiful, flat valleys. Many valleys are high enough to be cool and pleasant in the summer. Ranchers send cattle there to graze, and people spend vacations there. But in the winter, mountain valleys can be lonely places, very cold and full of snow.

God made the Rockies so high that they form a *continental divide*. Rain falling on the east side of the divide runs into rivers heading east toward the Atlantic Ocean. Rain falling on the west side of the divide runs into westward-flowing rivers, which run into the Pacific Ocean.

The Rocky Mountain States

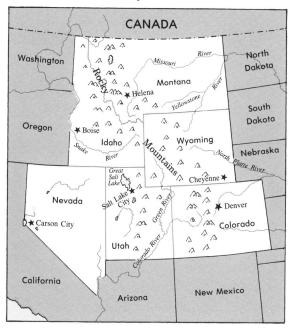

A small lake in the Rocky Mountains. Do you think these mountains have been given a good name?

In one large lower area west of the Rockies, called the Great Basin, rivers do not flow to the ocean at all. Some rivers dry up as they go along. Some are used for irrigation. Others flow into Utah's Great Salt Lake, which is more than four times saltier than the ocean. No fish live in the Great Salt Lake, but thousands of tons of salt are taken from the lake every year. In the Great Basin you can also find mountains, rugged hills, and canyons.

At the far western edge of this basin stands another wall of mountains, the Sierra Nevada. God made many of them as tall as the Rockies, or even taller. You will study them in the next lesson.

Mountains make most of this region *arid*. Winds that cross the country from the Pacific Ocean carry moisture they picked up from the water. As they rise up the sides of tall mountains west of the Great Basin, they become cooler. Cool air cannot hold as much moisture as warm air. Clouds form, and soon it begins to rain or snow. By the time the winds get over the tall mountain ranges, they have very little water for the thirsty lands on the other side. We say that these lands are in the *rain shadow* of the mountains.

Many areas of the rain shadow are too dry for farmers to raise anything except grass. Some are too dry even for grass, and only cactuses and the bushy **sagebrush** grow there. The Rocky Mountain area is the most thinly populated of the United States regions that you have studied so far. Only Alaska, far to the north, has fewer people per square mile.

What good can people get out of a country like this? Some people who live in this region have changed parts of it into farmland by using irrigation and fertilizer. Here and there are green or golden fields, watered by

Bales of hay stretch into the horizon on a Montana farm. Farmers in the Rocky Mountain States usually use irrigation to raise crops.

Irrigation circles in south-central Colorado. Barley, potatoes, and wheat are the major crops grown in this area.

streams that flow from the mountains. In many fields, water runs to the crops through irrigation ditches. In other places, long irrigation pipelines on wheels roll across the fields. One kind of pipeline moves around the center of a field the way a hand moves around a clock. A traveler flying across the country can count hundreds of huge dark green circles, irrigated by pipelines on wheels. Sagebrush grows only a few feet from the edges of the lush, irrigated fields.

Other people have found much good in the Rocky Mountain country just as it is. Where the land is not too dry for grass, ranchers graze cattle and sheep on huge ranches. In Montana and Wyoming there are more cattle and sheep than there are people.

Some western farmers practice ***dry farming***. Since they do not receive much rain or snow, they try to save all the moisture they receive. They make their furrows run across the slopes, rather than up and down, so that any rain that falls will not run

A windmill pumps water for cattle in the dry plains of eastern Colorado.

away. They farm only part of their land at one time, letting the other part lie *fallow* for a year to collect moisture between crops. They raise crops that do well in a dry climate, such as wheat.

Miners are glad this region is just as it is. They often find minerals in cold, dry, or rough parts of the world where no one else can find anything worthwhile. Do you remember the two C's that people find underground in the Southwest—copper and crude oil? They are the most important minerals of the Rocky Mountain States as well.

A few factories have been built in the Rocky Mountain States. But most factory owners would rather build factories close to big cities. Then they do not have to ship their goods as far to the people who buy them.

Just as in the Southwestern States, finding enough water for everyone in the Rocky Mountain States is a problem. Dams store water for farms and cities, but there is not nearly enough water for all the farmers who would like to irrigate. States have often argued over how much water each area should get. Colorado solved some of its problems by running tunnels from the rainy western side of Colorado to the dry eastern side, where most of the people of the state live.

The only state with a plentiful fresh water supply is Idaho. Sometimes people say water is Idaho's most important mineral. Perhaps you already know the crop Idaho is famous for—potatoes! Mothers bake some of them, but more than half of them are made into instant foods such as powdered mashed potatoes.

Study Exercises

1. Match these words with the definitions given below.

    passes   rain shadow   dry farming   sagebrush
    fallow   irrigation   continental divide

   a. Places where there are gaps in a mountain range.
   b. A ridge separating streams that flow toward different oceans.
   c. Farming practices that wisely use what little water is available.
   d. Watering crops.
   e. An area that receives little rainfall because of mountains standing in the way.
   f. Not used for raising crops.
   g. Bushy plants that grow in dry soil.

2. (a) What mineral is taken from a lake in the Rocky Mountain States? (b) What other minerals come from this region?

3. Which states have more cattle and sheep than people?

4. Which state is known for raising potatoes?

Gaining Geographical Skills

1. Trace Map J in the map section, and label it "The Rocky Mountain States."

2. Label the Rocky Mountains, the Great Basin, and the Great Salt Lake.

3. Label each state and its capital city.

Further Study

1. What change in temperature do you find as you go up a mountain?

2. What happens to the rain that falls in the Great Basin?

3. Why does it rain on the mountains more than on the land east of the mountains?

72. The Pacific Coast States

Glossary Words

fault   sequoia   suspension bridge
redwood   smog

California, Oregon, and Washington are quite a pleasant change from the dry Rocky Mountain States. The Lord gave these states some dry

The Pacific Coast States

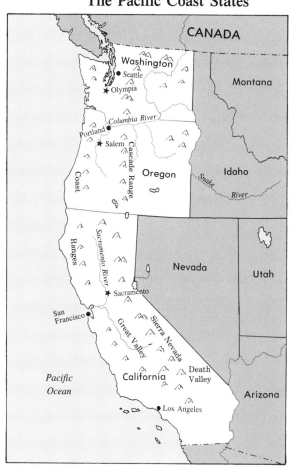

areas too, but He also gave them large forests and fertile plains. The Pacific Coast States are the greatest fruit-growing region in North America. Washington grows more apples than any other state. California produces more peaches and pears than any other state. Almost all the raisins produced in the United States come from California.

California is a big state with many resources. More people, bigger trees, and more kinds of minerals are found in California than in any other state. Californians also do more manufacturing and earn more money from farming than the people of any other state.

Let us study California from east to west. In eastern California stands the Sierra Nevada mountain range. A number of its snow-capped peaks are taller than many of the Rockies. The name *Sierra Nevada* means "snowy range."

In the Great Valley that runs north and south through much of California, almost any kind of crop can grow—from hay and potatoes to rice and cotton. Many oranges grow in the Great Valley.

Between the Great Valley and the Pacific Ocean are more mountains. The west coast of North America is not like the east, where long, gentle slopes run down to the sea. Here the rocky cliffs of the Coast Ranges tower above the shore. Between these coastal mountains, running north and south, are beautiful valleys. Farms and orchards do well here.

God gave southern California a warm, dry climate. Rain falls in part of southern California when other states are having winter. It has a dry season when other states are having summer. This climate, like that in Bible lands, is called a Mediterranean climate. So it is not surprising to learn that Californians grow olives, dates, and figs, just as people in Bible lands do.

Grapes are raised in this fertile California valley.

Some areas of southern California, such as Death Valley, are desert. Summer temperatures in Death Valley often reach 125°F. In the winter, people come here on vacations. They like Death Valley's mild winter temperatures.

Los Angeles, in southern California, is the second largest city in the country. Oil attracted people to Los Angeles. When the oil men moved in, other industries moved in too. Some of them were factories that used oil to make other products. Many people moved to Los Angeles to work in the factories. Others moved there because they enjoyed the warm, dry climate, the nearby beaches, and the snow-capped mountains.

Smaller cities have clustered around Los Angeles. The many cars and factory smokestacks give off fumes that sometimes fill the air with a thick yellow haze called *smog*. Smog can make people sick, and it can even kill plants. On the smoggiest days, the government tells factories not to burn fuel oil. People are asked not to drive their cars unless it is necessary.

San Francisco has cooler weather

The Golden Gate Bridge spans the San Francisco Bay. In the background is the city of San Francisco.

and more rain than Los Angeles. It is built on a peninsula that partly surrounds San Francisco Bay. The Golden Gate Bridge crosses the entrance to the bay. This bridge is one of the world's largest *suspension bridges*.

Spanish-speaking Mexicans make up a large part of California's population. Many Chinese, Japanese, Indians, and black people live in California. Often these people have a hard time finding work, and the work they do

find does not pay well. Many live in crowded, rundown houses. Those who cannot speak English have problems, such as finding a job, doing their shopping, or studying in school. But such people keep moving to California, because they hope to find better opportunities there.

The San Andreas *Fault*, runs through California. Sometimes the earth along the fault shifts suddenly, causing earthquakes. Today buildings are made to withstand even strong earthquakes. But when a severe one shakes a big city, there is still great damage.

The *redwoods* of California grow only in one part of northern California, and some Californians have never seen them. The tallest living things in the world, some of them stand more than three hundred feet tall. That is about ten times as tall as a good-sized house.

Giant *sequoias*, found on the western slopes of the Sierra Nevadas in California, do not grow as tall as redwoods, but their trunks are thicker. Several hundred of them have trunks more than ten feet thick. The world's largest tree (containing the most wood) is the General Sherman Tree. It is thought to be about 2,500 years old. Laws have been made to protect the sequoias and many of the redwoods. The value of seeing these trees is greater than the value of the wood if they were cut down.

The Cascade Mountains run like a backbone through Oregon and Washington. They keep much rain from falling on the eastern part of the two states. But between the Cascades and the low mountains near the coast lie fertile lowland valleys. Mild, moist winds from the Pacific Ocean blow across this valley region. Rain falls almost every day in winter, but the summer is a dry season. Almost every day is sunny.

Most people of Oregon and Washington live in these lowlands. Big cities such as Portland, Oregon, and Seattle, Washington, have sprung up there.

Massive redwood trees tower above the person who took this photograph.

Logs from the forests of Oregon traveling to a sawmill.

Oregon and Washington are as well-known for their forests as for their farms. Huge evergreen forests cover the mountains. Oregon and Washington produce much lumber. A large percentage of the nation's plywood (made of thin layers of wood glued together) comes from Oregon. The people of Oregon and Washington try to take care of their forests. They know that not only fire but insects and disease can destroy many acres of trees. Forest owners plant seedlings in areas where they have cut mature trees.

Farmers irrigate the drier eastern parts of Oregon and Washington. Water from the Grand Coulee Dam on the Columbia River irrigates thousands of farms. Farmers also produce crops that do not need much water. By now you should know enough about dry areas to guess that beef and wheat come from there. Because of irrigation, the dry land of the Columbia Basin is now much more beautiful and productive than when settlers first saw it.

<hr>

Study Exercises

1. Name six things in California that are more or bigger than in any other state.
2. Name each place or thing described below.
   a. Western mountains with peaks taller than the Rocky Mountains.
   b. A hot, dry place that may reach 125°F in summer.
   c. The second largest city in the United States.
   d. The bay whose entrance is crossed by the Golden Gate Bridge.
   e. A long, deep crack in the earth, found in California.
   f. The world's largest tree.
3. What product comes from Oregon's forests?

Gaining Geographical Skills

1. Trace Map K in the map section, and label it "The Pacific Coast States."
2. Label the Sierra Nevada, Coast Ranges, and Cascade Mountains.
3. Label the Great Valley and Death Valley.
4. Label each state and its capital city. Also label Los Angeles and San Francisco.

Further Study

1. (a) What kind of pollution sometimes interrupts factory work and causes people to stay home in California cities? (b) What other effects does it cause?
2. What has been done to improve the land of the Columbia Basin?

73. *Alaska and Hawaii*

Glossary Words

panhandle   pontoons   volcano

Alaska

The word *Alaska* makes people think of a big, icy state where Eskimos and polar bears live. They are partly right. In central Alaska, January temperatures average about -12°F, which is colder than in any other state.

Alaska has warm weather in summertime though. The warm summer is short, but the sun shines for long periods each day. Some vegetables and fruits grow even in central Alaska, where the sun shines about twenty hours a day.

Ocean breezes keep the temperature mild in some parts of southern Alaska. These areas receive more rain than snow, and the thermometer goes above freezing more often than below—even in January. Compared with inland areas, that is warmer than the winter temperatures of some places farther south.

Alaska is the biggest state in the United States, more than twice the size of Texas. But it has fewer people per square mile than any other state. More people would settle in Alaska if the winters were not so long. Winter days are short; people go to work in the dark and come home in the dark.

Alaska

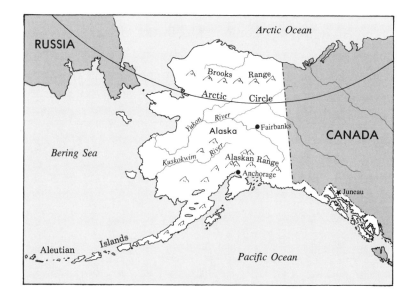

Even though Alaska has some difficult living conditions, it is actually a very valuable land. Remember, God has placed rich supplies of minerals in some of the most desolate lands. Oil has been discovered in both northern and southern Alaska. A pipeline runs from Prudhoe Bay in northern Alaska to Valdez in southern Alaska, where tanker ships can load the oil and haul it away. Other valuable minerals also come from Alaska.

Fishing is an important industry in Alaska. Boats like this catch large numbers of salmon and other fish.

The Alaskan pipeline carries oil from wells in northern Alaska to ports in southern Alaska.

Besides oil, remember three *F*'s: Forests, Fishing, and Farming. Alaskan forests are mostly evergreen trees. Sawmills cut the trees into lumber, and pulp mills make pulp for paper, cardboard, and other products.

Fishing is even more important, especially salmon fishing. The fish are canned or frozen at processing plants in cities near the coast. Alaska's many mosquitoes are good food for young fish. Perhaps there would be no salmon industry if there were no insects.

What about farming? Although you would hardly expect corn or wheat to grow in Alaska, potatoes, barley, oats, and other cool-weather crops do well. Animals are more important than crops. Milk is the most important animal product, and eggs and wool are also important. The fertile Matanuska Valley near Anchorage produces about three-fourths of Alaska's farm products.

The United States government values Alaska partly because it is so far away. From distant points in Alaska, men can keep watch over other parts of the world. The Alaskan mainland is only fifty-one miles away from Russia at its closest point. And if you measure from the farthest

American island to the closest Russian island, Russia and the United States are only two and a half miles apart!

In such a big state as Alaska, roads and railroads run long distances through mountains and empty, frozen areas. For small villages in out-of-the-way places, it is often easier to send an airplane in and out, carrying people and supplies. Bush pilots fly small planes to little airfields here and there. Many times they land on a lake or a river. The planes have *pontoons* that keep them floating. If the airplanes must land on snow or ice, they use skis. Alaskans have been called "the flyingest people under the American flag."

Alaska has a *panhandle* running southeast from its main body. It can easily be seen on the map in this lesson. But never try to pick up Alaska by the handle because the handle is not very solid! Islands make up a large part of it. The coast is very mountainous. Mountains in other parts of the world usually stand inland, but the mountains along Alaska's shore stand knee-deep in the ocean. That is why it rains so much in this part of Alaska; when sea breezes reach shore, the first thing they must do is rise over mountains. This causes rain.

The highest mountain peaks in North America are found in Alaska. Mount McKinley, at 20,300 feet, is

Airplanes help Alaskans travel and carry supplies across the many miles that separate some settlements. This airplane is equipped with pontoons.

highest of them all. Mount McKinley is in the Alaska Range, a range of mountains that curve around the southern part of Alaska. Another range, the Brooks Range, crosses the far northern part of Alaska.

Between the Alaska Range and the Brooks Range flows the Yukon River. The Yukon River begins in Canada and runs from east to west all the way across Alaska. It is Alaska's biggest river.

The Aleutian Islands stretch from Alaska nine hundred miles toward the west. They are rugged, cold, and foggy.

There are only three big cities in Alaska. The capital, Juneau (JOO noh), is in the panhandle. Strangely, it is the biggest city in the United States—if you count the square miles included in the city limits. But it does not have even as many people as Anchorage (You can remember that Anchorage is near the ocean by the word *anchor*.) The only big city in the heart of Alaska is Fairbanks.

Hawaii

God created Hawaii quite different from big, cold, empty Alaska. Lying farther south than Florida, Hawaii has warm weather the year round. Yet the ocean breezes keep it from becoming very hot. Palm trees and bright flowers—in fact, nearly any kind of plant—can grow here.

Hawaii is actually a group of islands in the Pacific Ocean. The islands contain mountains. Perhaps we should say that the islands themselves are mountaintops. The mountains are **volcanos** whose bottoms rest on the floor of the Pacific Ocean. Most of these volcanos no longer throw out fire and ashes. But a few of them are still active. One of them poured out enough lava in 1960 to destroy a nearby village. A highway takes visitors up to the crater of this volcano, where they can see hot lava bubbling.

Hawaii is known for its lovely palm trees, warm weather, and beautiful scenery.

Hawaii

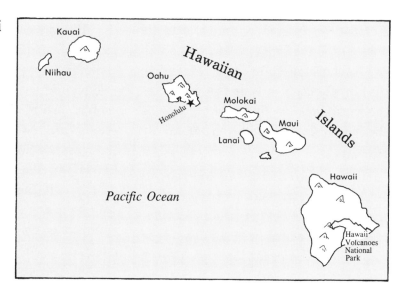

Kauai

Niihau

Oahu

Honolulu

Hawaiian

Molokai

Maui

Lanai

Islands

Hawaii

Hawaii
Volcanoes
National
Park

Pacific Ocean

The Hawaiian Islands are more than two thousand miles away from the United States mainland. This makes Hawaii very valuable to the United States. Ships and airplanes can stop at Hawaii on their way across the ocean. Many Hawaiians earn their living by working for the United States government.

How many islands does Hawaii have? Over a hundred. Most of them are too little for people to live on. Hardly anything grows on them. Anyone who tried to dig a well would get only salt water. Most Hawaiians live on only seven of the largest islands.

Being so far south, Hawaii grows much sugar cane and many pineapples. One pineapple company owns a whole island and has made it a big pineapple plantation. One fifth of the world's pineapple supply comes from Hawaii.

Pineapple harvest in Hawaii. Notice the pineapples near the bottom of the photograph.

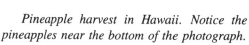

Hawaii also has some of the biggest cattle ranches in the world. One of the islands is practically all one big ranch.

The mountains in Hawaii, lying so close to the ocean, have much rainfall. The mountainsides toward the ocean breezes are much wetter than the sides away from the wind. Hawaiians irrigate dry parts of their land with water from the wet parts.

You would expect most people to live on Hawaii, the largest of the Hawaiian islands. But most Hawaiians live on Oahu (oh AH hoo), where the state capital (Honolulu) is found. Honolulu is the biggest city and ocean port in Hawaii.

Study Exercises

Write Alaska *or* Hawaii *for each word or phrase. For the items that fit both states, write* Alaska and Hawaii.

1. panhandle
2. many islands
3. pineapples
4. Eskimos and polar bears
5. tropical
6. Fairbanks
7. largest state
8. ocean breezes
9. far from the main group of states
10. palm trees
11. sugar cane
12. sawmills and pulp mills
13. short winter days
14. valuable to the United States government
15. stopping point for crossing the Pacific
16. vegetables, fruits, and flowers
17. cattle
18. highest mountain peaks in North America
19. Oahu
20. oil pipeline

Gaining Geographical Skills

Alaska

1. Trace Map L in the map section, and label it "Alaska."
2. Label Mount McKinley, the Alaska Range, the Brooks Range, the Yukon River, and the Aleutian Islands.
3. Label Juneau, Anchorage, and Fairbanks.

Hawaii

1. Trace Map M in the map section, and label it "Hawaii."
2. Label the seven largest islands of Hawaii.
3. Label Honolulu.

Further Study

1. How many hours of darkness do most Alaskans have on summer nights?
2. (*a*) How do ocean breezes affect the temperature in southern Alaska? (*b*) How do they affect the temperature in Hawaii?

Chapter 12 Review

Reviewing What You Have Learned

A. *Write a glossary word for each definition.*

1. A mineral containing a valuable substance.
2. A fuel made from coal and used in steel mills.
3. The making of products.
4. A mixture of smoke and fog.
5. The business of buying and selling goods.
6. The place along rivers where rapids stop ships.
7. Ground-up wood used to make paper.
8. A bank built along a river to prevent flooding.
9. Farmers that raise vegetables and fruit.
10. Dry, not having much rainfall.
11. A narrow strip of territory connected to a larger territory.
12. A crack beneath the earth's surface.

B. *Choose the correct answer to complete each sentence.*

1. The main industries in New England are ———.
   a. manufacturing, tourist trade, and fishing
   b. farming, fishing, and ship building
   c. government work, mining, and manufacturing

2. ——— is the largest city in United States.
   a. Washington, D. C.
   b. Chicago
   c. New York City

3. The largest river of United States is the ———.
   a. Colorado River
   b. Tennessee River
   c. Mississippi River

4. The country's main food supply comes from ———.
   a. the corn belt, wheat belt, and dairy belt
   b. citrus orchards of the South
   c. the Garden State

5. Many —— live in the Southwest.
   a. black people
   b. prosperous factory owners
   c. Indians and Spanish people

6. A continental divide is formed by the ——.
   a. rain shadow
   b. Rocky Mountains
   c. Mississippi River

7. —— are mountains in California.
   a. The Ozarks and Appalachians
   b. The Cascade Ranges and Rocky Mountains
   c. The Sierra Nevada and Coast Ranges

8. —— is the largest state in the United States.
   a. Alaska
   b. Texas
   c. California

9. Hawaii is a group of islands in the ——.
   a. Atlantic Ocean
   b. Pacific Ocean
   c. Gulf of Mexico

C. *Write* true *or* false.
   1. The New England States have much fertile soil.
   2. The nation's government work is done in Washington, D.C.
   3. Boll weevil damage led to better farming in the South.
   4. Cities around the Great Lakes ship most of their goods down the Mississippi River.
   5. Some people live in the Southwest because the dry weather is good for their health.
   6. The Great Salt Lake gets its salt from the ocean.
   7. Death Valley is heavily forested.
   8. The panhandle of Alaska is close to Russia.
   9. Hawaii has warm weather the year around.

Gaining Geographical Skills

1. Trace Map N in the map section, and label it "United States."

2. Label each of these regions, and color each group of states a different color from the regions next to it.

   The New England States   The Southwestern States
   The Middle Atlantic States   The Rocky Mountain States
   The Southern States   The Pacific Coast States
   The Midwestern States

3. Label each of these on the map: the Appalachian Mountains, the Rocky Mountains, the Mississippi River, the Atlantic Ocean, and the Pacific Ocean.

So Far This Year

Choose the correct answers. See how many you can give without looking back.

1. Match.
   a. Northeast Indians
   b. Southeast Indians
   c. Great Plains Indians
   d. Southwest Indians
   e. Intermountain and California Indians
   f. Northwest Coastal Indians
   g. Arctic peoples

   1. made large wooden houses, totem poles, and log canoes.
   2. included Inuit and Aleuts.
   3. included the best-known Indian tribe—the Iroquois.
   4. built pueblos and irrigated crops.
   5. were quick to learn white men's ways.
   6. lived in teepees and hunted buffalo.
   7. gathered seeds and nuts and made baskets.

2. Quebec was the first lasting (English, French, Spanish) settlement in North America.

3. The Pilgrims, Quakers, and many other groups moved to America in search of (an easy life, freedom of worship, gold).

4. (Slaves, Indians) did much of the work on large southern plantations.

5. The (Declaration of Independence, Constitution) describes how the United States government is to work.

6. Many Loyalists and Mennonites moved to (Canada, England, Georgia) after the Revolutionary War.

7. The colonists in (United States, Canada) obtained their independence gradually and peacefully from Great Britain.

8. Before the Civil War, many (Northerners, Southerners) were afraid the (Northerners, Southerners) would make them give up their slaves.

9. Many settlers moved to the Great Plains after the government started giving away (land, food) and railroad companies built (local, transcontinental) railroads.

10. The invention of (tugboats, steamboats) made travel upstream easier.

11. World War I was (longer, worse) than any war before it.

12. World War II ended soon after (Canada, England, United States) dropped atomic bombs on two Japanese cities.

13. Most North Americans are (richer, poorer) than many other people in the world.

14. Water draining into the Atlantic Ocean is separated by the (Continental Divide, Great Salt Lake) from water draining into the Pacific Ocean.

Mt. Robson, the tallest peak in the Canadian Rockies, is 12, 972 feet high.

CHAPTER 13

REGIONS OF CANADA

Regions of Canada

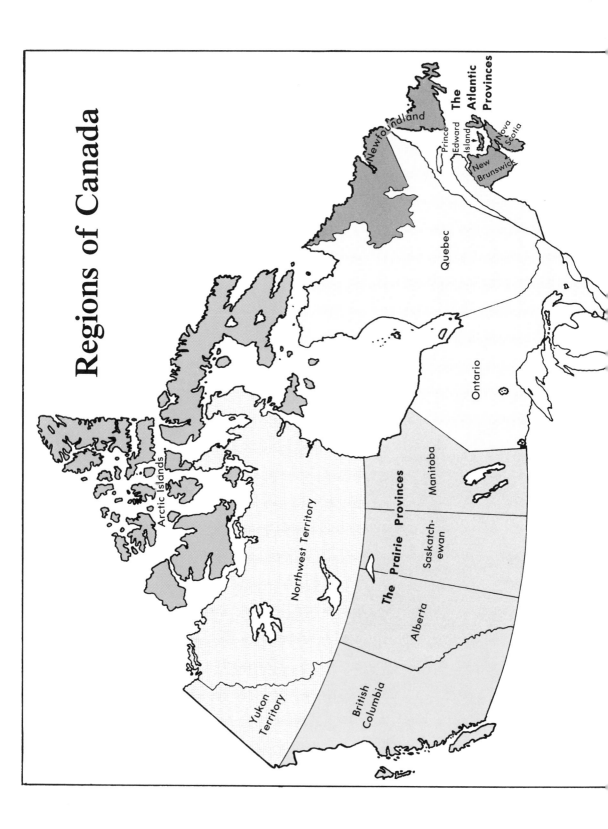

The Atlantic Provinces

The

Newfoundland

Prince Edward Island

Nova Scotia

New Brunswick

Quebec

Ontario

Arctic Islands

Northwest Territory

The Prairie Provinces

Manitoba

Saskatch-ewan

Alberta

Yukon Territory

British Columbia

74. The Atlantic Provinces

Glossary Words

condense   current   tide

continental shelf   maritime

The Atlantic Provinces are New-foundland, New Brunswick, Nova Scotia, and Prince Edward Island. Three of these—New Brunswick, Nova Scotia, and Prince Edward Island—are sometimes called the *Maritime* Provinces.

The sea helps to give these provinces an agreeable climate. Since they are farther north than Maine, you might expect them to be cold. But in winter the nearby ocean cools more slowly than the land. Winds from the ocean keep the temperature from dropping too low. Also, an important ocean *current*, called the Gulf Stream, flows past the Atlantic Provinces, bringing warm water from farther south. The Gulf Stream helps to warm the Atlantic Provinces.

Far to the north, a part of Newfoundland called Labrador misses the warmth of the Gulf Stream. In these parts of Labrador, snow covers the ground in September and does not melt until June. An ocean stream flows along the coast, but it is the cold Labrador Current. Sweaters feel comfortable in Labrador even in the warmest months.

Near the island of Newfoundland, the cold Labrador Current from the north meets the warm Gulf Stream from the South. Here the warm, moist air above the Gulf Stream is suddenly cooled. The moisture in the air *condenses* and becomes fog, which often settles in over the ocean and the shore.

The Atlantic Provinces

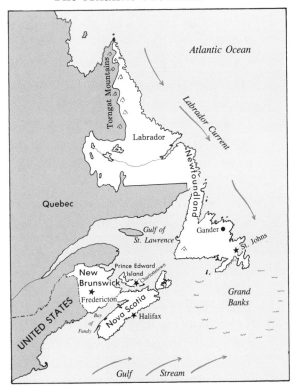

People living in the Atlantic Provinces enjoy many beautiful landscapes. God covered much of this land with mountains, hills, and evergreen forests. Streams, lakes, and ocean waters are never far away. Beautiful New Brunswick is called the Picture Province. This province has more forests than farms, but rich farmland can also be found, especially along the rivers.

The first valuable thing explorers discovered when they came to the Atlantic Provinces was fish—multitudes of them. They found so many fish because the ocean is different here than in many parts of the world. It stays shallow for a number of miles out from the shore, then drops off to the ocean floor. The shallow part, called a *continental shelf*, makes a good home for fish—cod, haddock, herring, salmon, and many others.

The richest fishing area is the Grand Banks. Fishing boats from around the world go there to fish. God gave the Atlantic Provinces a rugged coastline—just what fishermen like. The ocean inlets make good harbors where the fishermen can shelter their boats from ocean storms.

How do the fishermen catch the fish? Often they drag a big net behind their boat. Angling (using a rod and line) would be much too slow for the kind of fish most fishermen want. The fishermen do not want to catch all the small fish. Their nets are made with holes big enough to let the small fish escape. The small fish will grow until they are worth catching.

In several provinces, lobsters are the most important catch. Lobster fishermen set traps close to shore for these strange-looking creatures with big pincers. Perhaps you have seen live lobsters in stores or restaurants. People pay high prices for their tasty meat.

Not everything grows well in the Atlantic Provinces. In many places, the soil is poor. And the growing season is short. But farmers have learned that potatoes grow well there. Potatoes are Prince Edward Island's most important crop. Apples also do well in the Atlantic Provinces. In Nova Scotia, dairy farming is the most important kind of farming, and hay is the most important field crop. In Labrador, the climate is so cold that farming is hardly worthwhile.

Like people in many other regions, most people in the Atlantic Provinces earn their living through manufacturing. Knowing the natural resources of the region, perhaps you can guess what they manufacture—canned and frozen food from the fisheries and farms, and lumber and paper from the forests. The Atlantic Provinces produce much newsprint. They also manufacture other things such as ships, aircraft, and automobile parts.

In one way, the Atlantic Provinces

Lobsters are caught in traps like the ones stacked on these docks.

have an advantage over the parts of Canada farther inland. Ships going to cities in Ontario must wait until the ice breaks in the spring before they can sail up the St. Lawrence Seaway. But ships can visit the Halifax port in Nova Scotia the year round. This makes Halifax an especially busy port.

Newfoundland, as out of the way as it might seem, actually lies on the route from the United States to Europe. Though hard to imagine from a flat map, this is easy to see on a globe. Airplanes making flights across the Atlantic often stop to refuel at Gander in Newfoundland.

Newfoundland also has an important natural resource: great deposits of iron ore in Labrador. Some parts of Labrador are so rich that Quebec would have liked to own the land, but it was decided that the land belonged to Newfoundland.

Prince Edward Island is the smallest province. Since its name is so long, people often just call it P.E.I.

Why is manufacturing not the most important activity on Prince Edward Island? This province does not have minerals such as iron ore to use in industry. Being so small, it does not

Halifax is a busy port because ships can come and go even in the winter, when other Canadian ports are closed because of ice.

other nearby areas, it is mostly a gently rolling plain. The rich soil produces thousands of bushels of potatoes, as well as barley and other grains. Prince Edward Island has been called the Million Acre Farm.

The Bay of Fundy, between Nova Scotia and New Brunswick, is famous for its high *tides* that roll in from the sea twice a day. In some places the water level rises as much as forty or even fifty feet. When the tide goes out, little boats that had been floating along the shore rest on the ground. There is one good thing about the strong tides: they keep ice from forming in the bay, and this allows ships to go in and out of it all winter.

have large rivers to generate electricity either. Since electricity costs more on Prince Edward Island, businessmen would rather build factories elsewhere. Besides, people on the island have the problem of getting to and from the mainland. Ferries do run back and forth, and one ferry line even carries train cars. Still, depending on a ferry all the time is not handy. If goods were made in factories on Prince Edward Island, they would cost more because they would need to be transported to the mainland.

God made Prince Edward Island well suited for farming. Unlike many

Neat farms on Prince Edward Island.

Study Exercises

1. How is a rugged coastline helpful to the fishing industry?
2. Name the province that is noted for each of these industries: (*a*) potato farming, (*b*) iron ore mining, (*c*) hay and dairy farming.
3. Labrador is part of which province?
4. What is the ordinary way to travel from Prince Edward Island to other provinces?
5. What is unusual about the Bay of Fundy?

Gaining Geographical Skills

1. Trace Map O in the map section, and label it "The Atlantic Provinces."
2. Draw arrows in the Atlantic Ocean to indicate the Gulf Stream. Label the Grand Banks and the Bay of Fundy.
3. Label each province and its capital city.
4. Label Gander, Newfoundland, and draw a small airplane symbol next to it.

Further Study

1. Why does the ocean take so long to become cold near the Atlantic Provinces in winter?
2. What causes the fog near the Newfoundland shore?

75. Quebec and Ontario

Glossary Words

economic   escarpment   heartland

Quebec and Ontario are Canada's biggest provinces. Quebec, the biggest province, stretches as far from north to south as the distance between the New England States and Florida—1,200 miles.

Quebec and Ontario have larger populations than any of the other Canadian provinces. Most people who live in Quebec cluster in its southern part, along the St. Lawrence River. Most of Ontario's population lives close by in the southeastern corner of their province, which is the warmest

part. The most thickly populated areas of Quebec and Ontario, put together, make up what is called the *heartland* of Canada.

The heartland is one of Canada's smallest regions. Yet a large percentage of all the Canadians live there. The heartland includes Ottawa, the capital of Canada, and other big cities such as Montreal, Canada's largest city. Canada's heartland is its most important *economic* region; in other words, it is where most of Canada's business takes place. Why is this part

Quebec and Ontario

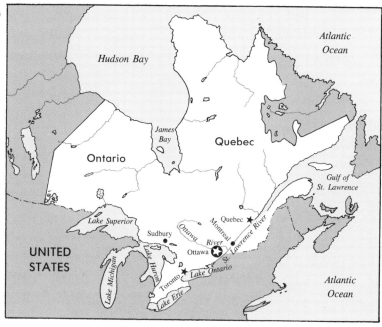

Ottawa is the capital city of Canada. It is located on the Ontario side of the Ottawa River, which flows between Ontario and Quebec. The Parliament buildings, where Canadian lawmakers meet, are in the lower left corner of this photograph.

of Canada so important? Why do so many people want to live here?

For one thing, this part of Canada has good water transportation. Ships can travel up the St. Lawrence River from ocean ports around the world. Some bring coffee, bananas, and other goods that Canada cannot produce for herself. Ships also carry away the lumber, paper, wheat, and other things that Canada sells to other countries.

Suppose you were exploring the St. Lawrence River, coming in from the Atlantic Ocean. About three hundred miles "up" the St. Lawrence (although you really would be traveling south), the river narrows. Here you would find Quebec, a city so old that the oldest part has a wall around it. It is the oldest city in Quebec. Most of the people in Quebec speak French.

Farther up the St. Lawrence stands another French city, Montreal. It is quite an unusual city; it is built on an island in the river, and in the middle of the city sits a mountain. The oldest part of Montreal has narrow streets, and a few of them are even paved with cobblestones. But Montreal also has some very modern areas. It has the largest "underground city" in the world, with over two hundred stores and restaurants below street level.

Just above Montreal on the St. Lawrence are rapids. That is why Montreal was built where it is. Ships that could sail up the river as far as Montreal had to stop and unload there. It was a busy spot.

Men often dreamed of building a canal around the rapids so that ships could sail on up the river. In the 1800's Canada built a shallow canal there. Later the United States and Canada worked together to build several canals and locks that made it possible for ships to sail all the way to

Quebec City is the capital of the province of Quebec. The French language, French-style buildings, and Catholic churches throughout the province remind visitors that this region of Canada was once controlled by France.

the Great Lakes. This passage is called the St. Lawrence Seaway. The St. Lawrence Seaway and the Great Lakes are the busiest inland water route in the world.

The St. Lawrence and its many neighboring rivers produce much hydroelectric power. The rivers tumble over waterfalls and through rapids. Because the water falls so rapidly, it has plenty of energy to turn generators. Some of the falling water is directed through turbines that spin electric generators. Imagine the power of the water that roars over Niagara Falls! Some of the water from the Niagara River is used to generate hydroelectricity—so much that it provides power for thousands of homes and factories.

Another reason people settled in the heartland of Canada was to farm the fertile soil. Southern Ontario has

a special blessing because large lakes that partly surround it help to keep the temperatures mild. Even though the winters are cold and snowy, crop-killing frosts do not come too early in the fall or too late in the spring.

Since you have studied other northern regions, perhaps you can guess what farm products are found in Quebec and Ontario. Hay grows well there, and that encourages farmers to raise cows and steers. Beef, milk, and milk products—butter, cheese, and ice cream—are important.

What fruits and vegetables would be important in Quebec and Ontario? Those that prosper in a cool climate, of course, such as apples and potatoes. Berries grow well too. Even fruits sensitive to cold, like peaches and grapes, grow near the western shore of Lake Ontario. Nearby is the Niagara

Escarpment, which protects the area from cold winds. There are many orchards in this area.

More maple syrup comes from Quebec than from anywhere else. Farmers go out into their "sugar bush" early in the spring when snow still lies on the ground. They bore little holes into maple trees and stick spouts into the holes. Then they hang covered buckets beneath the spouts. When the weather warms and the sap rises into the trees, some sap drips slowly into the buckets. Later the farmers gather the sap and take it to a shed, where they boil it into maple syrup.

Provinces with many people can manufacture many goods. Ontario has been called the Workshop of the Nation. Toronto and other nearby cities such as Hamilton have factories that make cars, farm machinery, stoves and refrigerators, and many other things. One tenth of Canada's manufacturing is done in Toronto.

The rest of Quebec and Ontario has no problem with overcrowding! Half of Ontario and most of Quebec is part of the rough, rocky Canadian Shield. In spite of its ruggedness, God made this area beautiful. The endless evergreen forests and thousands of lakes make beautiful scenery. Many

A dairy farm in Ontario.

Orchards near the shore of Lake Ontario avoid frost because the lake helps warm the air. Most other areas of Ontario and Quebec are too cool to raise fruit, except apples.

tourists visit the Canadian Shield.

But the rocky countryside has never attracted many farmers. Only a few spots in the Canadian Shield have good soil; in fact, some places are only bare rock. In the area farthest north, the climate is too cold even for trees to grow. Besides, during the summer, millions of mosquitoes breed in the many swamps.

Often land that looks rough and forbidding is hiding riches for diligent seekers to find. The great evergreen forests produce lumber, firewood, and especially paper. Quebec produces more paper than any other province or state in North America. Most of this is newsprint. Hidden among the rocks are many minerals such as iron and copper. Sudbury, Ontario, produces a fourth of the world's nickel.

Although the people of Quebec and Ontario speak different languages, the two provinces are alike in many ways. Both are huge. They share the St. Lawrence River, the heartland of Canada, and the Canadian Shield. They are good neighbors.

Study Exercises

1. —— is Canada's capital city.
2. —— is Canada's largest city.
3. —— is Canada's oldest city.
4. —— is Canada's greatest manufacturing city.
5. —— is Canada's greatest nickel center.
6. —— is the main language of Quebec.

Gaining Geographical Skills

1. Trace Map P in the map section, and label it "Quebec and Ontario."
2. Label the five Great Lakes, the St. Lawrence River, and the Gulf of St. Lawrence.
3. Label Niagara Falls.
4. Label each province and its capital city. Also label Ottawa.

Further Study

1. What is the heartland of Canada?
2. What is the Niagara Escarpment?
3. What is the Canadian Shield?

76. The Prairie Provinces

Glossary Words

chinook   elevator

The Prairie Provinces—Manitoba, Saskatchewan, and Alberta—are actually not all prairie. Vast areas in their northern parts are covered with evergreen forests. Even the prairie is not what it used to be. The land where buffalo once roamed is now divided into big square fields and is dotted with houses and striped with roads. Prairies are often imagined to be flat, but not nearly all the prairies are flat like a table top. In the western part especially, the prairies are rolling or hilly.

The Prairie Provinces become very cold in the winter. The northern prairies differ from the southern. The summers in the southern areas are warm enough for farmers to grow good crops. Farther north, the summers are too short and cool. Most people live in the warmer areas.

Sometimes a warm wind called a *chinook* (shi NOOK) swoops down across the Rockies. Chinooks have left their moisture on the western side of the Rockies, and by the time they reach the prairies they are so dry that they pick up moisture from the land. When chinooks blow in the summer, they dry out and damage the crops. In the winter they melt the snow and

The Prairie Provinces

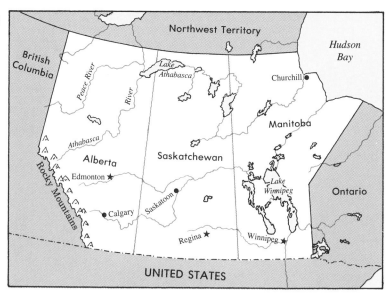

Wheat harvest

dry up moisture that would have soaked into the ground. But they do bring milder temperatures to the prairies for a few days.

Traveling west from Ontario, the first province you come to is Manitoba. Its biggest city is Winnipeg, the capital. Half of the people of Manitoba live there.

Many roads and railroads run through the Winnipeg area. The map in this lesson will show you why. Winnipeg lies on a narrow neck of land between the southern tip of Lake Winnipeg and the northern border of the United States. People traveling from

Large fields of wheat and other grain cover the Great Plains of Canada.

east to west have to pass through Winnipeg. Sometimes Canadians call Winnipeg the Gateway to the West. Winnipeg also has the largest stockyard in Canada and several large meatpacking houses. Mills in Winnipeg produce much flour. (Flour and meat—now you have an idea of what types of farms are in the Prairie Provinces.)

As you continue through Manitoba and on into Saskatchewan, you notice huge farms. Some are a square mile in size; some are several square miles together. A newcomer feels lost in the immense fields that stretch to the horizon. A grain *elevator* that looks as if it is a mile away might be three or four miles away.

God gave Saskatchewan a dry climate. Many crops do not grow well, even though the soil is rich and dark, even black. But wheat grows so well that more wheat is raised in Saskatchewan than in any other province. Prairie farmers raise spring wheat. At harvest time, combines reap the wheat and pour the grain into trucks. The trucks take the wheat to grain elevators, where it is stored in the tall bins. Elevators clean the wheat, dry it, and

Elevators clean and store the wheat. Some of it is carried by trains and and ships to many countries of the world.

grade it. Later the elevator will load the wheat into train cars. The train might take the wheat to a flour mill. Your bread, your pie crust, or the shredded wheat on your breakfast table may have come from wheat that once grew on a prairie farm.

The train might also take the wheat to a larger elevator at a seaport, where it will be loaded onto ships headed for other countries. People around the world like the high-quality Canadian wheat. Vancouver, a seaport where some of the grain is shipped, lies to the west of the Prairie Provinces in British Columbia. Thunder Bay, a great grain port on Lake Superior, lies to the east in Ontario.

The Prairie Provinces are too far from the ocean to have any big ports of their own—except one. This port is Churchill, where Manitoba touches the Hudson Bay. A map will show that Churchill is so far north that the port freezes shut in the winter. Ships can use it only from July to October. But while it is open, many shiploads of grain are loaded there.

Besides wheat, plains farmers raise barley, hay, and other crops. Much of their earnings come from beef cattle. Minerals have been found under the plains. The most important mineral is oil; Alberta produces more petroleum and natural gas than all the other provinces together. Most of the oil and gas flows through underground pipelines for hundreds of miles. Some of it flows two thousand miles to eastern Canada.

What about the parts of these provinces that are not prairie? The Rocky Mountains begin in western Alberta. Many people visit the Rockies, especially the parks, to marvel at the majesty of the tall, snow-capped mountains.

The Canadian Shield runs through Manitoba and northern Saskatchewan and even touches a northern corner of Alberta. The Canadian Shield and other northern areas are dotted with many evergreen and poplar forests, rocks, lakes, and rivers.

By far, the most precious natural resource of the Prairie Provinces is neither lumber nor oil, but their good soil. In some places on the prairies, the rich, dark topsoil is quite thick. The soil feeds everyone, and God expects farmers to take good care of it.

Study Exercises

1. What is a chinook?
2. What is a grain elevator?

3. Name three great grain ports that ship wheat from the Prairie Provinces, and name the provinces in which they are found.

4. Which province produces most of Canada's petroleum and natural gas?

5. Which province produces the most wheat?

Gaining Geographical Skills

1. Trace Map Q in the map section, and label it "The Prairie Provinces."

2. Shade the northern half of the area green to represent forest.

3. Label Lake Winnipeg.

4. Label the Prairie Provinces, their capital cities, and Churchill.

Further Study

1. Why is Winnipeg called the Gateway to the West?

2. (a) What effect does a chinook have on the temperature? (b) What effect does it have on the moisture?

77. British Columbia

Glossary Word

plateau

When you think of British Columbia, think of mountains! As you go west through Alberta, you come to the Rocky Mountains some distance before the British Columbia border. The men who tried to build the first railway through the Rocky Mountains must have felt like ants trying to build a trail over a rock pile. The railroad men did find a few lower passes suitable for railroad tracks. Today these passes are used by trains, buses, trucks, and cars traveling to British Columbia.

British Columbia has many more mountains than just the Rockies. You hardly cross the Rockies before you see another range of mountains just ahead. This is the Columbia Range. Beyond it lies a *plateau* full of hills and low mountains. And just before you reach the Pacific Ocean, you must find your way through the high Coast Ranges.

The mountains cause different parts of British Columbia to be either wet or dry. Ocean breezes bringing moisture from the Pacific are raised

British Columbia

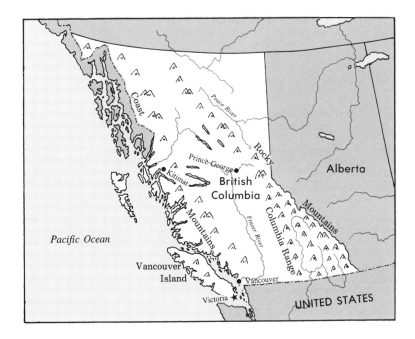

as they cross the Coast Ranges. The rising air cools, producing rain. On the eastern side of the Coast Ranges the breezes are no longer so moist. As they cross the plateau farther inland, no big mountains cause rain. Some areas on this plateau receive enough rain, but other parts are desert dry. Sagebrush covers the brown hills, and only a few evergreen trees grow here and there. In some parts there are no trees at all. Where the land is irrigated, green fields look like gems on a brown carpet.

A lake in the Rocky Mountains of British Columbia.

British Columbia is a land of contrasts. Some areas have beautiful, well-watered farms where dikes must be used for protection from floods; in other places, farmers can grow crops only by using irrigation water. Most places in British Columbia have cold, snowy winters; yet the southwest corner is green the year round!

Next to mountains, the second most important thing that affects British Columbia's climate is the Pacific Ocean. Besides bringing rain, the ocean also helps keep the temperature mild, especially along the coast. A warm ocean current called the Japan Current keeps western British Columbia surprisingly warm for as far north as it is. Most British Columbians live in the southwest corner, where the most pleasant weather is. Notice on a map how close together the cities lie. The largest city in British Columbia is Vancouver.

Vancouver Island is the most important island off the coast of British Columbia. It has the mildest weather in Canada, and the southern end is especially mild. Victoria, the capital of British Columbia, was built here.

Interestingly, the city of Vancouver is not on Vancouver Island. It lies close by on the mainland, next to a good harbor. The harbor is ice-free all year, something very important to a northern country such as Canada. Roads and railroads from across Canada end in Vancouver.

Vancouver has the largest harbor in western Canada.

British Columbia produces almost two-thirds of Canada's lumber. Some loggers use chain saws to cut down trees. Where the slopes are not too steep and the trees are not too big, machines on caterpillar tracks move through the forests, using huge hydraulic shears to cut down trees. The machines lay the trees in neat piles. Other machines drag the trees to a landing where workmen cut off the branches and saw the logs to the right lengths. Then they are loaded onto trucks.

Since long, crooked fingers of the sea run miles inland, some loggers float the logs out to the coast. There men tie the logs into rafts or put them on barges that take them to the sawmill.

Traveling through the forests and seeing the millions of trees, you might think that they would never all be cut down. But even the greatest natural resources can be destroyed. (Think of the huge forests that once covered the eastern United States.) Young trees need to be planted where big ones have been cut down. Foresters are learning more about fertilizing trees and thinning them to keep them from crowding each other. They want trees to grow as fast as they are cut down, so that their children will also have plenty of lumber and paper.

The foresters keep a sharp watch for fires. Some of them are stationed in fire lookouts on mountaintops, where they can look across the mountain ranges for smoke. Some fly airplanes across areas through which thunderstorms have passed, to see where lightning might have struck. If a fire begins, firefighters haul tanks of water as close as they can to spray on the fire. Others saw down trees near the edge of the fire or push them down with bulldozers to keep the fire from spreading. Airplanes may also spray the fire with water or fire retardant. Everyone, firefighter or not, must do his part. Signs along roads tell people how serious the danger of fire is so that they know when to be especially careful.

Compared to the forest land, British Columbia does not have much farmland. But much of what it does have is very good. In the northeastern area, farmers raise grain and cattle. In the southwestern corner near Vancouver, dairy products are important because grass and hay grow well in the rainy climate and many people nearby use milk. In the sunny southern plateau, farmers in the dry belt irrigate their crops. The Okanagan Valley has thousands of

Bumper boats pushing logs from the forests of British Columbia.

orchards and is well-known for its apples and other fruits.

Fishermen catch so many fish that British Columbia is a leading fishing province. This helps make Canada one of the world's most important fishing countries. The most valuable fish is salmon. Perhaps you have eaten sockeye or pink salmon, or one of the other kinds.

Other important fish are herring and halibut. Fishermen catch herring close to shore, using nets. But to catch halibut, fishermen must go far out to sea and use lines and hooks. Halibut are large fish, weighing as much as two hundred pounds.

Kitimat, one of British Columbia's most interesting cities, was built for one main reason—to make aluminum.

The men who planned the aluminum factory at Kitimat had to plan much more than the factory. Making aluminum takes much electricity. Where would the electricity come from? Far away, a river flowed toward the east, away from Kitimat. The river was dammed and its water backed up until it filled several lakes. The lakes rose so high that water began to flow from them in a new direction—west! Water from the lakes now rushes through a ten-mile-long tunnel to a power plant inside the mountain, where it generates electricity. The electricity travels through wires about fifty miles to Kitimat, where it is used to make aluminum. Perhaps some of the products you use were made of aluminum from British Columbia.

―――――――― Study Exercises ――――――――

1. What is important about each of these cities of British Columbia? (a) Vancouver (b) Victoria (c) Kitimat
2. What is the most important island off the coast of British Columbia?
3. What is done with the forest land after the loggers have cut down the trees?
4. What is the most valuable fish processed in British Columbia?

Gaining Geographical Skills

1. Trace Map R in the map section, and label it "British Columbia."
2. Label the three mountain ranges that run through British Columbia.
3. Label Vancouver Island.
4. Label British Columbia, its capital city, Vancouver, Kitimat, and Prince George.

Further Study

1. Why does British Columbia have some very wet land and some very dry land?

2. How do the people of British Columbia protect their forests from fire?

78. The Yukon and the Northwest Territories

Glossary Words

muskeg	tree line
permafrost	tundra

The Canadian Northlands is one of the most interesting areas in Canada to learn about. But most people would not like to live there.

Surprisingly, not much snow falls in the Northlands—only a few inches each winter. It is too cold to snow much. Some areas of the Northlands are as dry as a desert. But the little snow that does fall never melts until summer. For nine or even ten long winter months, savage winds whip the snow back and forth across the barren land. Huge drifts pile up be-side buildings in the lonely villages. And the temperature drops to forty below zero or colder.

In northern Canada, winter days are very short and winter nights are very long. In late December, the parts farthest north have no daylight at all, only darkness—even at noon. During those bitter winter nights, people cannot do much outside. Even those who have lived in the Northlands for years get restless and tired of staying indoors. They say they are getting "cabin fever."

The Yukon
and the
Northwest Territories

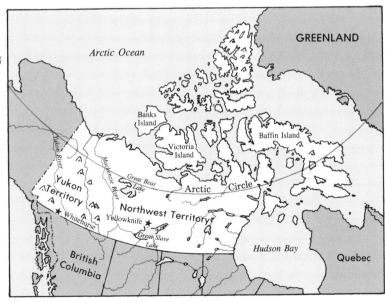

Those winter storms of the Canadian Northlands are more important to weathermen in the United States than most people realize. After the storms build up in the Northlands, they move south across North America, bringing cold and snow. Weathermen at stations far to the north watch the weather and help weathermen farther south predict what might be coming their way.

Does northern Canada have any summers at all? Oh, yes. Summer days may be so warm and sunny that people do not even need sweaters. Grass grows, flowers bloom, and insects fill the air. People in some areas can raise potatoes and cabbage. Although summers are short, the days are long. In fact, north of the Arctic Circle the sun never sets on the longest days of summer. Northern Canada is often called The Land of the Midnight Sun.

Yet even in the summer the ground only thaws on top. Below the surface of the thawed ground lies *permafrost*, ground that always stays frozen. Water from rain and melted snow cannot seep down through, so it lies on top of the ground in puddles and in swamps called *muskegs*. There are so many lakes that some of them have not even been named.

The Canadian Northlands are empty and lonely. Just the hugeness of the region helps to make it so. The Canadian government spends millions of dollars each year rescuing people who get lost or whose boats or airplanes have engine trouble far from towns or telephones. Scattered across the north are a few villages and towns. Yellowknife, the capital of the Northwest Territories, has about ten thousand people in it. That is small compared to the biggest cities of southern Canada, where people live by the hundreds of thousands!

Few roads cross the Northlands. Airplanes take people in and out of the little towns and bring them the goods they need. Children in some areas fly to school. But then they live at school for quite a while before they fly home.

Yellowknife, the capital of Northwest Territories, is one of the few towns in northern Canada. It is located on the shore of Great Slave Lake.

Not all shipping requires the expense of flying. Another way to transport supplies is by river. Many boats and barges use the Mackenzie, a giant river longer than the Mississippi. The River of Disappointment, as it was called, has turned out to be a blessing after all. Other rivers that flow into the Mackenzie also carry boats to distant places. And the Yukon River, which flows through Alaska, allows boats to come into Canada from the Pacific.

Travel is harder in the Northlands than it is farther south, and goods are more expensive. Think of how much more difficult travel must have been for pioneers who walked behind dog sleds, and what they must have had to do without.

If you were traveling north into the Yukon and the Northwest Territories, you would first pass through huge evergreen forests. But as you travel north, especially in eastern Canada, you would notice that gradually the trees are shorter and farther apart. A tree as old as your grandfather might be no taller than you are. Still farther north, you would find only the hardiest trees, growing in low places near streams. Finally the trees would disappear, and only empty plains and bare mountains could be seen.

Most Indians live south of the *tree line*. The Eskimos like the wide,

A prospector near his cabin in Yukon Territory. Minerals provide an important source of income for the northern Canada territories.

empty spaces farther north. In Eskimo schools the teachers pass around leaves in their classrooms so the children can touch them, perhaps for the first time in their lives.

But the land north of the tree line, called *tundra*, is still not bare of plants. Mosses, low shrubs, and lichens grow among the stones. Bright flowers may bloom for a few weeks each year. In summer, much of the tundra reminds you of a wet pasture full of huge clumps of ground covered with plants. If you try to walk on the humps, you are likely to slip off into the soggy ground between. This land, so full of wet spots, makes a perfect breeding ground for mosquitoes and

Much of the Yukon is covered by mountains.

furs. In turn, the white men gave rifles to the Inuit. The Inuit hunted still more animals. Finally the animals became scarce, and the Inuit who tried to hunt in the old way could not find enough game. The old way began to change.

Today most Inuit live in wooden houses with stoves and glass windows. They wear modern clothing, and their sleds are pulled by snowmobiles. They live more comfortably than their ancestors did.

The changes for the Inuit have been both good and bad. The first white men brought diseases that spread rapidly among the Inuit, and many of them died. Alcoholic beverages became another cause of serious trouble.

One of the biggest recent problems is that many of the Inuit are unable to find jobs. They depend on the government to give them money for everyday living. But some of the people are learning crafts such as making soapstone carvings. Others work at jobs such as mining or fishing. Some are going to school to learn new skills.

The Canadian government has helped some Inuit build canneries. The Inuit can the meat of seal, shark, whale, and walrus. This helps them have more food available during the winter, when game may be harder to find. Also, they hope to sell canned

black flies—billions of them! People slap at them, and herds of caribou sometimes plunge into rivers to escape them.

Things have changed in the Northlands. The Eskimos, or Inuit, probably feel the changes most of all. For years and years they wandered, fishing and hunting with spears and with bows and arrows. Then came sailors in whaling ships. Some of the Inuit helped the sailors. Others trapped animals for men who wanted to buy

Long ago, the Inuit lived in igloos during the winter. When there was no snow, they lived in tents made from seal or caribou skins.

whale, seal, or walrus meat to other parts of Canada or to the United States. Perhaps the food that Inuit eat every day will become a treat to people in other lands!

In some ways, the Inuit are different from most North Americans. Their ancestors made their homes in North America long before the Europeans arrived. They have learned to live in a cold, barren land where many people could not survive. But in one way the Inuit are like everyone else in the world. All peoples need to hear the Gospel, whether they live in cold lands or warm lands, neighboring lands or faraway lands. God wants every person "to be saved, and to come unto the knowledge of the truth" (1 Timothy 2:4).

Study Exercises

1. How do the northern winter storms affect the rest of North America?

2. Why is northern Canada called the Land of the Midnight Sun?
3. What is permafrost?
4. What plants grow on the tundra?

Gaining Geographical Skills

1. Trace Map S in the map section, and label it "The Yukon and the Northwest Territories."
2. Label the Great Bear Lake, Great Slave Lake, and Mackenzie River.
3. Label each area and its capital city.
4. Label the Arctic Circle.

Further Study

1. Why does not much snow fall in the Northlands?
2. What kinds of work are available in the far north?
3. What do all peoples need to hear?

Chapter 13 Review

Reviewing What You Have Learned

A. *Write a glossary word for each definition.*

1. A steep cliff separating two levels of land.
2. An area of high, level land.
3. Located on or near the sea.
4. Wet, spongy ground.
5. The part of the year when crops can be raised.
6. A steady flow of water within a larger body of water.
7. A building where grain is stored.
8. The northern limit for trees to grow well.
9. The rise and fall of the oceans twice each day.
10. A shallow part of the ocean near a continent.

B. *Choose the correct answer to complete each sentence.*

1. The —— is a rich fishing area.
   a. Gulf Stream
   b. Grand Banks
   c. St. Lawrence Seaway
2. Labrador is part of the province of ——.
   a. Nova Scotia
   b. Quebec
   c. Newfoundland
3. —— is the largest province of Canada.
   a. British Columbia
   b. Ontario
   c. Quebec
4. Much of Canada's population and business is found in the ——.
   a. Heartland of Canada
   b. Northwest Territories
   c. Canadian Shield

5. The Prairie Provinces produce a large part of the world's ———.
   a. automobiles
   b. wheat
   c. lumber

6. ——— is called the Gateway to the West in Canada.
   a. Vancouver
   b. Prince Edward Island
   c. Winnipeg

7. British Columbia is a province of ———.
   a. lakes
   b. mountains
   c. prairies

8. Leading industries in British Columbia are ———.
   a. farming and tourism
   b. logging and fishing
   c. manufacturing and printing

9. Northern Canada is the Land of the ———.
   a. Midnight Sun
   b. Maritime Provinces
   c. Frozen Volcanoes

10. In the Northland people travel mostly by ———.
    a. snowmobiles and horses
    b. skis and dog sleds
    c. airplanes and boats

C. *Write* true *or* false.

   1. Labrador is rich in iron ore deposits.
   2. Ottawa is the capital of Canada.
   3. The St. Lawrence Seaway connects the Atlantic Ocean and the Pacific Ocean.
   4. The Canadian Shield is a good farming area.
   5. Alberta, Manitoba, and Ontario are the Prairie Provinces.
   6. Chinooks bring warm, dry air.
   7. Vancouver is the most important city on Vancouver Island.
   8. The most valuable fish caught in British Columbia is herring.

9. Huge machines on caterpillar tracks cut down trees on the tundra.

10. Permafrost is a lower level of ground that never thaws.

Gaining Geographical Skills

1. Trace Map T in the map section, and label it "Canada." Label the provinces and territories.

2. Label the capital cities of the provinces, territories, and the nation.

3. Label the Great Lakes, Gulf of St. Lawrence, Hudson Bay, and Atlantic and Pacific Oceans.

So Far This Year

Choose the correct answers. See how many you can give without looking back.

1. North America is in the (Northern, Southern) and (Eastern, Western) hemispheres.

2. Canada is (smaller, larger) than the United States, but it has (fewer, more) people.

3. (Christopher Columbus, Amerigo Vespucci) discovered America while trying to find a new route to the Far East.

4. The first lasting English settlement in North America was (Boston, Jamestown, Philadelphia).

5. The French settled lands (north, south) of the English colonies.

6. The American colonists fought to be independent because they felt that the taxes and laws of (Great Britain, Pennsylvania, Virginia) were unfair.

7. The United States took a large area in the Southwest from (Great Britain, France, Mexico).

8. The (Civil War, Revolutionary War) started after the Southern states seceded from the United States.

9. The Emancipation Proclamation helped the North to win the Civil War by stating that the slaves would be (captured, freed).

10. (Kansas, Oklahoma, Texas) was the last big section of Indian land to be taken by white settlers.

11. In 1867, (two, four, seven) Canadian colonies joined to form the new country of Canada.

12. (Stagecoaches, Trains, Pony express riders) eventually replaced canal boats.

13. During the Great Depression, many people (lost their jobs, invested their extra money).

14. The United States entered World War II after (Germany, Japan, Russia) bombed Pearl Harbor in Hawaii.

15. One of the most important modern inventions is the (computer chip, microwave oven, satellite).

16. Only —— knows exactly what will happen in the future.

17. (Los Angeles, New York City, Washington, D.C.) is the capital of the United States.

18. The (Mississippi, Ohio, Tennessee) River is the largest river in the United States.

19. The (Grand Banks, Gulf Stream, St. Lawrence Seaway) connects the Great Lakes and the Atlantic Ocean.

20. (Montreal, Ottawa, Quebec) is the capital of Canada.

21. The large wheat farms of Canada are in (Quebec and Ontario, the Prairie Provinces).

22. Most of British Columbia is covered with (mountains, tundra).

Rules for Neat Maps

1. Use printing, not cursive writing, for all words on the map.
2. Print all words horizontally except the names of rivers and mountain ranges. A river or mountain range name should follow the course of the river or mountain range.
3. Use all capital letters for the names of countries, states, provinces, and large bodies of water. Capitalize only the first letter of each word for cities, lakes, rivers, and land regions.
4. Color bodies of water blue. Make all coloring strokes horizontal, not vertical or every which way.
5. To color countries, states, or provinces, use a color that is different from the color of any area beside it. Do not use any color that is too dark for the lettering to show.

Table of Contents

Map A

North America (Lesson 1)
The First North Americans (Chapter 2 Review)

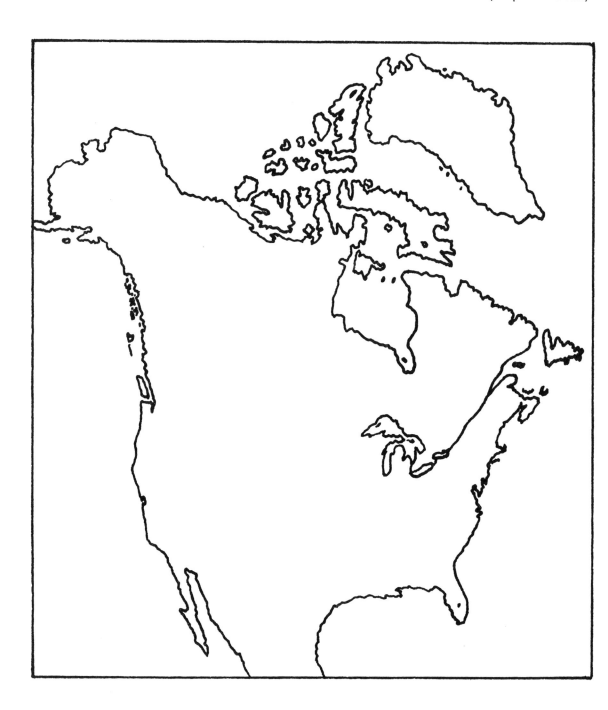

Map B

United States (Lesson 2)
Westward Expansion (Lessons 36, 37, 38)
Trails to the West (Lessons 38, 39, 40)

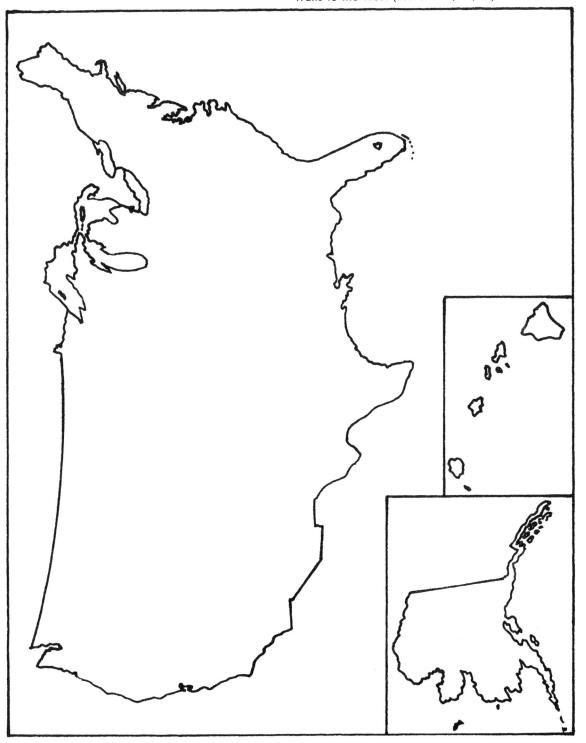

Map C

Canada (Lesson 3)
Canada Expands Westward (Lesson 50)

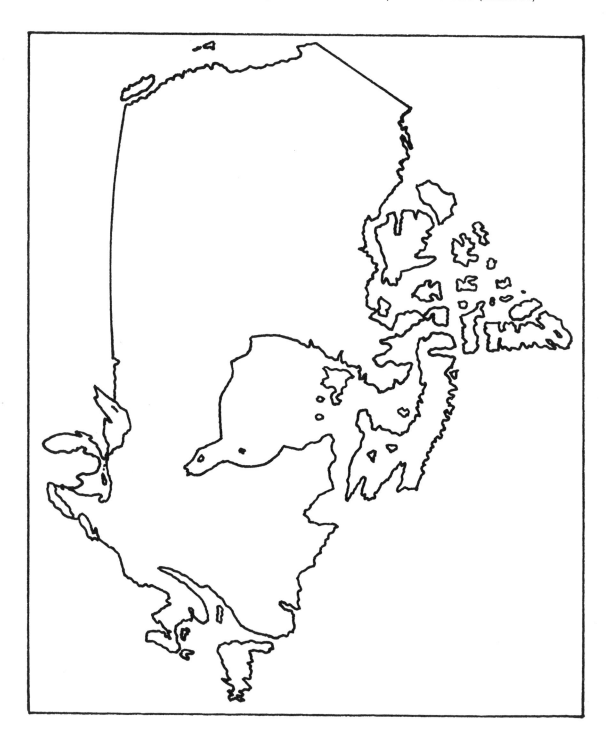

Map D

Early American Settlements (Lessons 17, 20)
French and English Settlements in North America (Chapter 4 Review)
North America after the Revolutionary War (Lesson 33)

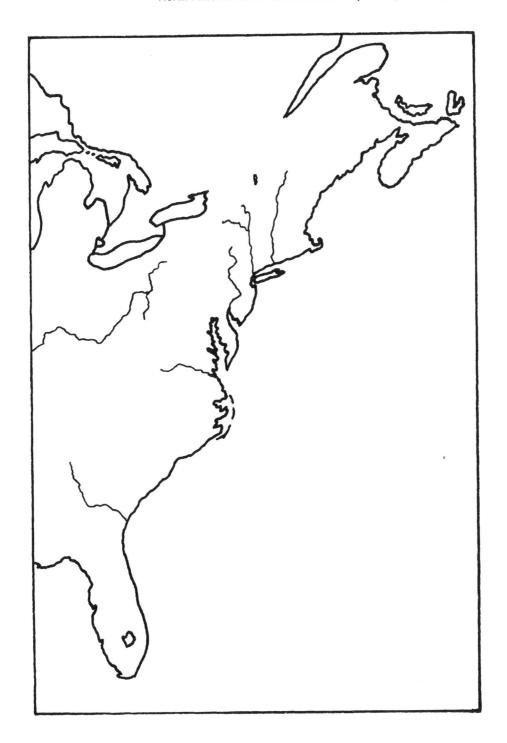

Map E

The New England States (Lesson 66)

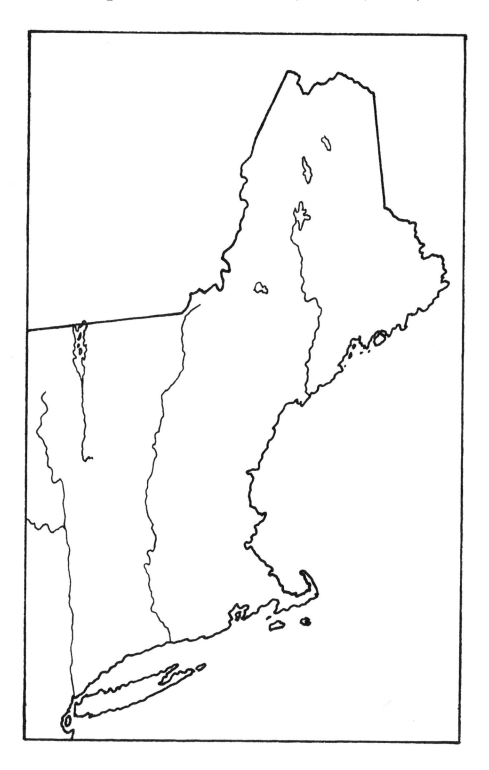

Map F

The Middle Atlantic States (Lesson 67)

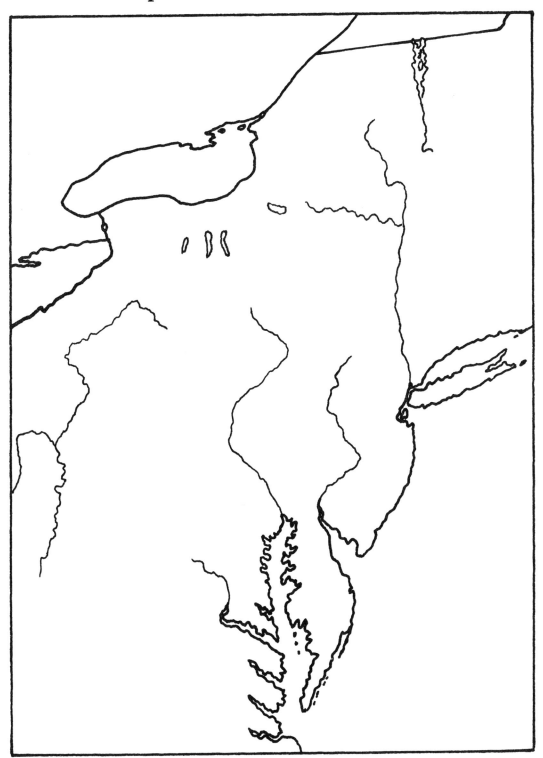

Map G

The Southern States (Lesson 68)

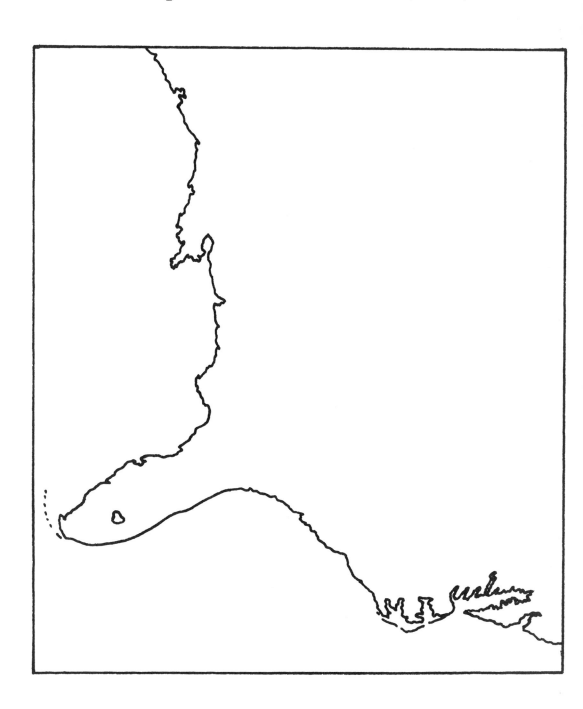

Map H   The Midwestern States (Lesson 69)

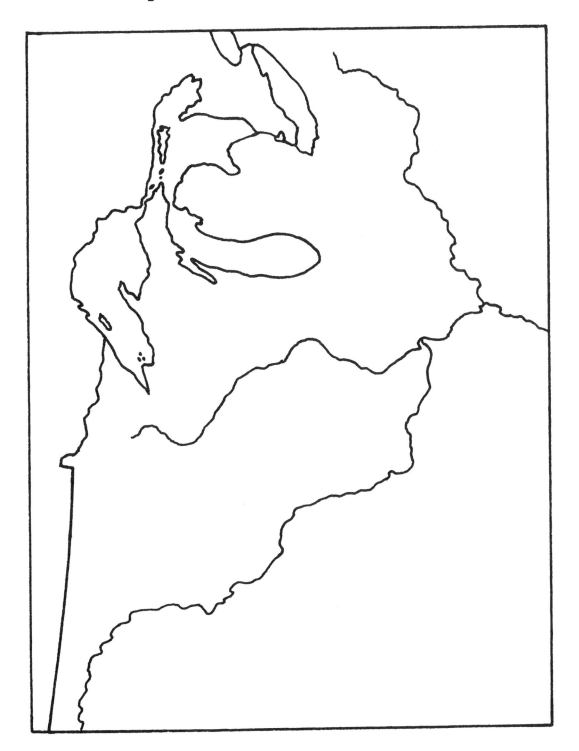

Map I

The Southwestern States (Lesson 70)

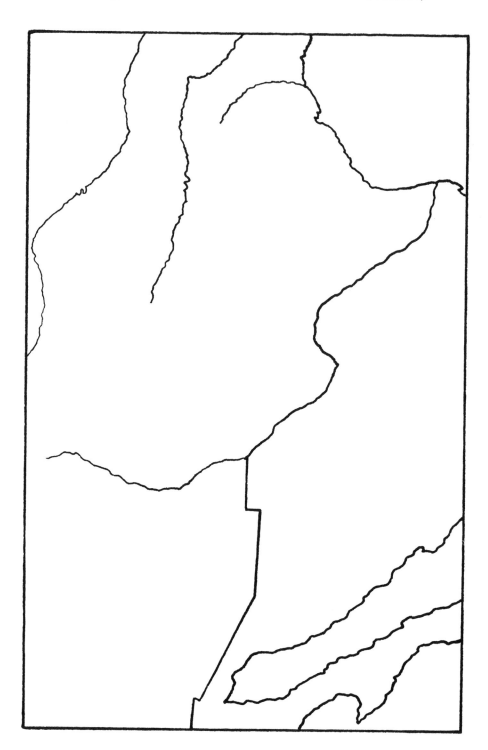

Map J

The Rocky Mountain States (Lesson 71)

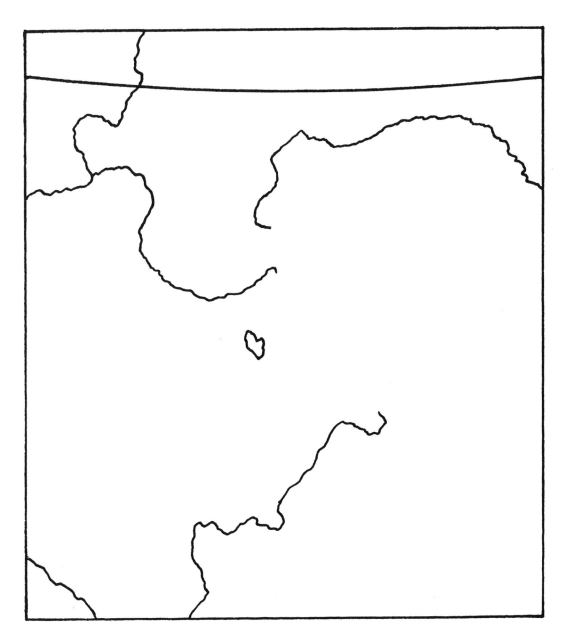

Map K   The Pacific Coast States (Lesson 72)

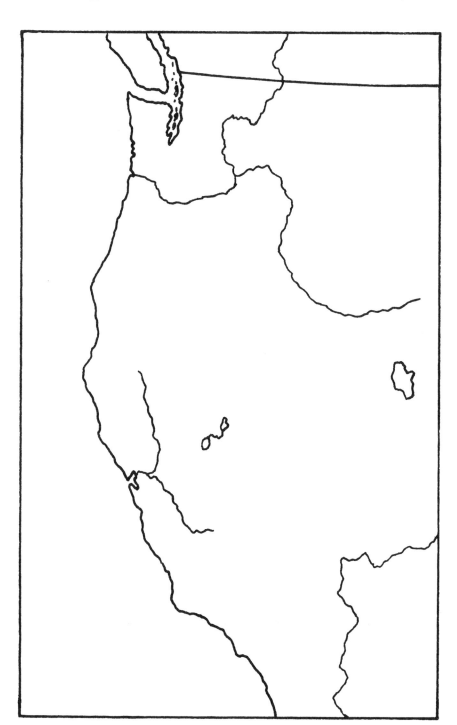

Map L

Alaska (Lesson 73)

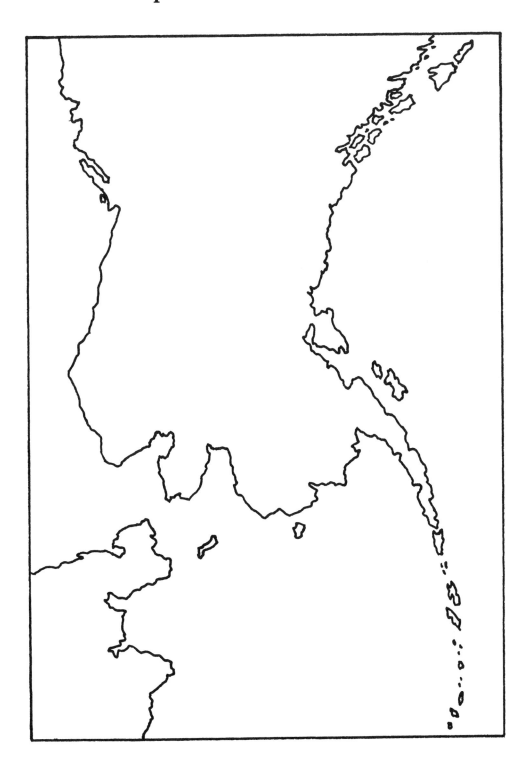

Map M

Hawaii (Lesson 73)

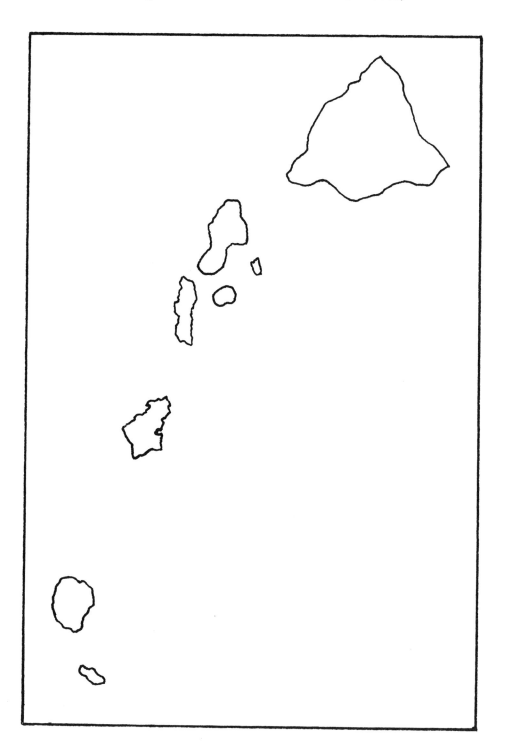

Map N

United States (Chapter 12 Review)

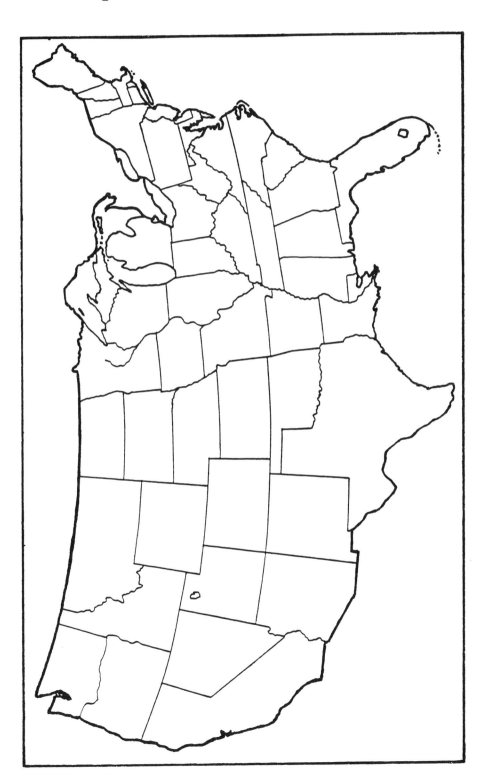

Map O

The Atlantic Provinces (Lesson 74)

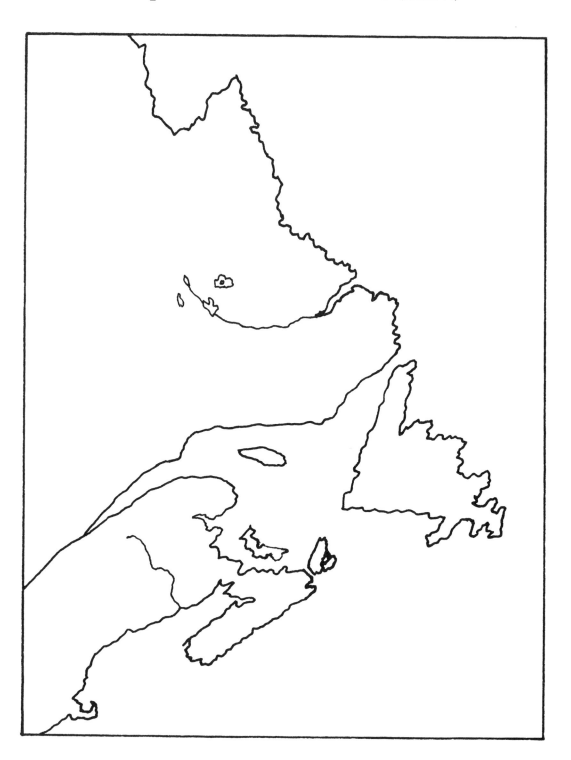

Map P

Quebec and Ontario (Lesson 75)

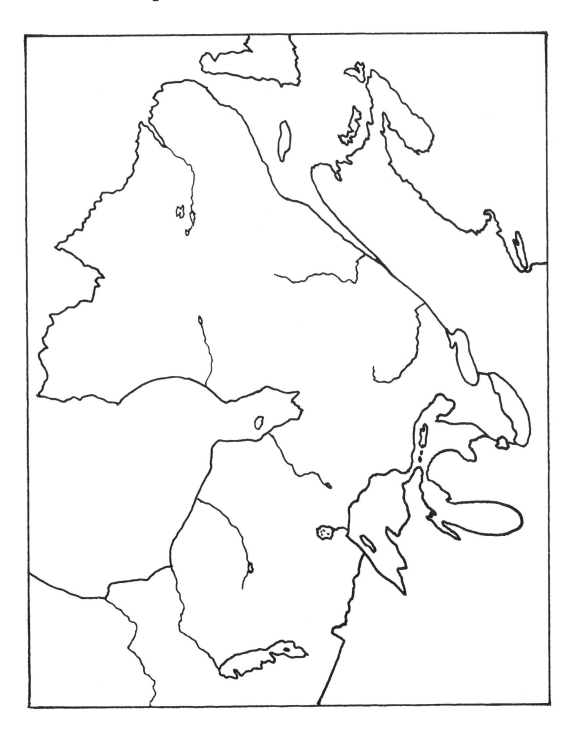

Map Q

The Prairie Provinces (Lesson 76)

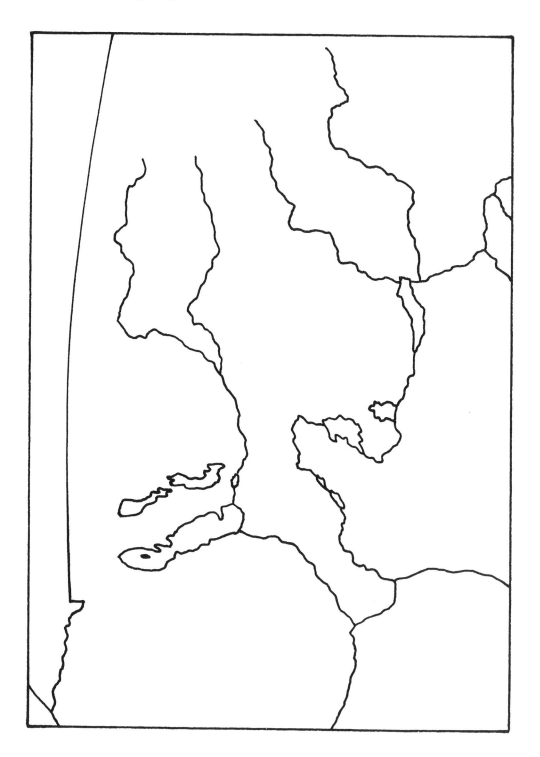

Map R

British Columbia (Lesson 77)

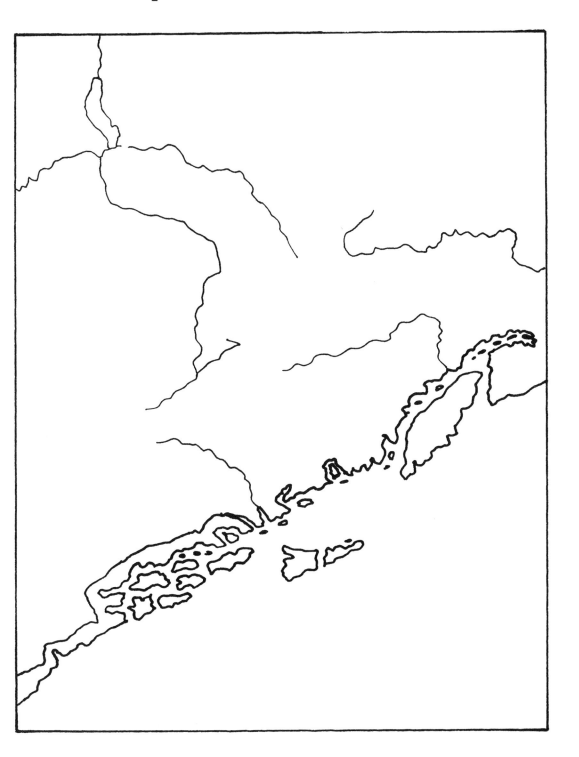

Map S   The Yukon and the Northwest Territories (Lesson 78)

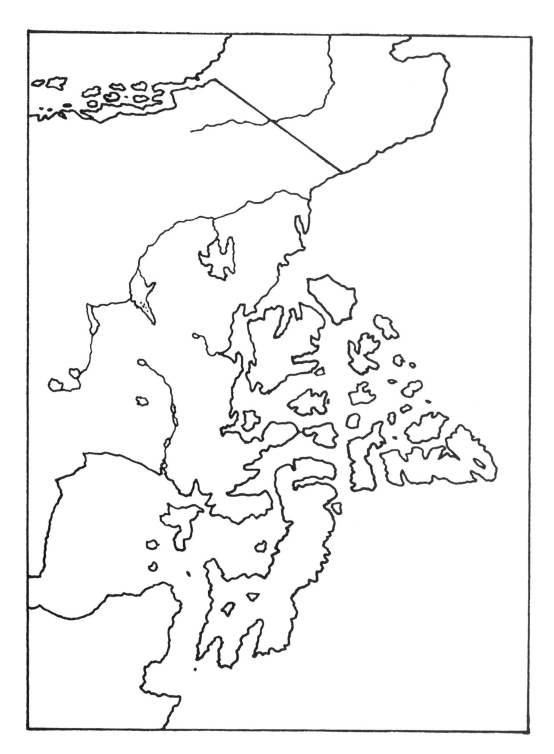

Map T

Canada (Chapter 13 Review)

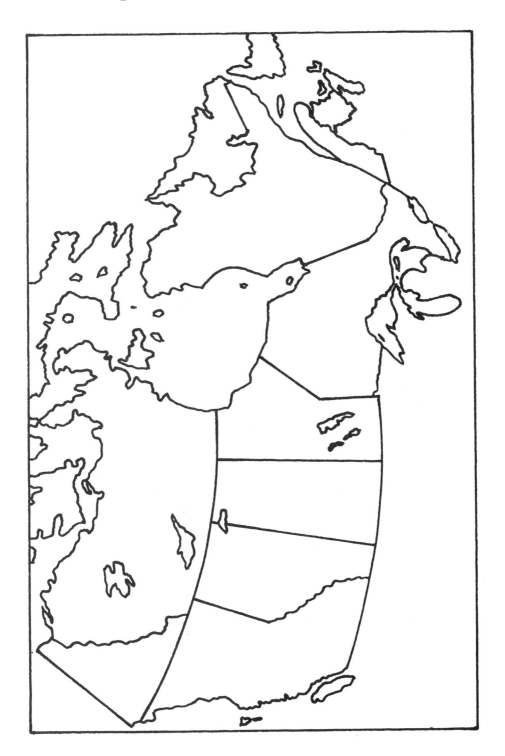

Glossary

This glossary gives the meanings and pronunciations of the glossary words listed in each lesson. The numbers in brackets show which lessons list them.

The definitions tell only how the words are used in this book. Use a dictionary if you want to find other meanings for the words.

Most of the words have been respelled within parentheses to show how they are usually pronounced. Accented syllables are printed in capital letters.

abolish (uh BOL ish) To do away with. [44]

adobe (uh DOH bee) 1. A brick made of clay and dried in the sun.   2. Clay used to make bricks. [8]

Aleuts (AL ee oots) The native people of the Aleutian Islands. [11]

allies (AL ize) Nations that have agreed to help each other. [57]

amendment (uh MEND munt) A change in a law. [32]

America (uh MER i kuh) The name given to the lands in the Western Hemisphere. [13]

Amish (AH mish) A church that separated from the Mennonites in 1693, led by Jacob Ammann. Historically, the Amish beliefs have been similar to early Anabaptist doctrine (see Anabaptists). [12]

ammunition (am yuh NISH un) Bullets and gunpowder. [29]

Anabaptists (an uh BAP tists) Christians who believed that the New Testament is to be obeyed and practiced in daily life, and that only true believers in Jesus Christ, not babies, should be baptized. Other Bible teachings they held included loving their enemies, not holding government office, and not swearing. The first Anabaptists, called Swiss Brethren, left the state church in 1525 at Zurich, Switzerland. The Anabaptists led by Menno Simons became known as Mennonites, and those of Moravia became known as Hutterites. [12]

antiseptic (ant uh SEP tik) A germ killer. [51]

Appalachian Mountains (ap uh LA chee un) The mountain ranges in eastern North America. [2]

Arctic (ARK tick) The area around the North Pole. [1]

Arctic Islands (ARK tick EYE lunds) Several hundred Canadian islands in the Arctic Ocean. [3]

arid (AR ud) Dry, not receiving much rainfall. [71]

armistice (AR mi stis) An agreement to stop fighting. [57]

assassinate (uh SAS uh nayt) To kill an important person. [45]

assembly line A line of workers who assemble a product piece by piece as the product moves through a factory. [34]

Atlantic Coastal Plain (at LAN tik KOH stul) An area of flat land along the eastern coast of the United States. [2]

atomic bomb (uh TOM ik) An extremely powerful kind of bomb. [59]

basin An area of land that has a low center surrounded by higher ground. [39]

bauxite (BAWK site) A mineral that contains aluminum. [40]

bituminous coal (bi TOO muh nus) A soft coal that burns well and gives off much smoke. [68]

boll weevil (bohl WEE vul) A small insect that destroys cotton crops by laying its eggs in cotton bolls. [68]

border (BOR dur) The boundary of a country. [3]

boycott (BOI kot) To refuse to buy from or sell to someone as a way of protest. [29]

Canadian Shield (SHEELD) A large rocky area of Canada covered by only a thin layer of soil. [3]

canal (kuh NAL) A man-made waterway used by boats or for irrigation. [52]

card To clean and straighten fibers in preparation for spinning. [34]

Central Plains A large area of fairly level land in central North America. [2]

chinook (shi NOOK) A warm, dry wind that blows down from the Rocky Mountains. [76]

circuit rider (SUR kit) A preacher who rode from settlement to settlement, preaching at each one. [24]

citrus fruit (SIT rus) Oranges, lemons, grapefruit, and related fruits. [68]

civilization (siv uh li ZAY shun) An advanced way of life. [35]

civil war (SIV ul) A war between people of the same country. The American Civil War was fought between the northern states and the southern states. [45]

Coast Ranges A range of mountains along the western coast of North America. [2]

coke A fuel made from soft coal, often used in making steel. [68]

Cold War A conflict between nations without actual fighting. [60]

colony (KOL uh nee) A newly settled area, governed by the country from which the settlers came. [14]

combine (KOM bine) A machine that cuts, threshes, and cleans grain. [55]

communism (KOM yuh niz um) A system of government in which property and goods are owned and controlled by the state. [60]

compromise (KOM pruh mize) A way of agreeing about differences, in which each side gives up some demands. [32]

computer chip (kum PYOO tur) A tiny man-made square of material that has thousands of electronic circuits, used in computers and other modern electronic equipment. [62]

concentrate (KON suhn trayt) Juice that has been thickened by the removal of some of its water. Water is added to the concentrate before it is used. [68]

concentration camp (kon suhn TRAY shun) A prison camp for enemies of a country. [59]

condense (kun DENS) To become more dense, to form into a vapor. [74]

Conestoga wagon (kon i STOH guh) A heavy covered wagon that was used by American pioneers. [33]

Congress (KONG gris) The assembly of lawmakers. In the United States, Congress is made up of the Senate and the House of Representatives. [32]

conscientious objector (kon shee EN shus ub JEK tur) A person who believes it is wrong to fight in a war. [57]

conserve (kun SURV) To avoid wasting something by using it carefully. [56]

constitution (kon sti TOO shun) A document that describes how the government of a country is to work. [32]

continent (KON tuh nunt) One of the seven large areas of land on the earth. [1]

continental divide (kon tuh NEN tl) A ridge of mountains that separate streams that flow into one ocean from streams that flow into another ocean. [71]

continental shelf (kon tuh NEN tl) A shallow part of an ocean near a continent. [74]

cotton gin (JIN) A machine that removes seeds from cotton. [34]

cradle (KRAYD l) A frame fastened on a scythe, used to catch grain as it is cut. [55]

credit (KRED it) Trust given to a customer for the future payment of goods instead of requiring immediate payment. [58]

crop rotation A method of improving farmland by not planting the same crops year after year in the same soil. [56]

cult (KULT) A religion that follows a false teacher. [39]

current (KUR unt) A steady, regular flow of water within an ocean. [74]

Declaration of Independence A document stating why the American colonists wanted to be independent, signed by the members of the Second Continental Congress. [30]

delta (DEL tuh) The fan-shaped area that is formed from soil that settles near the mouth of a river. [68]

democracy (di MOK ruh see) Government in which ordinary people, not kings, rule the country. [32]

depression (di PRESH un) A time when jobs are hard to find, wages are low, and businesses make little money. [58]

descendant (di SEN dunt) A child, grandchild, and so forth, who has descended from a certain person or family. [33]

draft To require persons to fight in the armed forces. [57]

drought (DROUT) A long period of dry weather. [56]

drugs Strong medicines that are harmful if used wrongly. [64]

dry farming A way of farming dry land without irrigation by carefully using the water that is available. [71]

dugout (DUG out) A shelter dug in a hillside and roofed with sod. [47]

economic (ek uh NOM ik) Having to do with making, selling, and using goods. [75]

elevator (EL uh vay tur) A building where grain is stored. [76]

Emancipation Proclamation (i man suh PAY shun prok luh MAY shun) President Lincoln's announcement that the Southern slaves would be free on January 1, 1863. [45]

emigrant (EM i grunt) A person who leaves one country to settle in another. [33]

empire (EM pire) A government ruling over various groups of people or nations. [28]

epidemic (ep i DEM ik) A widespread outbreak of disease. [57]

equator (i KWAY tur) An imaginary line running around the earth between the Northern and Southern hemispheres. [1]

erosion (i ROH zhun) The wearing away of the earth's surface. [56]

escarpment (i SKARP munt) A steep ridge or cliff separating two levels of relatively flat land. [75]

Eskimo (ES kuh moh) A native person from a group of peoples living in the Arctic, also called Inuit. [11]

Fall Line The boundary between coastal plains and hills, the place where rapids and waterfalls stop seagoing ships. [67]

fallow (FAL oh) Plowed but not seeded during the growing season. [71]

fault (FAWLT) A crack beneath the earth's surface. [72]

forty-niners Persons who took part in the California gold rush of 1849. [40]

freedmen Persons who have been freed from slavery. [46]

friar (FRY ur) A man who spends his life teaching the Roman Catholic religion and trying to do good works. [15]

Frigid Zone (FRIJ id) The extremely cold area around the earth's poles. [1]

frontier (frun TIR) The area along the edge of a settled region. [24]

ghost towns A town left empty when its inhabitants moved away. [40]

Great Basin A region in the western United States that is lower than the surrounding areas. Much of the rainfall drains into low-lying areas within the Great Basin rather than out to an ocean. [2]

Great Valley of California A large valley in California between the Sierra Nevada and the Coast Ranges. [2]

growing season The part of the year when crops can be raised. [66]

gulden (GOOL dun) The basic unit of Dutch money. [18]

harbor (HAHR bur) A protected place for ships to anchor. [18]

hardwood The wood from a broad-leaf tree, usually harder than the wood from a cone-bearing tree. [68]

harpoon (hahr POON) A spear with a barb near its point, used for hunting seals, whales, and large fish. [11]

headdress (HED dres) A covering or ornament for the head. [7]

heartland (HAHRT land) An important, central part of a country. [75]

hemisphere (HEM i sfeer) 1. Half of a sphere or ball. 2. Half of the earth. [1]

homestead (HOHM sted) Government land gained by living on it. [47]

hornbook An early one-page reader that was protected by a thin sheet of horn. [22]

House of Representatives (rep ri ZEN tuh tivs) The branch of the United States Congress in which states are represented according to population. [32]

Hutterite (HUT ur ite) An Anabaptist church that was started in Moravia in 1528, later named after their leader, Jacob Hutter. Historically, Hutterite beliefs have been similar to early Anabaptist doctrine, except that they work and live together in isolated colonies (see Anabaptist). [57]

igloo (IG loo) A dome-shaped Eskimo house, often made of snow and ice. [11]

immigrant (IM i grunt) A person moving into a new country. [63]

immune (i MYOON) Not likely to catch a disease. [51]

import 1. (im PORT) To bring goods into a country.   2. (IM port) Goods that have been brought into a country. [56]

indentured servant (in DEN churd) A person who agrees to work for a certain amount of time, often to buy passage to America in colonial days. [22]

independent (in di PEN dunt) Free from the control or rule of others. [16]

indigo (IN di goh) A plant from which blue dye can be obtained. [25]

Industrial Revolution (in DUS tree ul rev uh LOO shun) Changes that occurred when factories began making goods that had been made at home. [34]

inflation (in FLAY shun) A rapid rise of the price of goods. [61]

interest (IN trist) Money paid for the use of borrowed money. [58]

Interior Plains (in TIR ee ur) A large area of fairly level land in central North America. [3]

Inuit (IN yoo it) An Eskimo word meaning "the people"; what the Eskimos call themselves. [11]

invade (in VAYD) To enter by force in order to conquer or steal. [43]

invest (in VEST) To spend money in order to gain profit. [58]

Iron Curtain The heavily guarded border in Europe between the Communist countries and the free countries, especially during the Cold War. [63]

kayak (KY ak) A one-man Eskimo canoe made of a frame with skins stretched tightly over it. [11]

levee (LEV ee) A bank built along a river to help prevent flooding. [68]

liberty (LIB ur tee) Freedom from the control of others. [29]

lock A section of a canal with gates that control the water level, used to raise or lower ships. [52]

long house The long wooden dwelling of the Iroquois Indians. [5]

loom A machine used to weave cloth. [34]

Louisiana Purchase (loo ee zee AN uh) The large area of land between the Mississippi and the Rocky Mountains that the United States purchased from France in 1803. [36]

Loyalist (LOI uh list) A person who remained loyal to Great Britain during the American Revolution, also called a Tory. [31]

manufacturing (man yuh FAK chur ing) The making of products. [66]

maritime (MAR i time) Located on or near the sea. [74]

massacre (MAS uh kur) The violent killing of a large number of people. [29]

mechanical reaper (mi KAN i kul REE pur) A machine invented to reap grain. [55]

melting pot A place where immigrants from different countries learn to accept the same way of life. [63]

Mennonite (MEN uh nyt) A church named after Menno Simons, an early leader among the Anabaptists in the Netherlands and Germany. Historically, Mennonite beliefs have been similar to early Anabaptist doctrine (see Anabaptist). [12]

Mexican Cession (MEKS i kun SESH un) The territory ceded to the United States from Mexico after the Mexican War. [37]

migrate (MY grate) To move from one area and settle in another. [41]

minerals (MIN ur uls) Valuable natural substances that are neither plants nor animals. Minerals are usually obtained by mining. [40]

minutemen (MIN it men) American colonists who were ready to fight the British at a minute's notice. [29]

muskeg (MUS keg) Wet, spongy ground. [78]

natural resources (NACH ur ul REE sors iz) Water, minerals, trees, soil, and other useful supplies God has created. [56]

newsprint (NOOZ print) Cheap paper that is used for newspapers. [66]

nomadic (noh MAD ik) Wandering around from place to place. [7]

nonresistant (non ri ZIS tunt) Refusing to use force to protect oneself. [27]

ore (OR) A mineral that is mined for the valuable substance it contains. [40]

palisade (pal i SAYD) A protective wall of logs set upright in the ground. [5]

panhandle (PAN han dl) A narrow strip of territory connected to a larger territory. [73]

pass A narrow gap in a mountain range. [71]

pasteurize (PAS chuh rize) To heat a liquid for a certain length of time in order to kill germs. [51]

pemmican (PEM i kun) Dried meat that has been pounded into powder and then mixed with fat and berries and shaped into small cakes. [7]

perishable (PER i shuh bul) Likely to spoil. [67]

permafrost (PUR muh frawst) Ground that is frozen all year. [78]

persecution (PUR si kyoo shun) The mistreatment or torment of someone for his beliefs. [12]

Piedmont (PEED mont) The hilly land between the Appalachian Mountains and the Atlantic Coastal Plain. [2]

Pilgrims (PIL grums) A group of people who had separated from the Church of England and established the first permanent colony in New England. [16]

pinyon nut (PIN yohn) The edible seed of the pinyon pine tree. [9]

pioneer (py uh NEER) One who settles in a frontier area. [24]

plantation (plan TAY shun) A large farm on which crops are grown. [25]

plateau (pla TOH) A high, fairly flat area of land. [77]

pollution (puh LOO shun) The condition of being dirty or harmful because of impurities and poisons. [69]

polygamy (puh LIG uh mee) The practice of having more than one husband or wife at a time. [39]

pontoons (pon TOONS) Floats attached to an airplane for landing on water. [73]

pony express A system of carrying the mail by riders on fast ponies. [53]

populated (POP yuh late ed) Filled with people. [24]

potlatch (POT lach) A feast given by Northwest Coastal Indians to show their wealth. [10]

precipitation (pri sip i TAY shun) Moisture that falls to the earth in the form of rain, snow, hail, sleet, etc. [69]

president (PREZ i dunt) The highest officer in the United States government. [32]

prime minister (prime MIN i stur) The highest officer in the Canadian government. [50]

prospector (PROS pek tur) One who searches for valuable minerals such as gold. [40]

province (PROV ins) A division in some countries, such as Canada. [3]

pueblo (PWEB loh) An Indian village of adobe houses built together as one building. [8]

pulp Moist, ground-up wood that is used to make paper. [66]

Puritans (PYOOR i tnz) A group of people who wanted to purify the Church of England. Some Puritans started a settlement at Boston, Massachusetts. [17]

Quakers (KWAY kurz) A persecuted group of people who wore simple clothes, would not fight, and would not join the Church of England. They were the first settlers in Pennsylvania. [19]

race A group of people with the same ancestors. [59]

rain shadow An area that receives little rain because of mountains that block moisture-bearing winds. [71]

ration (RASH un, RAY shun) To limit the amount one can buy. [59]

raw materials Natural products that can be used to make things. [56]

redwoods Giant evergreen trees that grow in California. [72]

repeal (ri PEEL) To do away with a law. [29]

represent (rep ri ZENT) To speak or act for someone else. [14]

representative (rep ri ZEN tuh tiv) 1. A type of government that is controlled by officials chosen by the people.   2. A person who has been chosen to represent a group of people. [14]

reservation (rez ur VAY shun) Land set aside for Indians. [9, 49]

reservoir (REZ ur vwor) A body of water backed up by a dam to provide water for future use. [8, 70]

retreat (ri TREET) To back away from an enemy. [30]

revolt (ri VOLT) To rise up in rebellion against leaders. [29]

revolutionary (rev uh LOO shuh ner ee) Having to do with a complete change in government. [30]

rights Freedoms that are protected by law. [32]

robot (ROH bot) A machine that can do jobs automatically. [62]

Rocky Mountains A range of high mountains running north and south in western North America. [2]

sagebrush (SAYJ brush) A shrub that grows in the dry lands of western North America. [71]

satellite (SAT l ite) An object in space that revolves around the earth. [62]

scurvy (SKUR vee) A disease caused by lack of vitamin C. [15]

scythe (SYTH) A mowing tool with a long curved blade fastened to a long handle. [55]

secede (si SEED) To break away from a group, to stop being a part of. [45]

Second Continental Congress (kon tuh NEN tl KONG gris) A group of men that met to discuss the problems in the American colonies at the beginning of the Revolutionary War. [30]

Senate (SEN it) The branch of the United States Congress in which each state is represented by two members. [32]

sequoia (si KWOI uh) Giant evergreen trees that grow in California. Giant sequoias have thicker trunks than California redwoods, but they do not grow as tall. [72]

sharecropper A farm worker who shares the crops he raises with the owner of the land. [46]

Sierra Nevada (see AIR uh nuh VAH duh) Mountain range in eastern California. [2]

slavery (SLAY vuh ree) The practice of owning people and forcing them work. [25]

slums Very poor, crowded areas in cities. [65]

smog A mixture of smoke and fog. [72]

society (suh SY i tee) A community of people with similar ideas. [64]

sod A layer of soil filled with the roots of grass and other plants. [47]

soddy (SOD ee) A house made of sod. [47]

softwood The wood from a cone-bearing tree, usually softer than the wood from a broad-leaf tree. [66]

sphere (SFEER) An object shaped like a ball. [1]

spinning jenny (JEN ee) An early spinning machine that could spin several threads at a time. [34]

spring wheat Wheat that is planted in the spring and harvested in the fall. [48]

stagecoach (STAYJ kohch) A horse-drawn vehicle that was used to carry passengers and mail. [40]

standard parts Parts that are made exactly alike so they will fit on similar products. [34]

state church A church approved and controlled by government leaders. The Catholic church was the first state church, but other state churches were later started in some countries. State churches have often persecuted those who would not accept their teachings. [12]

steppes (STEPS) Large plains in Russia. [48]

stock Part ownership of a company. [58]

stockholder A person who owns a share of a company. [58]

surrender (suh REN dur) To give up to an enemy in war. [30]

suspension bridge (suh SPEN shun) A bridge that is held up by cables. [72]

telegraph (TEL uh graf) A device for sending messages by electric signals through wires. [53]

Temperate Zone (TEM pur it) The region half-way between the equator and one of the earth's poles, having a comfortable climate. [1]

tepee (TEE pee) A cone-shaped tent used by Indians. [7]

territory (TER i TOR ee) A part of a country that is not a state or province, but has some government of its own. [3]

textile (TEKS tile) Woven or knitted cloth. [34]

threshing machine A machine used to separate grain from straw. [55]

tide The rise and fall of the oceans twice each day caused by the pull of the moon and the sun. [74]

time zone One of twenty-four zones around the earth. Clocks are set with a one hour difference from one zone to the next. [1]

topsoil The fertile top layer of ground. [56]

Torrid Zone (TOR id) The hot region of the earth near the equator, also called the Tropics. [1]

Tory (TOR ee) A person who remained loyal to Great Britain during the American Revolution, also called a Loyalist. [31]

totem pole (TOH tum) A pole with carved or painted animals or other symbols to represent a family or tribe. [10]

tourist (TOOR ist) A person who travels for pleasure. [66]

trade The business of buying and selling. [69]

trading post A station or store in a thinly settled area where goods can be bought, sold, or traded. [15]

transcontinental (TRANS kon tuh NEN tl) Reaching across a continent. [47]

transportation (trans pur TAY shun) The moving of goods or people from one place to another. [52]

travois (truh VOI) Two poles fastened to a dog or horse and used as a sled. [7]

treaty (TREE tee) An agreement between two or more countries or groups of people. [19]

tree line The northern limit for trees to grow well. The region north of the tree line is mainly tundra. [78]

Tropics (TROP iks) The hot region of the earth near the equator, also called the Torrid Zone. [1]

truck farmers Farmers who raise vegetables and fruit for the market. [67]

tundra (TUN druh) A treeless plain in the arctic regions where a few plants can grow during the summer, but the ground below the topsoil is permafrost. [78]

Underground Railroad A plan used by people who hated slavery to secretly help slaves reach freedom in Canada. Kind people along the routes hid the slaves until they could direct them on to the next "station." [44]

Union (YOON yun) The group of states that make up the United States. During the Civil War the North was called the Union. [45]

vaccination (vak suh NAY shun) A method of helping a person resist a dangerous disease by placing germs from a milder disease in his body. As the body fights off the mild disease, it also builds up resistance to the more dangerous disease. [51]

vegetation (vej i TAY shun) The plants of an area. [70]

Viking (VY king) One of the daring seamen who lived in what is now Denmark, Norway, and Sweden. [13]

volcano (vol KAY noh) A mountain with an opening from which hot rock has come. [73]

wampum (WOM pum) Beads made from shells and used as money by some of the Indian tribes. [5]

wigwam (WIG wom) An Indian dwelling made by covering a rounded pole frame with hides or birch bark. [26]

winter wheat Wheat that is planted in the fall and harvested the next spring or early summer. [48]

Map Index

General Index

Photo Credits

Alaska Division of Tourism: 377, 378

Brickman, Jim: 356

Butcher, Solomon D./Nebraska State Historical Society: 239

Deere and Company: 349

Engstrom, Eric G.: 122 (from *Husbandmen of Plymouth* by Darrett B. Rutman, Beacon Press)

Florida State Archives: 347

General Motors Corporation: 317

Henry Ford Museum/Greenfield Village: 179 (#B88772), 315 (#PO3449)

Historic Urban Plans: 101, 105

J. I. Case: 355

Kaschub, Norma: 8, 17 (bottom), 373

Library of Congress: 31, 32, 39, 41, 42, 43, 46, 47, 49, 50, 54, 57, 58, 64, 66, 67, 72, 75, 78, 80, 83, 84, 88, 89, 90, 93, 94, 96, 98, 100, 102, 104, 112, 119, 120, 125, 130, 131, 136, 140, 146, 150, 162 (center), 167, 174, 178, 187, 192, 194, 199, 202, 209 (top), 212, 218, 222, 226, 227, 229, 231, 240, 241, 243, 245, 247, 260, 261, 264, 269, 270, 272, 279 (bottom left), 286, 294 (top right), 296, 298, 299, 314 (bottom left), 320, 361

Martin, Michael S.: 16, 24

McDowell, Robert: 344

Metropolitan Toronto Library Board: 183, 289

Miller, Evan: 388

National Archives of Canada: 35 (bottom), 52, 116, 129, 166, 168, 249, 250, 251, 294 (top left)

National Archives of United States: 128, 176 (bottom right), 279 (bottom right), 290, 293

National Museums of Manitoba: 35 (top), 53

Ontario Archives: 139

Oregon Historical Society: 195 (#OrHi1643)

Photri: front cover, back cover, 1, 17 (top), 28, 162 (bottom), 209 (bottom), 258, 301, 302, 306, 312, 321, 332, 336, 338 (top right), 341, 342, 343, 348, 350, 354, 359, 362, 365, 366, 371, 372, 374, 379, 380, 398, 399, 400, 403 (top), 408, 409, 410, 416

Roark, Tom: 79 (Jamestown-Yorktown Foundation), 117 (Huronia Historical Parks), 124, 153, 154 (Independence National Historical Park Collection), 162 (top), 265

Rod and Staff Publishers, Inc.: 158

San Antonio Convention and Visitors Bureau: 191

Schueler, William L.: 97

Tom Stack and Associates: 367 (top)

Tourism Canada: 21, 22, 115, 314 (bottom right), 393, 394, 397, 403 (bottom), 404, 414, 415, 417

USDA: 360 (Fred S. Witte), 367 (Soil Conservation Service)

Vermont Travel Division: 337, 338 (top left)